The Urban Book Series

Series Advisory Editors

Fatemeh Farnaz Arefian, University College London, London, UK
Michael Batty, University College London, London, UK
Simin Davoudi, Newcastle University, Newcastle, UK
Geoffrey DeVerteuil, Cardiff University, Cardiff, UK
Karl Kropf, Oxford Brookes University, Oxford, UK
Marco Maretto, University of Parma, Parma, Italy
Vítor Oliveira, Porto University, Porto, Portugal
Christopher Silver, University of Florida, Gainesville, USA
Giuseppe Strappa, Sapienza University of Rome, Rome, Italy
Igor Vojnovic, Michigan State University, East Lansing, USA
Jeremy Whitehand, University of Birmingham, Birmingham, UK

Aims and Scope

The Urban Book Series is a resource for urban studies and geography research worldwide. It provides a unique and innovative resource for the latest developments in the field, nurturing a comprehensive and encompassing publication venue for urban studies, urban geography, planning and regional development.

The series publishes peer-reviewed volumes related to urbanization, sustainability, urban environments, sustainable urbanism, governance, globalization, urban and sustainable development, spatial and area studies, urban management, urban infrastructure, urban dynamics, green cities and urban landscapes. It also invites research which documents urbanization processes and urban dynamics on a national, regional and local level, welcoming case studies, as well as comparative and applied research.

The series will appeal to urbanists, geographers, planners, engineers, architects, policy makers, and to all of those interested in a wide-ranging overview of contemporary urban studies and innovations in the field. It accepts monographs, edited volumes and textbooks.

More information about this series at http://www.springer.com/series/14773

Lucia Capanema Alvares
Jorge Luiz Barbosa
Editors

Urban Public Spaces

From Planned Policies to Everyday Politics
(Illustrated with Brazilian Case Studies)

Editors
Lucia Capanema Alvares
Programa de Pós-Gradução em
  Arquitetura e Urbanismo
Universidade Federal Fluminense
Niterói, Rio de Janeiro
Brazil

Jorge Luiz Barbosa
Programa de Pós Graduação em Geografia
Universidade Federal Fluminense
Niterói, Rio de Janeiro
Brazil

ISSN 2365-757X   ISSN 2365-7588 (electronic)
The Urban Book Series
ISBN 978-3-319-74252-6   ISBN 978-3-319-74253-3   (eBook)
https://doi.org/10.1007/978-3-319-74253-3

Library of Congress Control Number: 2017963844

© Springer International Publishing AG, part of Springer Nature 2018
This work is subject to copyright. All rights are reserved by the Publisher, whether the whole or part
of the material is concerned, specifically the rights of translation, reprinting, reuse of illustrations,
recitation, broadcasting, reproduction on microfilms or in any other physical way, and transmission
or information storage and retrieval, electronic adaptation, computer software, or by similar or dissimilar
methodology now known or hereafter developed.
The use of general descriptive names, registered names, trademarks, service marks, etc. in this
publication does not imply, even in the absence of a specific statement, that such names are exempt from
the relevant protective laws and regulations and therefore free for general use.
The publisher, the authors and the editors are safe to assume that the advice and information in this
book are believed to be true and accurate at the date of publication. Neither the publisher nor the
authors or the editors give a warranty, express or implied, with respect to the material contained herein or
for any errors or omissions that may have been made. The publisher remains neutral with regard to
jurisdictional claims in published maps and institutional affiliations.

Printed on acid-free paper

This Springer imprint is published by the registered company Springer International
Publishing AG part of Springer Nature
The registered company address is: Gewerbestrasse 11, 6330 Cham, Switzerland

Foreword

Any critical discussion of urban public spaces requires that it be done through multidisciplinary perspectives. This is expertly done by Lucia Capanema Alvares and Jorge Luiz Barbosa in Urban Public Spaces: From Planned Policies to Everyday Politics—Brazilian case studies. As the world's population has become increasingly urban, we have witnessed a reduction of urban public spaces. Whether this is because of government action or inaction or advances in information technology, we are seeing a reduction in the amount of opportunities for public interaction. To truly understand the many dimensions of how people use urban public spaces and how public policies (directly and indirectly) affect the availability and use of such spaces, we must explore this fascinating area of inquiry through discussions in such interrelated topics as public policy, urban design, architecture, economics, environmental studies, sociology, landscape architecture, and urban planning.

It is important we acknowledge that urban public spaces are more than simply the parks in a city. There are many types of spaces. They can be community gardens, public markets, public buildings, streets, shopping malls, schools, public squares, plazas, parking lots, etc.

As illustrated by the various contributors to this book, there is a myriad of benefits associated with urban public spaces. Their availability can help create a sense of community by offering people an opportunity to come together for various reasons such as recreation, supporting community commercial efforts, viewing art displays, having concerts and dances, and even protesting. They might start out one way and then act as a conduit for something else. They may start as temporary spaces for one purpose and then evolve into permanent spaces with multiple purposes. This goes along with the notion that cities are not static entities. They evolve over time and, as such, urban public spaces evolve as well. Conversely, a lack of urban public spaces can cause conflict and a lack of trust in government.

The various chapters in the book clearly show that citizens and government may have differing views about urban public spaces. Citizens may feel that government economic development policies are forcing them to relocate to areas with little urban public spaces. As such, the citizens will need to be creative in developing their own public spaces. This is clearly evident in the case of favela residents. To these residents, government policies that worsen inequality heighten tensions between the government and the citizens.

This is a powerful book that offers readers unique insights into the creation, availability, and use of urban public spaces in Brazilian cities. It is a timely and significant addition to the research on urban public spaces. It is a well-researched and documented book that should be read by practitioners, faculty, students, and citizens interested in understanding of issues associated with urban public spaces.

San Diego, USA

Roger W. Caves
Professor Emeritus of City Planning
San Diego State University

Preface

Dear reader, this book presents a collection of contributions about the public space in different theoretical, conceptual, and methodological approaches. The styles are plural for multiple reasons, among them the questions that mobilize the writers as they read the public space in the contemporary city and the intellectual interlocutions they seek in each original writing context. Despite those differences, what prevails is an understanding about the relevance of analyzing the uses and appropriations of the city by social subjects and groups as they represent difference. The similarities between the chapters can also be noticed, and this is no coincidence. The authors understand the city as a place to share life experiences; as such, places of public use should be thought of and understood as concept and as social practice. Together, they suggest a scope of research centered on observation, description, and analysis of the city and of the political actions that enhance the public spaces as locus of the public sphere.

In opposition to the analysis that identifies the fall of the public man in the city, either due to violence, to urban models of self-enclosure in the form of private condominiums and shopping centers, or to limited mobility, we depart from the premise that the city is a public space created and lived in contradictory forms and conflicting processes. Hence, rather than seeing it as something in extinction or decay, we see the need to understand the complex constitutive dynamics of citizenship exercise. To build new ways of thinking, the public space is, therefore, to propose an understanding of the social, economic, and environmental conditions as a path to comprehend the struggles and demands for equity and dignity in the contemporary urban world.

This volume is about understanding, contextualizing, and carrying out critical analyses of the policies intended and/or implemented by the various public and private actors in urban public spaces, as well as the daily, or eventual, politics exercised by the organized civil society and by citizens. There are undoubtedly a myriad of actors to consider in their multiple roles and in their multiple space–temporal scales of events.

The intrinsic objective is to unfold an understanding of urban public spaces that not only recognizes, but also values the differences, inequalities, and the multiple forms of exclusion and segregation in the city. These are all factors of affirmation and/or denial of an urban citizenship imposed on the inhabitants of contemporary cities. The goal here is to ask ourselves about the social relations, institutions, concepts, and practices that contribute either to a city of utopia where all differences take place or to an accentuation of inequalities, segregation, and exclusion; it is, at last, to understand how each city brings these marks to its public spaces and how the latter conforms equalities/inequalities that produce conflict and/or cooperation.

The very concept of urban public spaces is open and under construction within the encounter of landscape studies and the social sciences, and based on physical, environmental, and social practices, aiming at a transdisciplinary wish.

In landscape studies, urban open spaces are defined as spaces free of buildings, all of them: backyards, gardens, streets, parks, forests, and urban beaches or empty spaces. They form a pervasive fabric, without which one cannot conceive the existence of cities; they are everywhere, more or less processed and appropriated by society. In the social sciences, public spaces take the character of meeting places, sites of individual and collective manifestations, struggle, conflict, and symbolic appropriations, while social practice intrinsically brings the public sphere realm—the very *vita activa*—that can only happen in public spaces. Physical and environmental practices, on the other hand, point out that urban open spaces systems can be fairly complex, given other juxtaposed systems, as circulation and infrastructure, and/or socioeconomic and cultural systems, ranging from land values to memories.

It is in the meeting point of such studies and practices that the concept emerges. In this volume, urban public spaces will mean those places of free access to the people, falling mostly in areas free of buildings, but not limited to them. They are the public sphere locus, where one can observe social interactions as well as the relationships between built and free elements, and between people, goods, and natural flows.

Despite the newly spread ideologies arguing that the informational era cancels distances, transforming the world into a "global village," urban public spaces will always constitute a concrete wholeness in which society develops itself; this development is indeed a socio-spatial process: There is no history or technique detached from concrete spaces. The public life sphere is realized in concrete spaces as it has been demonstrated worldwide by recent popular movements (such as the "Arab Spring" and the numerous "Occupy" protests).

A critical perspective also requires contextualization of UPS policies and practices under the capital and labor structure; rather, and using the ideas of Lefebvre, Harvey, and others, the struggle being waged in urban space is ultimately between capital in its various forms and labor. Large contractors, the financing system, multinational corporations, real estate speculators, and a whole myriad of capitalist actors have and exert direct and indirect interests in the city and, therefore, in urban public spaces. At the other side is the work force, which has in space not only its production means, but also its reproduction means, depending on itself to exert

Preface

many of their activities and survive. The third major component of the equation is the State, which, although theoretically could support any side, has consistently sided with capital.

In order to approach such a daring goal, some of the most important authors working with urban public spaces in Brazil were asked to share this endeavor with the editors. The book is divided into two complementary parts; the first one is about people: It discusses how humans express themselves in spacetime and how differences are dealt within the encounter, individually and/or collectively, more genuinely or more manipulated by the mainstream media and the corporate capital. While all four chapters, to different degrees, picture hegemonic situations pushing citizens to edgy positions, they all argue for a city of rights and envision a way out of the current settings through cultural expressions and appropriations of our urban public spaces. The second part is about space. And people. The three authors discuss how public policies toward urban public spaces can hinder or help appropriation, participation, and care for these spaces, either by promoting/restraining the encounter or by totally disregarding space as a basis for the right to the city.

It is from the perspective of the content and practice meetings that Lucia Capanema Alvares and Jorge Luiz Barbosa open the collection with the Chap. 1 "A Multidimensional Frame for Analyzing Urban Public Spaces Policies and Politics". They examine, under the logic of the appropriation of open public spaces, how citizens conform the city and how the city conforms the inequalities of places, possibilities, and behaviors. As an analytic tool, they offer a model with four local content dimensions—socioeconomic, sociocultural, socio-environmental, and political-administrative, and an external dimension. Through these dimensions, they explore how people relate to the chores of organizing daily life activities while engaging in conflicts that confront inequalities in their meeting places, and in the sites of individual and collective manifestations, of struggles, and of symbolic appropriations of public spaces; all of them process inherent to late capitalism now in vogue (led by large corporations, globalization, and the tourism industry). The authors seek to debate the concepts and social practices that contribute to a city of utopia, where all differences can be seen and dealt within public spaces and where free individuals can present themselves and engage in a *vita activa*.

Ana Fani Alessandri Carlos focuses on the presence of the body in the public space through sociocultural demonstrations. Chapter 2 "The Power of the Body in Public Space: The Urban as Deprivation of the Right to the City" analyzes the process of occupying streets and squares in Brazil as a means to reaffirm the public space; this process unfolds itself into struggles for the city, driven by the need to appropriate urban space in order to accomplish "another life", in which the deprivation of rights experienced by a significant part of society can be overcome. The diverse forms of occupation can be interpreted as the capacity to resist in daily life and in opposition to the hegemonic production and reproduction of capital.

Jorge Luiz Barbosa and Ilaina Damasceno Pereira, in their Chap. 3 "Reinventing Public Spaces: Politics of Oneself and Politics with Many Others", analyze public space as a set of multiple powers and acts of self-disclosure spatially situated that becomes real when social subjects seek political recognition. These powers are expressed in being, in living, in experiencing, in being-in-the-world, and in self-disclosing vis-à-vis the material and symbolical socio-spatial conditions of men and women in their diverse urban experiences. In the authors' arguments, political action gains the meaning of living in society, because subjects affirm their own differences in the possibility of the others' differences. They bring to surface a debate on public spaces where the presence of subjects in the city—with their struggles and demands for visibility, and their consequent differences affirmation—can be the guarantee unit of shared rights.

In Chap. 4 "A Cornered Democracy: The Echoes of the 2013 Demonstrations in Rio de Janeiro and the Architecture of a Crisis", Lia Beatriz Teixeira Torraca innovates in her critical assessment by considering the geopolitical dimension of public spaces, especially when discussing the violent conditions of exclusion of differences and of the different considered undesirable. In the visible and invisible walls that impede and separate social subjects, the relations of exception that fragment society and shatter cities are inscribed. The author also draws attention to the power of art and culture to overcome a democracy trapped by urban inequalities. The public spaces occupation movements in Brazilian cities, highlighting those that took place in July 2013 and their consequences to the country, demonstrated a crisis of the urban order and of reality construction by the mainstream media, bringing new political perspectives to the resignification of public spaces and of the political democracy itself.

Ângelo Serpa's, Chap. 5 "Leisure and Work in Contemporary Urban-metropolitan Space: Perspectives, Tendencies and Utopias", assumes the premise that the production of leisure spaces is dialectically and inseparably linked to the production of work spaces in the current context. The author seeks to characterize the economic, political, social, and cultural transformations of capital–work/work–leisure relationships in the contemporary world, starting from the consolidation of the industrial society and the modern era. He then presents a specific case study of working-class neighborhoods in Salvador and Feira de Santana which concerns the work and leisure of micro-entrepreneurs, small business owners, and consumers. Mainly based on the concepts of "creative idleness" and "telework", the discussion is amplified to think about the changes in capital–work/work–leisure relationships and their impacts on the public spaces of our cities and metropolises.

Eugênio Fernandes Queiroga, in his Chap. 6 "Open Public Spaces and the *vita activa*", dwells on the public relevance of open public spaces in Brazil's large- and midsized cities in contemporary settings. Distinguishing the concepts of public sphere, public spaces, and open spaces, the author presents a system of concepts that allows a better understanding of the theme, providing useful insights into the potentiality of multi-functional (and temporary) space-times that can be applied toward the development of public policies genuinely interested in improving the quality of urban spaces. Through examples across the country, he stands up for an urban planning paradigm that is more inclusive, more distributive, and more participatory.

Vera Regina Tângari presents, in the Chap. 7 "Open Space Systems in Rio de Janeiro: The Public and Private Spheres Reflected in the Urban Landscape", preliminary results of her team research project on the role of open spaces in the urban landscapes. These spaces have an important role in the shaping the urban morphology, in the urban fabric layout, and in the definition of centralities that focus around and along the circulation and permanence systems: streets, avenues, squares, and plazas. On the other hand, they are determined by the contradictions of a process of occupation that expresses the high concentration of income and resources in some sectors and areas, and the omission of public governance in others. These contradictions result in an imbalance in the supply, accessibility, and appropriation of open spaces by the population, directly affecting the quality of the physical environment and the conditions of sociability that can occur in open spaces, and more specifically those belonging to the public sphere.

Cristóvão Fernandes Duarte, Chap. 8 "The "Reinvention" of the City Through the Favelas" addresses the importance of popular territories in the cultural production and the vitality of Rio de Janeiro. The author indicates that while favelas started as temporary and precarious settlements they became, in less than a century, large popular neighborhoods, endowed with great cultural visibility and showing a clear critical consciousness regarding the segregationist and excluding processes associated with their origin. The author discusses the resistance demonstrated in favelas, and their accepted leading role in the production and reproduction of spaces for the poor in the city of Rio de Janeiro. According to the author, the solution is to recognize that favelas legitimately represent the "re-invention" of the city itself, understood as a place for gathering and exchanging among different individuals.

If in the 1970s self-help and auto-construction meant opening the door to governments' withdrawal from investing in slums, in postindustrial times, marked by worldwide neoliberal policies of accumulation by dispossession, as Harvey has put it in several occasions, and the withdrawal of most international aid (including that coming from foreign NGOs), Duarte sees now a different, bottom-up solidarity that actually turns slums into livable and viable places. Opposing the forced evictions paradigm, the slums that are able to stay put provide a living example of the social potential of conflicts by proposing a dialogue with the formal city and by gaining support from various sectors. In so doing, they recreate spaces of political and economic life in the city and re-establish the public sphere. Not relinquishing their fair share of public investments, the oldest and therefore better-established slums are telling us that the Third World poor do not need advice or direction, but respect for and confidence on their way of being in the world.

In the last chapter, testing the proposed model as a privileged analytical tool, Lucia Capanema Alvares tries to unveil how the content chapters are knitted together in real life and how Brazilian urban public spaces stage global phenomena in their own Third Worldliness, sometimes mimicking them, sometimes surprising us all.

As "the insights to be gained from the standpoint of the global South have increasing relevance for radical planning in the era of global neoliberalism" (Miraftab 2009, p. 33), we, together with the authors, hope all readers will enjoy this trip to urban public spaces in Brazil.

Niterói, Brazil

Lucia Capanema Alvares
Jorge Luiz Barbosa

Contents

**1   A Multidimensional Frame for Analyzing Urban
Public Spaces Policies and Politics** 1
Lucia Capanema Alvares and Jorge Luiz Barbosa

Part I   About People

**2   The Power of the Body in Public Space: The Urban
as a Deprivation of the Right to the City** 27
Ana Fani Alessandri Carlos

**3   Reinventing Public Spaces: Politics of Oneself
and Politics with Many Others** 43
Jorge Luiz Barbosa and Ilaina Damasceno Pereira

**4   A Cornered Democracy: The Echoes of the 2013 Demonstrations
in Rio de Janeiro and the Architecture of a Crisis** 57
Lia Beatriz Teixeira Torraca

**5   Leisure and Work in Contemporary Urban-Metropolitan
Space: Perspectives, Tendencies, and Utopias** 73
Ângelo Serpa

Part II   About Spaces. And People

6   Open Public Spaces and the *Vita Activa* 91
Eugênio Fernandes Queiroga

**7   Open Space Systems in Rio de Janeiro: The Public
and Private Spheres Reflected in the Urban Landscape** 109
Vera Regina Tângari

8 The "Reinvention" of the City Through the Favelas 127
Cristóvão Fernandes Duarte

**9 In the Guise of a (Global) Comprehension: A Multidimensional
Analysis of Urban Public Spaces Through Selected Authors** 141
Lucia Capanema Alvares

Index 159

Contributors

Jorge Luiz Barbosa Programa de Pós Graduação em Geografia, Universidade Federal Fluminense, Niterói, Rio de Janeiro, Brazil

Lucia Capanema Alvares Programa de Pós-Gradução em Arquitetura e Urbanismo, Universidade Federal Fluminense, Niterói, Rio de Janeiro, Brazil

Ana Fani Alessandri Carlos Department of Geography, University of São Paulo, São Paulo, Brazil

Cristóvão Fernandes Duarte FAU-UFRJ, Rio de Janeiro, Brazil

Ilaina Damasceno Pereira Afro-Brazilian Studies Center, Rio de Janeiro State University, Rio de Janeiro, Brazil

Eugênio Fernandes Queiroga Faculty of Architecture and Urbanism, University of São Paulo (FAU-USP), São Paulo, Brazil

Ângelo Serpa Department of Geography, Institute of Geosciences, Federal University of Bahia, Salvador, Brazil

Lia Beatriz Teixeira Torraca Federal University of Rio de Janeiro, Rio de Janeiro, Brazil

Vera Regina Tângari Federal University of Rio de Janeiro, Rio de Janeiro, Brazil

Chapter 1
A Multidimensional Frame for Analyzing Urban Public Spaces Policies and Politics

Lucia Capanema Alvares and Jorge Luiz Barbosa

Abstract This introductory chapter proposes a new reading of everyday politics as exercised by citizens in their Urban Public Spaces appropriations in face of governmental policies for such spaces. It takes on a model with four non-exhaustive dimensions—socio-environmental, socioeconomic, sociocultural, and political–administrative—and their relations with the external dimension, considering their interscalar and intersectorial character. Departing from Milton Santos' new geography, it also considers other contributions, especially regarding place and identity, the public sphere, and capital, labor and their forms and fractions. The concept of Urban Public Spaces (UPS) is itself still under construction, being structured within landscape studies, social sciences, environmental and land use practices, social practice, and a wishful trans-disciplinarity. In this chapter, the operating UPS concept that emerges means spaces accessible to the people that lie, most times, in open areas free of buildings, but are not restricted to them; they will be more environmentally relevant when forested, economically relevant when superposing infrastructure or located at prime real estate plots, culturally relevant when associated to citizens' identities, and socially relevant when they help to create or maintain a public sphere.

Keywords Urban Public Spaces · Public policies · Hegemonic city
Popular appropriations · Urban identities

L. Capanema Alvares (✉)
Programa de Pós-Gradução em Arquitetura e Urbanismo,
Universidade Federal Fluminense, Niterói, Rio de Janeiro, Brazil
e-mail: luciacapanema@gmail.com

J. L. Barbosa
Programa de Pós Graduação em Geografia,
Universidade Federal Fluminense, Niterói, Rio de Janeiro, Brazil
e-mail: jorgebarbosa@vm.uff.br

© Springer International Publishing AG, part of Springer Nature 2018
L. Capanema Alvares and J. L. Barbosa (eds.), *Urban Public Spaces*,
The Urban Book Series, https://doi.org/10.1007/978-3-319-74253-3_1

1.1 Introduction

Urban studies seem to miss a multidisciplinary method to analyze Urban Public Spaces as places of *vita activa*, as producers and products of the difference society, as some authors have been demanding and others have been trying to reach. Within this perspective, this book analyzes, under the logic of Urban Public Spaces (UPS) policies and appropriations, how public policies conform the city and how the latter conforms unequal places, imaginaries, behaviors, identities, conflicts, and segregations. These questions, while regarding UPS more specifically, also seem to echo Ouriques's (1998) and Miraftab's (2009) urge toward considering Urban Planning vis-à-vis invited and invented spaces of insurgent citizenship. A decade ago, Irazábal, introducing her "Ordinary Place/Extraordinary Events" book, stated that "no study [had] explicitly scrutinize[d] the development of democracy and citizenship in physical urban space" (2008, p. 2) and sought to "interrogate the fate of the link between public spaces and the construction of citizenship and democracy in this era" (2008, p. 3). In so doing, her book does not focus, however, on the everyday uses of UPS; rather, it looks at how key urban spaces—like Mexico City's Zócalo and other central squares in Latin America—house political activism: the presented chapters "focus particularly on the moments in which 'cracks' in the lifeworld have given way to transitions from making life processes to making history episodes—on extraordinary events in otherwise ordinary places" (pp. 3–4). As in Irazábal, the current book looks at Urban Public Spaces from a multidisciplinary stand point, but here we otherwise seek to offer an analytical tool to understand how the everyday politics of difference are shaped by institutional policies and how they shape concrete spaces, answering, in a complementary way, her plead for more "literally 'grounded' perspective[s]" (p. 1).

This study's theoretical framework adopts as one of its main principles Milton Santos' new geography. In so doing, it starts with understanding space as a whole, as a social instance, at the same level of economic, cultural, ideological, and political instances; as such, social dialectic is not only established in space, but is undertaken with space.

Phenomenological relations, true geographies of perception, are established in places, a perception that permeates the individual's cultural universe, his or her psychological and historical conditions, and the image construction of place imposed on the self. The framework also considers other contributions, especially regarding the place scale and in search of symbolic meanings, for they do not lead to losing sight of the dialectic and systemic perspective proposed by Milton Santos' theory of space. In addition, the adoption of a critical frame requires the contextualization of political practices in Urban Public Spaces from the perspective of capital and labor in its various forms and fractions.

This volume proposes a fresh reading of Urban Public Spaces representations, imaginaries, appropriations, and conflicts taking as its basis a model of four non-exhaustive dimensions and their relations with external aspects: a socioeconomic dimension, a sociocultural dimension, a socio-environmental dimension, and a political–administrative dimension. Unlike the analytical model presented here, of a positive nature and in that sense particularly discussing how public spaces have been shaped by different actors in the Third World, the comprehensive model proposed by Carmona et al. (2003) focused on Urban Design and had a normative goal; as such, it depicted how different aspects of real life influence the design process itself and how this latter can conform quality public spaces. Whereas the authors saw the urban processes as shaped by local, global, market, and regulatory aspects, which influenced the "substantive dimension[s] of urban design—'morphological', 'perceptual', 'social', 'visual', 'functional' and 'temporal'" (p. vii), in the present volume, we dive into the local urban context to investigate how the different dimensions of real life can be systematically understood and thought of, aiming at questioning, and hopefully subsidizing efforts toward structural change, the very aspects Carmona et al. rightfully "accept[…] as givens" in "individual urban design projects" (p. 36). Despite the different focus and aims, their book also discusses the external and internal governmental, social, economic, cultural, and environmental impacts on urban design.

Urban Public Spaces will be more environmentally relevant when they are vegetated or represent residual spaces, economically when they overlap infrastructure lines or can be considered of real state interest, culturally when conforming citizens identities, socially when they conform the public sphere, and administratively when they become the subject of plans and projects. But since public spaces can only exist in a dialectical relation with society, all thematic dimensions are herein called "socio". Most aspects can and do overlap in Urban Public Spaces. The external factors come to complete the equation, as all that happens at the local scale is subject to and in tune with the world.

1.2 Urban Public Spaces (UPS), Everyday Life, Conflicts, and the Public Sphere

This work understands public spaces as commonly used places like streets, squares, parks, public buildings, and all collectively appropriated spaces where public sphere actions are carried out, whether publicly or privately owned. They may even exist without a physical and tangible support, considering that public institutions—like judicial courts—and cyber spaces are now important, collectively appropriated, spaces for citizen manifestation.

The concept of **Urban Public Spaces**, notwithstanding, is still open and structured within landscape studies, the social sciences, physical and environmental practices, social practice, and a transdisciplinary wish. In landscape studies, urban free spaces are defined by Magnoli (1982) as the spaces free of buildings; all of them: backyards, public or private gardens, streets, avenues, squares, parks, rivers, forests, wetlands and urban beaches, or unnoticed urban voids; such spaces may also form a pervasive fabric without which one cannot conceive the existence of cities; they are everywhere, more or less processed and appropriated by society; they usually represent the highest percentage of city land, even among the most populous metropolises (Magnoli 1982).

In the social sciences, public spaces take the character of meeting places, sites of individual and collective manifestations, struggle, conflict, and symbolic appropriations. Social practice intrinsically brings the public sphere issue—the very *vita activa's* sphere that can only happen in public spaces.

Geophysical and social and environmental practices, on the other hand, point out that urban free spaces systems are fairly complex, given their interrelation with other systems that can be juxtaposed on them (circulation, urban drainage, environmental comfort, leisure, imaginaries and memories, conservation and environmental improvement, to cite a few).

It is in the meeting point of such studies and practices that the concept—open and under construction—emerges in this study: In a first approaching attempt, Urban Public Spaces (UPS) will mean those tangible spaces of free access to the people, mostly falling in spaces free of buildings, but not limited to them. They are the spaces where one can observe the relationships between built and free elements, between people and goods flows, and the social interactions.

Human life manifests itself in space on an everyday basis, revealing each society's conflicts and contradictions at different historical moments. The production of the quotidian in postmodernity reproduces an urban way of life that highlights mass culture and globalization forces (Carlos 1996) by standardizing procedures and practices that tend to homogenize individuals' behaviors and demands. According to Heller (2004) the duality between each person's particular individuality and the very generality of being human—present in every individual and characteristic of human beings—is currently exacerbated, overwhelmingly demonstrated in the production of UPS, as they show the coexistence, not always peaceful, between public and private spheres, between the contemporary and the traditional, between individuals, groups and the collective, as previously discussed, among others, by Mauss (1979) and Vernant (1990) concerning societies in general.

The possibilities of transgressing apparently consolidated models are exposed in daily life through small and spotted expressions that reveal individualities and/or recover traditional practices common to different social groups; moreover, it is in everyday life that people create new forms of sociability, conflicting or not, generating places of encounter and unforeseen appropriations that renovate UPS. Places are spaces of resistance, where different rationalities—the systemic (more institutionalized, structured, and hierarchical rationality) and the communicative (most popular, free, and horizontal)—meet and get in conflict (Habermas 1981). As such, they are spaces of state and citizen action, spaces of industrial capitalist production/reproduction maintenance, and also territories of the new, of conflict.

Bauman (2007) describes Urban Public Spaces (UPS) considering the dichotomy generated by fear and its counterpart, the social possibilities of encounter with the other: "a meeting of strangers is a locus of endemic and incurable unpredictability. Not suppressing the differences, in fact [UPS] celebrate them"

(Bauman 2007, p. 102–103). While the modernist ambition proposed the annihilation and the leveling of differences, without ever accomplishing such a feat, the postmodern trend deepens and "calcifies" them, through separation and mutual estrangement.

One century before Bauman, Simmel (1903) already highlighted the importance of social interactions, i.e., of spaces that require individuals to form a unit-antagonism society; the philosopher understood sociability as self-regulation of the individual in their dealings with others. In Simmel, human life manifests itself in daily life when conflicts and contradictions of each society in its different historical moments are revealed. Conflict, the elementary form of socialization between individuals, is an inseparable part of the unity-antagonism dialectic, leading to the sociological significance of the subject in cooperation with the other. For the author, man brings hostility and friendliness to others as forms of transcendence. Social struggles would be like deed or legal conflicts, when personality and fights may be set apart and the process can result in purely objective decisions, even if people are subjectively entangled. Personal aggravation within the conflict decreases without a reduction in the conflict intensity; rather, the conflict becomes more conscious, focused, and proactive, because individuals find themselves fighting for a vast cause, beyond personal concerns. Under a Durkheimian or organic perspective, conflict could be considered as "antibiotic" or defense mechanism of social cohesion, a social disease inhibitor; although conflicts may seem an affront to order and incitement to chaos, these phenomena would act as to avoid chaos and the dismantling of the social system.

Whether offering the dialectical antagonism-unity construction possibility as referred in Simmel (1903), the Durkheim's social cohesion (1979), or Bauman's (2007) exposure to difference that makes fears disappear, conflicts seem to propose an antithetical dialogic and constructive role facing the dominant structures most commonly represented by the state.

The city shows its slits, its longings through multiple ways and conflicts. It is in daily manifestations of conflicts that our societies create and recreate the public sphere and also in which the social dynamics of urban open spaces can be found and read. Yet, according to Katz (1984), it is in the collective manifestation that the subject tests his/her acquired skills and capacity for critical and continued action toward his/her inclusion in decision-making processes, where the subject exercises direct democracy and political action. Moreover, it is the collective subject that gives life to participatory budgeting, to urban councils and neighborhood associations, among others forms of citizen participation.

The public sphere life is, in Hannah Arendt's words (1991), the very sphere of the *vita activa*, of political actions understood in a broad sense, involving cultural production and citizen construction as fundamental parts of our own civilization histories. In the public sphere differences and divergences have, or could have had, the possibility to present themselves as discourses, paving the way for their recognition and inclusion in the political game; public interest and public good, socially constituted by unequal power relations, would then have to face collective interests conflicts.

It is worth noting that the public good notion cannot be misunderstood as the common good notion; the first one is the result of a dialectic political construction which takes place in the public sphere, while the second was produced as a ruling classes' ideology. The public sphere constitutes itself inside a freedom realm, within the cultural instance; the private sphere, on the contrary, relates itself primarily to a needs list, and as such to an economic instance.

1.3 Capital, Labor, the State and Their Fractions at Diverse Scales—A Critical Perspective

The struggles fought in urban spaces are, ultimately, struggles between capital in its various forms and labor. Powerful developers, the financing system, multinational corporations, real estate speculators, and a whole set of capitalist actors have and exert direct and indirect interests in the city and therefore in UPS. At the other end of the spectrum is labor (in its various fractions), which depends on space not only as its production means, but also as its means of reproduction, depending on it to realize most of its activities and its survival means (reminding ourselves that urban structure and infrastructure elements are physically overlaid with UPS in most cases). The third major component in the equation is the state, which could theoretically approach either side, but has systematically sided with capital.

Ribeiro (2006) cites Milton Santos to remind us there is an alternative system being conceived out in the streets, in opaque spaces, in new communication forms, facing the dominant projects for our large cities. The proposition consists of a system based on alternative rationalities that can be identified, for example, in the new space ownership forms developed by social movements and diverse labor fractions. In order to understand quotidian and place, the author argues for a greater involvement with the complexity of social life, either due to its interscale character or to its hybridism. According to Torres Ribeiro, one cannot understand the underlying social fabrics through models uprooted from their social practices, for they are deeply connected to their labor and capital fractions.

Fernández and Brandão (2010) argue that scales, given their heuristic capacity, are essential elements of multidimensional analysis that may account for the complexity of socio-spatial transformation processes; both shaping and shaped by social struggles' and routines' processes, scales would not be reifiable instances, since they result from unstable social constructions complementary to the concepts of network, territory, and place within the complex spatial dynamics configuration. In Swyngedouw, "[t]he scaling of everyday life is expressed in bodily, community, urban, regional, national, supranational and global configurations" (1997 p. 144); according to Vainer (2002, p. 28), "since cities do not exist loose in the air, the domination and accumulation forms that characterize them cannot be perceived without a regard at their regional, national and increasingly international articulations". Also in Swyngedouw (2010), the interescalar perspective is more sensitive to globalization processes spatiality, to the centrality of political dominance and to the shifting and changing power relationships and geometries. Along the same Marxist critical theory line taken up by Harvey, the author points out that as capital expansion always is the dominant factor, capital will sometimes side with nation states, sometimes subordinate the latter siding with local instances and their networks, in a dynamic process that gives rise to a set of new spatial scales, constituting what he calls glocalization. These processes often take place and/or involve UPS.

1.4 Urban Life: Symbolic and Identity Aspects, Imaginaries, and Bourdieu's Habitus

When describing UPS based on the social possibilities of encountering the other, Bauman (2007) elects "difference" as a key city feature; UPS are places of encounter with the different, of individual identity construction; as much as in Simmel (1903), the sociological significance of the subject would take place in the public sphere. If on the one hand public spaces lead to feelings of repulse, on the other hand, the attraction they exert over individuals may work to overcome or neutralize such repulsion:

> Public spaces are places where strangers meet and therefore are condensations and encapsulations of all city life defining features. It is in public spaces that urban life, with everything that separates it from other forms of human co-habiting, reaches its fullest expression, together with its most characteristic joys and sorrows, premonitions and hopes. [...] Fear and insecurity are relieved by the preservation of differences and of the ability to move freely around the city. [...] It is the exposure to difference that, with time, becomes the main factor of happy cohabitation, making the urban roots of fear disappear. (Bauman 2007, pp. 102–103)

UPS perception according to subjective processes is diverse and individual, as it comes from relational experiences between the city and the subject. Space identification and appropriation begin with the perception of physical, environmental, social, and cultural elements, hence developing a personal experience with the human psychological, emotional, and sensorial elements that can create place recognition and individual bonds, imaginaries, and memories (Lynch 1999).

Serpa (2013) sees two different processes of UPS apprehension and appropriation: On one level is the everyday perception, through which individuals have a basic reading of the city in which they move; on another level there would be a more experienced and elaborated reading, leading to the subject's cognition of places and to place appropriation according to his/her possibilities in the encounter with the different, through an identitarian process.

Identification with UPS seems to be also influenced by membership to social class fractions, when subjects share social behaviors, habits, values, and social position. In building his field concept, Bourdieu proposes the habitus as a "system of the social order constitutive differences" (Bourdieu 1987) in which the ownership of financial and cultural capital will dictate structural hierarchies of actions and symbolisms; in this case, objective possibilities conform imaginaries and subjective expectations, the latter conditioned by the subject's perceptions of his/her own social position. According to the author (2001), personal identity would come from each individual's complex and multiple representations/imaginaries of reality, given his/her position in the urban habitus, which is made of the following symbolic power criteria: (1) hierarchies, authorities, and relative positions of the subject; (2) material properties and capital; (3) prestige, reputation, and fame; (4) ethnic and religious affiliation, dwelling location; (6) principles of social division; (7) present and future collectivities. Bourdieu also seems to understand habitus as a result of class trajectories, as he makes a clear distinction between middle classes' habitus—based on freedom of consumption—and working classes' habitus—based on consumption needs. Bourdieu also sees the possibility of social production of individualities under the existing social structures logic.

Coming from a Gramscian perspective, Serpa speculates that the subordinated classes' fractions "produce subdominant or alternative cultures when facing ruling classes hegemonic strategies of cultural production" (Serpa 2013, p. 148). In so doing the subordinated classes would be exercising a desire to subvert Bourdieu's habitus: Fractions of the subordinate classes would be ultimately challenging power structures through different space appropriations, as Miraftab has also noted when looking at the Cape Town anti-eviction campaign prior to the 2010 Soccer World Cup: "In Gramscian terms, they launch a war of positions" (Miraftab 2009, p. 33). Finally, according to Serpa, different class fractions' spaces of representation (spaces "of complex cognitive structures" resulting from both the everyday perception and an elaborate environmental cognition) "contain and also express the struggles and conflicts [of such fractions] for the domination of these places conception's strategies" (Serpa 2013, p. 176). Thus, in Serpa, the conception of popular spaces reveals the underlying conflict between dominated class fractions' and hegemonic imaginaries.

1.5 Towards a Multidisciplinary Analytical Model

One of this books endeavors is to systematize the most important, as well as the presently vivid discussions and influences, on and from Urban Public Spaces, starting with the disciplinary considerations in environmental studies, in the social sciences, and in the architectural/landscape field, passing through everyday life, conflicts, and the public sphere matters, together with spatial symbolic and identitarian aspects, and taking a critical perspective to understand the dissimilar powers of capital, labor, state and their fractions at diverse scales.

Ultimately trying to understand the form–content or the social reality in human space—albeit provisional and always renewed—as Santos demands, this study proposes, as a first instrument, the systematization of the above-mentioned aspects

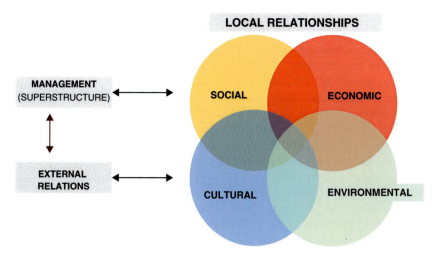

Fig. 1.1 Local relationships model

at the local relations scale. It builds on the model designed by Tourism scholars (Beni 2002; Boullón 2005), to whom places are necessarily structured by local social, economic, environmental, and cultural relations; these relations are permeable and overlay each other to some extent, forming an inseparable whole. The set of local relations would be in constant exchange with the external environment and under the influence of a superstructure given by the political–administrative dimension (Fig. 1.1).

Departing from this model, we seek a rereading of relations manifested in UPS anchored in four non-exhaustive dimensions and their relationships to external influences (in their current most relevant aspects) and administrative aspects. Considering the understanding of form–content, we assume that all local dimensions must be formulated within the social sphere; hence, they can be reduced to the socioeconomic, the sociocultural, and the socio-environmental dimensions, plus the political–administrative dimension (considering structural issues). Adding the external influences on local issues, interscalarity processes emerge as fundamental (as the scale theories here contextualized demand), while the processes inherent to late capitalism now in vogue (large corporations, globalization, and the tourism industry) seem to complete a parsimonious equation.

1.5.1 The Socioeconomic Dimension

This dimension concerns, in the first place, aspects of land use and real estate speculation that structure capital flows and investments in urban areas, and are largely structured by transport axes—the true urban expansion axis. Transportation structures are the major determinants of mobility and porosity which, in their turn, will determine most of our urban inequalities. The reproduction of capital via real estate speculation and/or major transportation projects is also the cause of most violations of human rights cases intrinsic to the urban environment (housing, freedom of movement, and information).

According to Harvey (1982), capitalism needs a mass of resources continuously built for its expansion. The construction of spaces is itself contradictory, tense, and conflicting: on the one side there are the direct and indirect agents of land appropriation along with the capital connected to construction works and the capital in general; on the other is labor, to whom the built environment is both a good for consumption and a medium of reproduction. While free public spaces are for people consumption, their increasing privatization represents the spatialization of socioeconomic interests and conflicts. Needless to remind, the expansion of the built environment corresponds to the retraction of the natural environment, creating a clear conflict between socioeconomic (in itself questionable and unequal) and socio-environmental valuations.

The (re)construction of the environment occurs either through changes in land uses or through structural and imaginal changes, both continuously creating real estate surplus value in the cities and their peripheries. The restructuration of the production systems since the last quarter of the twentieth century has accentuated social inequalities, making way to a series of changes in the urbanization processes. Dialectically, urban changes and socioeconomic inequalities have broadened the social and environmental impacts in the territory. As a worldwide process, this construction/reconstruction processes strongly affected the global South urbanization, contributing, among other things, to the expansion of a disperse urbanization (Reis 2006), to the formation of megalopolitan structures and to the dissemination of fortified enclaves (Caldeira 1997).

As Bauman points out, the restructuration of the territory (which management has already become a burden to governing structures) and the businesses they generate have become ephemeral, and the capital now seeks "deterritorializable" instruments for its own actualization, such as mega-events and tourist structures, that can be built and unbuilt within months. This process establishes a fast and worldwide game of "real estate bubbles", as if it was a typhoon that quickly lands in and takes-off from different territories turning the land ownership logic around in cities that can best serve the capital interests. What remains, after the mega-events, are great socioeconomic, environmental, and sociocultural losses for the hosting populations (as can be seen in modern Olympic cases); as the processes include numerous forced evictions for urban renewal projects and humongous local debts, local residents disapprove of them and manifest themselves against the events.

The opening of new transport routes entails and complements the strategic plans of spotted land valorization: New corridors enable the colonization of free and/or green public spaces in the city's fringes, as well as they require the removal of population groups along their margins in numbers well superior to the strictly needed. In both cases, they make room for land speculation. Carefully designed, these corridors—particularly in the global South metropolises—link large facilities to each other and/or to marketable areas, making their way through established and vernacular neighborhoods that house the poor. In such cases they become "park-avenues" with wide border lanes for future use. New corridors thus create a socioeconomic surplus in their places of origin and destination and in their paths—a surplus that is evidently taken by real estate speculation together with the construction industry and international corporations. The process devalues socioculturally and socio-environmentally the cities, which lose their identity and environmental quality by promoting the pasteurization of the urban imagery and an inadequate use of preservation areas in their fringes.

Transportation networks are also the major determinant of physical mobility within cities and the porosity of its various parts. While physical and informational mobilities have been widely studied, porosity—rate and distribution of environmentally qualified open spaces available and accessible (including through public transportation) to varying flows of people, activities, and demonstrations from different backgrounds (Secchi 2014)—is a new and extremely important concept in studies related to inequality in cities, to the space capital (Soja 2010) and to the right to the city (Lefebvre 1991).

Objects of UN human rights resolutions, accessibility and mobility as well as the freedom to come and go in Urban Public Spaces, have been threatened by major transportation projects and their planned collaterals: "social cleansing", forced evictions, and reappropriation of urban land targeted for new developments. The consequent peripherization of communities away from their networks of economic, social, and cultural insertion, usually relocated in neighborhoods that lack public services such as health centers and schools, only deepens inequalities, deranges daily lives and turns assimilation into society almost impossible. Transportation planning itself may contribute to low mobility rates if it favors certain corridors designed to serve privileged segments of the population, denying adequate transportation modes to the majority, especially in their home-work-home routes and for those fractions of labor that depend on built spaces, infrastructures and facilities to produce and reproduce capital.

Land use and real estate, together with transportation planning through new expansion axes, are inexorably linked to promoting inequality in the above-mentioned cases and when their structural, imaginal, and legal changes cause the privatization or otherwise repress the use of Urban Public Spaces. In so doing, the state and its partners reverse urban mobility priorities and violate a number of human rights.

1.5.2 The Sociocultural Dimension

This dimension relates primarily to past and present sociabilities and identities in the public sphere, given the appropriations and uses of UPS. As it relates to the social structures in the city, it can be investigated according to its role in the industrial capitalism—by providing leisure and amenities to workers—and under its symbolic and identity sharing character (present in landscapes, squares, parks, and main axis and urban central spaces, when they are appropriate for public use) that complement the practical aspects of the city and becomes the glue, the unity that establishes collective memories.

Besides being keys to understanding the mobilized collectives and sociabilities established by different groups and classes of each locality, conflicts and appropriations also point to the structural, concrete and segregated/segregating functions found in urban spaces; moreover, they lead us to the fundamental question of the public sphere epistemological dialectic, in which the proper formation of public spaces is cause and, systematically, fruit of citizen action. It is in the manifestation of everyday conflicts and of space appropriations that the social dynamics through which our societies create and recreate the public sphere can be found and read, as the latter are the locus of the popular cries in the city. Macedo, Robba and Queiroga cite Arendt (1991) to rescue the Aristotelian concept of *vita activa* and its relationship to Urban Public Spaces. In Arendt, the public life sphere is the sphere of the *vita activa*—broad political action that concurs fundamentally for the construction of citizenship and civilizations.

Places are spaces of resistance, where the different rationales, systemic and communicational, meet and confront (Habermas 1981). Thus, in addition to spaces of capitalist industrial production/reproduction maintenance, they are territories of the new, of conflict. In Bourdieu, "it is the relationship between the distribution of agents and the distribution of goods in space that sets the value of different regions of the reified social space" (Bourdieu 1997, p. 161). Hence the interest in the various dialectic relations set by the various segments, or fractions of society, with different urban places, particularly with UPS, which are privileged places of urban action, of shaping the public sphere. As previously shown by Brazilian studies on urban conflicts (see Capanema Alvares et al. 2012), while the dwelling units of those who engage in "right to the city conflicts" are mostly located in places with difficult access to goods and services, the goods located in the rioting spots and regions—more central—add market and symbolic value to the "reified social space", advancing segregation and a priori setting apart subjects that only meet in the conflict manifestations.

Both favelas' and the new Occupy movements that propose a series of UPS appropriations and express themselves through conflicts in spaces, really offer themselves as the possible dialectical construction based on Simmel's antagonism-unit, as the Durkheimian social cohesion, and/or as the possible disappearance of fear by exposure to the different in Bauman. The mobilization and the reunion of social movements reach, beyond a convergence of interests, an ideological and evaluative scope in which all participants perceive themselves as members of a group that represents greater ideals and objectives than the individual yearnings. As Simmel proposes, personal aggravation can be reduced and the social struggle character is intensified; conflict becomes more conscious, focused and proactive. The wide, supra-personal, cause also reduces the possibility of dissolution and desertion of the group. Through association and articulation, publicity of their struggles, manifestation of conflicts, judicial and legislative suits, and through planning initiatives, the new Occupy movements in UPS have managed to refresh and re-signify the popular struggle against hegemonic interests (Szolucha 2017); particularly in the Global South, these struggles have had an anti-colonial character (Miraftab 2009, p. 44). They provide a living example of the social potential of conflicts by proposing the dialogue and by gaining support from various sectors. In so doing, they also recreate spaces of political life in the city and reestablish the public sphere.

From a sociocultural point of view and in a critical perspective, leisure and amenities fruition are necessities of capital (as shall be discussed by Serpa in this volume). Ouriques (2005), taking from Marx, Adorno, Horkheimer, Benjamin, Mandel, Thompson, Lefebvre, Castel, Arendt, Mészáros, Morin, Debord and Kripendorf among others, makes a genealogy of leisure and demonstrates how, since the mid XIXth century, the masses leisure is shaped as to expropriate them from their free time, to repress traditional manifestations, to promote well-behaved fruition, obeying the religious order and principles and, above all, fomenting capitalist production. Leisure differs from idleness because it does not suppress labor; rather, it complements labor with "doing" something in the free time and presupposes it:

> Amusement under late capitalism is the prolongation of work. It is sought after as an escape from the mechanized work process, and to recruit strength in order to be able to cope with it again. But at the same time mechanization has such power over a man's leisure and happiness, and so profoundly determines the manufacture of amusement goods, that his experiences are inevitably after-images of the work process itself. (Adorno and Horkheimer 1947; London 1997, p. 137)

According to Krippendorf (1989) the leisure industry was created in the postwar contemporaneity; by consuming in his/her leisure time, the laborer is reproducing the capital expansion logic. In Arendt (1991), the more time the laborer has, the more eager his/her consumption will be, in line with the thinking of Adorno and Horkheimer. For Morin (1990), leisure is the possibility of inclusion in the "mass consumption society" and the enjoyment of amenities for realization of leisure in free public spaces has as its principle the consumption of landscapes, which become commodities. In Lefebvre, the environment is a consumer product for recreation: "nature becomes an exchange value and a commodity: it is bought and sold, [...] becoming the leisure ghetto" (Lefebvre 1991, p. 116).

Thus, paraphrasing Ouriques (2005), "[leisure] should be studied in the context of progressive commodification of all aspects of life, of control and appropriation of all possible spaces [by] capital." The question that remains is to what extent and under what conditions, Urban Public Spaces can also serve as non-commodified spaces for the realization of idleness and *vita activa* and to what extent they are already subdued to the logic of capital. As we shall see later, tourism and the attraction of mega-events and megaprojects have been radically commodifying UPS to create the city spectacle, which configures the conflict between the interests of globalized capital and the use of leisure spaces for the existence, the cultural rescue, and the identity sharing of the various social groups cohabiting in the city.

Symbolic and identity aspects incorporate some of the most important functions of landscapes, squares, parks, and of major urban axes:

> It is men who attribute a value to the stones and all men, not only archaeologists and literati. We must therefore take into account, not the value itself, but the attribution of value, no matter who does it and to what end it is done. In fact, the value of [a space] is that which is assigned to it by the whole [...] community. It is therefore necessary to dispense with what seems obvious and see how, in all cultural levels, assigning value to visual data occurs. (Argan 1995, p. 228.)

As Castro (2002) postulates, landscape goes beyond the real-world offered by nature; the author indicates that landscape incorporates the real-world to become culture through representation, as Argan argues. According to her, representation, as a cognitive structure internalized by individuals, "constitutes an indispensable guide of specific behaviors' regulations" (Castro 2002, p. 123). In an ideological perspective and aligning us to Milton Santos' thoughts, for whom the dialectics of the space happens between space itself and society, this reasoning leads us back to the problem of the conformation of individuals by public spaces, and of spaces by individuals: Lacoste, Cosgrove, and also Barque, propose that landscape is manipulated by conscious and dominant, hegemonic, actors; "[as landscape is] impregnated with symbolic aesthetic value, it also becomes a political problem, since both itself and its value are socially produced" (Castro 2002, p. 124).

The same critical reasoning leads us to the relationship between symbolic value, social production of space and the culture of the spectacle (Debord 2011). There is an intangible consumption of the spectacle landscape, which can "be appropriated without being a property and consumed without being spent" (Ouriques 1998, p. 79). The new state communications policies adopt the "urbanism-spectacle" in designing and constructing new landscapes—impregnated with symbolic aesthetic value—in order to become fundamental attractions within the select group of cities that may be targets of the international capital. Regarding tourism, a theme that will still be discussed under the external dimension, Rodrigues highlights how leisure places are commodified and have their symbolic relations altered: "the spaces of, and for, tourism constitute a complex commodity since they are in and of themselves a commodity. It is the natural environment, or the social production, incorporated into another commodity, but as part of the same consumption/production of the space" (Rodrigues 1996, p. 56). According to the author, other commodities that use the very physical landscape of the commodified spaces as their base to become real and concrete, modify them, provoking changes in the social and symbolic relations among residents, places and forms of leisure (the "London Eye" would be a good example of this phenomenon along the Thames riverbank). As already pointed out by Souza and Capanema Alvares (2012), the way in which new spaces are presented communicates their character; they are not representative of the local cultures, but spectacular landmarks of the city that is renewed. The consumption of these commodified spectacle spaces ends up conforming a new *modus vivendi* in the cities, as they become part of the citizens imaginary, and citizens anxiously wait and receive with curiosity the innovations, in an apparent consensual approval. "We think that myth-images are a domesticated language to "hail" urban interventions, to seduce citizens, contrary to the stimulation of any action that could effectively build citizenship" (Sanchez 1999, p. 124). At the other end of the spectrum, individuals and collectives seek to express themselves in counter-hegemonic movements, as previously discussed based on the work of Arendt, and then Torres Ribeiro's and Serpa's.

The sociocultural conflict established at the symbolic level can be located within the rationalities perspective proposed by Habermas: on the one hand, civil society —bearer of a communicative rationality—and on the other, government and capital, both operating with an instrumental rationality, respectively constituting and deconstructing the public sphere. The instrumental rationality tries—through a technocratic ideology—to prevent the problematization of power by the communicational rationality in all processes, conflicts, consensuses and absences: political decisions that affect the community are transformed into technical problems, solved by a few experts, leading to the depoliticization of the masses and the penetration of the state in the social and economic spheres. Public space, an instance in which opinions are formed, becomes the privileged stage of the symbolic dispute: "ideologies reach their goal of preventing the discursive thematization, excluding from public communication themes and motivations considered inconvenient to the power system [by preventing] the birth of problematized discourses" (Habermas 1980, p. 21).

1.5.3 The Socio-environmental Dimension

Under this dimension, one must minimally consider the green areas, the infrastructure lines that overlay/underlay them endangering or enhancing the quality of urban life, and the residual spaces, vegetated or not (which are often located in fringe belts), given their potential. Basic actions of preservation, conservation, restoration, and/or intervention, as well as toward making these areas adequate to the promotion of social and environmental justice, should be considered, since environmental issues are not restricted to natural and rural areas and should be promoted at all times and places in order to reduce social pressure on the natural environment. Green areas have great environmental value because they not only allow the reproduction and circulation of fauna and flora in the urban environment but also improve local microclimates, in addition to their potential for landscape ecology; on the other hand, they have socioeconomic valuation insofar as they constitute positive externalities that can be used for real estate speculation.

Urban vegetated grounds, in general, balance the hydraulic underground and on-the-ground flows, hold soil movements, absorb noise and, as a filter of water and atmospheric pollution, provide microclimates conducive to habitability, places of conviviality, and iconographic value. The associated water resources also help to drain residues and waste, value the urban scene, and offer its banks as walkways, bike paths, and spaces for sports and leisure (Magalhães 2004). Categorizing UPS according to their environmental qualities, we can enlist: (1) the parks, which are public spaces specifically intended for mass recreation, able to incorporate conservation policies, and with a morphological structure independent from the surroundings; among its functions are active recreation, social integration, and public health. They also integrate ecological systems and can protect species at risk (Macedo and Sakata 2002). (2) The squares, which are urban public and open spaces intended for the recreation and the conviviality of the population, accessible to citizens and free of vehicles. Their functions, in central areas, are to soften the climate, improve air quality and sunstroke, promote pedestrian meeting, leisure and rest, and articulate motor-free circulation; in residential areas, they are passive and active leisure areas, providing children's recreation, leisure, and cultural coexistence among different people (Robba and Macedo 2002). (3) The street, especially in metropolises and big cities, conform a fundamental space for vehicles and the implantation of infrastructure, which lends it economic value; on the other hand, it traditionally is the locus of the *vita activa*, with great sociocultural value, especially in the peripheries where there is no sufficient and adequate equipment for the poor's coexistence and leisure, or in city centers, where conflicts are demonstrated, as discussed by Capanema Alvares et al. (2012). And finally, (4) the residual spaces which are composed of drainage lines, tracks bordering the waterways, right-of-way lines, great engineering works residual spaces, etc., which have some economic value while potentially usable and socio-environmental value as they may present the necessary characteristics to become green corridors. The tracks bordering waterways, similarly to parks, have sociocultural valuation. There also are the Fringe Belts, gaps in the growth of a residential or commercial area that appear as fringes temporarily unoccupied on the urban periphery. They are residual and fragmented spaces forming a whole structured by axes or lines of fixation that can be rivers, slopes, hills, and even social barriers such as shantytowns and slums. They have socio-environmental and socioeconomic value, given their systemic and real estate potential (Conzen 2001). All residual spaces seem to be potentially the target of land conflict, as they are often occupied by subnormal housing in the global South cities—denoting the quantitative and qualitative housing deficits.

Although they have no environmental value in the strict sense, built public spaces often have aesthetic value per se and/or in the composition of the urban environment. In addition to sometimes take the character of architectural icons they are also traditional locus of the *vita activa* of great sociocultural value—see, for example, areas such as the Colosseum and the Roman Forum in the history of that civilization.

The preservation—long-term protection of the species; the recovery—return to an undegenerated condition; the restoration—approximation to the original condition; or the intervention—according to new proposals for public open spaces, will always imply political choices and conflicts of interest. According to, and expanding from, Macedo (1999), among the topics and questions for a contextualized choice among these actions one has to consider: (1) the functional characteristics and susceptibilities due to anthropic action in the geomorphological support —soil, subsoil, drainage, aquifers; (2) the climatic characteristics and possibilities of adaptation of living communities; (3) the characteristics of the ecosystems, their value in the social context, and their potential to society; (4) social and cultural values assigned to the site and their implications for the survival of the species and forms of social behavior; (5) the patterns of human occupation—size, scaling, trends, and expansion possibilities; (6) the processing degree of the existing environmental infrastructure and the convenience of its transformation in the short and medium term, and its potential for utilization and survival within any kind of use and exploitation process; (7) the landscape morphological structure components within the different forms of occupation: residential, industrial, commercial, infrastructural, leisure, etc.; (8) The uniqueness factors such as the landscape value per se or the unity of an architecture landscape whole; (9) bearing legislation and projects; and (10) the stakeholders, mainly the ability of communities and institutions to get involved and to participate.

Socio-environmental justice envisions the need to work the environmental issue not only in terms of conservation/recovery/restoration/intervention, but also in terms of distribution and justice; this is the necessary conceptualization to approach and frame popular struggles for social and human rights, for collective quality of life, and for environmental sustainability into one dynamic (Moura 2010). Here the environmental, social, and ethical dimensions of sustainability and development, often dissociated in discourse and practice, are integrated. The achievement of social and environmental justice has, therefore, a substantive dimension, related to the distribution of benefits, risks, and encumbrances, as well as a procedural dimension, related to the participation of the affected population in the decisions regarding environmental policies that accrue on them (Nusdeo 2006). Social pressures on the natural environment are exercised by the entire population, but in the global South, the populations that live in more precarious conditions are the ones most obliged to use natural resources and dispose of their waste in unsustainable forms, since they are not commonly served by networks of water supply, energy, and collection of liquid and solid waste, and to occupy residual spaces of environmental relevance that are left out of the formal real estate market. Often these movements and needs are tolerated or ignored by the state, which sees irregular and informal housing as a cheap way to solve the housing problem. Also the peripheral populations that do not have leisure facilities will press with more intensity the natural landscapes, the areas of legal conservation and natural resources in general. At the other extreme there are the high-income groups, although fewer in number, who appropriate environmental positive externalities, like being in the midst of native forests, along clear streams and or enjoying unique sights.

1.5.4 The Political–Administrative Dimension

This dimension basically regards government structures and public policies relating to the three above-mentioned dimensions; The political–administrative frame in Brazilian cities is dictated by the 1988 Federal Constitution since its adoption and regulated by the City Statute since 2001; together they have enacted what has been called the municipal-lead constitution, very decentralized in terms of duties and taxes. But a number of duties and competences overlap in the constitution, especially concerning urban matters, creating a rather confusing legal scenario (Capanema Alvares 1992). In relation to UPS, important courses of action seem to be city entrepreneuring—widely adopted model which focuses on neoliberal management of the city as if it were a private, for profit, enterprise with market interests—resourcing to hygienists policies to "clean" the most visible and marketable spaces, and city marketing, which uses UPS to promote exclusionary policies and the administrators' images.

The overlapping with the socioeconomic and the sociocultural dimensions is clear, since both policies appear as economic and cultural forces imposed by an instrumental rationality. For Habermas,

> the submission of political decisions to a minority [...] means at the same time the depletion of practical activity in all instances of society (political, social and even economic) and the penetration of the State (the political instance) in the two others (social and economic instances), which are increasingly submitted to management. (Habermas 1980, p. 16)

Local governments are investing increasing volumes of resources in the recreation of urban images and in development projects that may become attractive to investors and tourists. Multinational entrepreneurs and managers want to see their brands associated with the modern image of the city or country in which they will be located, requiring large investments from administrations (Kotler et al. 1996). According to Ribeiro (2006), the economy imposes itself on politics and the market onto the state. By acquiring a business character, the city follows the market rules, losing its dimension of territory of democracy exercising (Arantes et al. 2000).

Neoliberal local administrations thus understand citizen participation, social movements, and manifested conflicts in UPS as threats to private interests that may be more convenient and rewarding for public authorities; as it is worth keeping the central city aesthetically pleasing through the relocation of poor communities to the urban fringes, the state, represented by local and state administrations, quietly acts through court injunctions, misled urban design projects, geological risk skewed reports, withdrawal of public services, threats and the like to promote low key evictions and "clean" landscapes and public spaces without harming its political image (Capanema Alvares et al. 2013). Afterward, it uses city marketing strategies to bargain the consequent vacant areas with the big capital.

City marketing (also discussed under the external dimension section) finds, in the head politicians of neoliberal local and/or regional administrations, its big allies, as the promotion of cities corresponds to the promotion of its leaders. Political marketing joins city marketing to create public images of public men and women and catapult them to higher levels of ambition and power.

Local governments adopt a series of other actions and intervention strategies in the territory and in the landscapes—from the insertion of architectural icons and requalification of the urban structure and infrastructure (which brings in its bulge the chosen territories for "cleansing") to the construction of strategic partnerships, the attraction of mega-events and the formulation of legal or paralegal instruments, as synthesized by Bessa and Capanema Alvares (2014). Often these instruments constitute ad hoc, exceptional legislation; as ANCOP reminds us, they are "decrees, provisory measures […] and an infinite tangle of sub-legislation pieces such as ordinances and resolutions that build an institutional exception" (ANCOP 2012, p. 10).

An act of exception is the act that aims to legalize disrespects to the law, that is, to consolidate or authorize exceptional measures making them the norm. The exception, in and of itself, becomes institutional when a network of national, state, and/or municipal executive acts "regulate" deregulating, giving legal form to what cannot have legality (Agamben 2004), in order to abolish individual and collective rights and to create different groups of citizens. "The law suppresses the law to the extent that certain guarantees and individual and collective rights are abolished by law, exposing citizens to the imminent risk of violent and legally justified death" (Duarte 2007, w/p). Institutional exceptions have been enacted in UPS in a number of situations, as discussed by ANCOP (2012): In the case of giving homeless cold showers while they sleep in the nights of Belo Horizonte, capital city of the state of Minas Gerais, in the case of "picking" homeless against their will off of noble areas and transporting them to poor and far away suburbs in Rio and, as shown by Capanema Alvares (2014), in the case of confiscating merchandise and arresting street vendors in Rio de Janeiro, through the municipal program "Shock of Order."

1.5.5 The External Dimension

Among the most relevant aspects of the current urban picture are the interscale characteristics of phenomena such as capital flows and public policies, all largely submitted to global capital and world corporations; business-led, event-led, and other types of tourism, understood as the material counterpart to volatile monetary flows, have become a primary mean for rotating resources and investments in the global game.

As already mentioned, multinational entrepreneurs and managers want to bring their organizations into places with at least apparent quality of life and of the environment; local governments, anxious to attract international capital, adopt strategic planning, spending large sums in the recreation of the urban image and in the construction of attractive projects for investors and tourists (Kotler et al. 1996; Beni 2002). According to Hazan (2003), in contemporary times architectural icons stand out not only for their monumentality and scale but also for the fact that they are designed by world-renowned architects who, due to their international recognition, begin the city marketing and globalizing processes in the designing phase of the projects. Arantes states that icons have been used as "merchandise publicity-forms, with the new economic supremacy sponsoring the well-designed symbols that celebrate its triumph" (Arantes 2000, p. 226). Thus,

> Capital in person is now the major producer of new urban spaces, which it fully requalifies. This way, public spaces and the physiognomy of cities have been determined or dictated to a large extent by business strategies with state support and endorsement. (Arantes 2000, p. 226)

Urban open spaces resulting from this designing model become hyperspaces—with no history, no identity, no local character—spaces which only frame equipment and facilities in the city spectacle (Cruz 2002; Debord 2011); instead of building the public sphere and strengthening identities, they enhance mass consumption.

The 1990s intensification of the globalization phenomenon corresponded to a bigger competitiveness between cities, as well as to the intensification of unequal and concentrated income levels; the experiences of popular survival were swept away from the public spaces, which needed to be "clean" and "orderly" (Ribeiro 2006). Then again, counter-hegemonic movements come to occupy major squares and UPS inspired by the Wall Street and the Arab Spring movements in the twenty-first century.

Fernández and Brandão (2010) propose a critical analysis of regional development departing from social classes' fractions at different scales; they state that it is necessary to understand, based on the capitalist logic within its own historical and concrete expressions in space-time, both the history and the diverse trajectory paths undertaken by the development discourse. There is a need to treat spatial scales dynamically when thinking about structural processes. In order to do so, they also see the need to adopt labor division as a social and basic explanatory category to approach endogenous and exogenous factors as determinants of socioeconomic-political-historical-theoretical institutional and territorial processes. In space-time, the processes of intersectoriality, interregionality, and interurbanity reveal mediations and concrete forms with which social reproduction in space is manifested.

Intersectoriality represents the interactions and economic ramifications in their links and networks regarding production, consumption, distribution, and circulation of goods. Interregionality represents "structural coherences in terms of production, distribution, exchange and consumption" (Harvey 2005, p. 89) converging, during a given period, to the production of regionalities and their interconnections; the concept is fundamental for understanding integration processes of the markets and inter- and intra-regional competitiveness. Finally, interurbanity represents the formation of an urban sociability at different layers and levels, as a privileged locus of social reproduction of material life, considering that the urban network is present in different scales and in agrarian and urban structures.

Tourism is the fastest growing industry in the world (according to the World Tourism Organization, in 2013 international tourism generated US$1.4 trillion in export earnings) and stands today as a key strategy for the attraction of population and economic flows; the occupation and consumption of areas of historical and cultural interest in tourism have been considered as objectives of excellence by local, regional, and national governments. Holder (in Ruschmann 1997) argues that tourism begins with small and elitist tourist flows in places of unparalleled attractiveness evolving to mass tourism, with degradation of the destination and loss of attractiveness, bringing economic decline, unplanned land occupation, abandoned equipment, and a culturally uprooted population. As an outside influence, tourism has become an important factor in the characterization and appropriation of public open spaces: If on the one hand it allows the citizen to enjoy the infrastructure and the quality of life generated for the tourist, on the other hand the disaggregation of local identities and of the social fabric, the peripherization of communities, stress, and consumerism will certainly have deleterious effects. Under the sociocultural dimension, the clash between external cultures and local culture can culminate in a valorization of identities, as it can, more commonly, corrupt values, pasteurize, or spectacularize the cultural aspects present in UPS.

In an effort toward systematizing the most important issues currently concerning UPS representations, imaginaries, appropriations, and conflicts, we propose the consideration of the aspects herein discussed and summarized in Table 1.1. As the main objective of the model is to offer a transdisciplinary framework with which researchers may systemize UPS issues and widen their dialogues with academia and practitioners, we shall, as a second step, come back to it in the last chapter and see how well it works as a tool to analyze and bridge the arguments made by our authors.

Before we move on to the content chapters, we would like to argue, echoing Milton Santos, that it is necessary to understand that society acts on materiality and

Table 1.1 Set of local relations and aspects to consider

Socioeconomic dimension
Land use and real estate speculation—capital expansion, segregation
Transport axes, expansion axes—mobility and porosity
Housing and work—human rights
Sociocultural dimension
Appropriations, uses, expressions of the self—sociability, public sphere, *vita activa*
Leisure, labor, and amenities—different class fractions
Landscape and identity—symbolic aspects and segregation
Spectacle, conflicts, and social movements—spatial distribution
Socioenvironmental dimension
Green areas, infrastructural lines, and residual spaces—potentialities
Preservation, conservation, restoration, and intervention
Environmental social justice
Pressures on the natural environment
Political–administrative dimension
Cities entrepreneurship
Hygienists policies
Political and city marketing
External dimension
Interscalarities, glocalization
Global capital and large corporations hegemony
Tourism

Source The author's

on itself concomitantly: "Dialectics [...] is not between society and landscape [as a visible accumulation of the past of man], but between society and space. And vice versa" (Santos 1996, p. 110).

What is intended is a comprehension of the urban that not only recognizes, but also values the differences, the inequalities, the multiple forms of exclusion and segregation in the city as factors of the affirmation and/or the denial of a citizen urbanity to which the inhabitants of contemporary cities are subject to. The objective here is to unveil the social mechanisms, institutions, concepts, and practices that contribute to a city of Utopia where all differences take place, or to the accentuation of inequalities, segregation and exclusion; it is to understand how each city brings its marks to its public spaces and how public spaces create conflict-producing inequalities or free individuals to present themselves and engage in a *vita activa*.

References

Adorno TW, Horkheimer M (1947) Dialectic of Enlightenment. London (1997)

Agamben G (2004) Estado de Exceção. Boitempo, São Paulo

ANCOP—Articulação Nacional dos Comitês Populares da Copa (2012) Megaeventos e Violações de Direitos Humanos no Brasil. Dossiê da Articulação Nacional dos Comitês Populares da Copa. ANCOP, Rio de Janeiro

Arantes O (2000) O Lugar da arquitetura depois dos modernos. Edusp, São Paulo

Arantes O, Vainer C, Maricato E (2000) A cidade do pensamento único: desmanchando consensos. Vozes, Petrópolis

Arendt H (1991) A condição humana (5th edn). Forense Universitária, Rio de Janeiro

Argan GC (1995) Arte e crítica de arte (2nd ed). Editorial Estampa, Lisboa

Bauman Z (2007) Vida líquida. Jorge Zahar, Rio de Janeiro

Beni MC (2002) Análise Estrutural do Turismo (7th edn). Senac, São Paulo

Bessa ASM, Capanema Alvares L (2014) A Construção do Turismo: Megaeventos e outras estratégias de venda das cidades. C/Arte, Belo Horizonte

Boullón RC (2005) Os municípios turísticos. Edus, Bauru

Bourdieu P (1987) Choses Dites. Éd. de Minuit, Paris

Bourdieu P (1997) A Miséria do Mundo. Ed. Vozes, Petrópolis, RJ

Bourdieu P (2001) O Poder simbólico. Bertrand Brasil, Rio de Janeiro

Caldeira TPR (1997) Enclaves Fortificados: a Nova Segregação Urbana. Estudos Cebrap, São Paulo, vol 47, pp 155–176

Capanema Alvares L (1992) Brazilian metropolises: A planning challenge. Memphis State University (master thesis)

Capanema Alvares L, Bessa ASM, Guimaraes AC, Rodrigues RF, Tolentino S (2012) Mouvements sociaux à Belo Horizonte: conflit et associativité comme forme de récréation de la sphère publique dans le domaine de l'habitation (2006–2010) In: Métropoles des Amériques en mutation. Presses de l'Université du Québec, Montreal

Capanema Alvares L, Medeiros MGP, Paiva LR (2013) O paradigma neoliberal e os megaeventos: como a Copa e as Olimpíadas servem à produção de cidades mais excludentes no Brasil. In: XV Encontro Nacional da Associação Nacional de Pós Graduação em Planejamento Urbano, 2013, Recife. Anais do XV Encontro Nacional da Associação Nacional de Pós Graduação em Planejamento Urbano, vol 01

Capanema Alvares L (2014) Espaços livres públicos (ELP): uma análise multidimensional de apropriações e identidades. In Espaço e Cultura, n. 36 July–December

Carlos AFA (1996) O Lugar no/do Mundo. Hucitec, São Paulo

Carmona M et al (2003) Public places—urban spaces: the dimensions of urban design. Architectural Press, Burlington

Castro IE (2002) Paisagem e turismo. De estética, nostalgia e política. In: Yázigi E (org) Turismo e Paisagem. Contexto, São Paulo

Conzen MP (2001) The study of urban form in the United States. In: Urban Morphology, vol 5 (1)

Cruz RCA (2002) As paisagens artificiais criadas pelo Turismo. In: Yázigi E (org) Turismo e Paisagem. Contexto, São Paulo

Debord G (2011) A sociedade do espetáculo. Contraponto, Rio de Janerio

Duarte A (2007) Sobre a biopolítica: de Foucault ao século XXI. Cinética, Ensaios Críticos, 2007. Available in http://www.revistacinetica.com.br/cep/andre_duarte.pdf. Accessed on 03 May 2015

Durkheim E (1979) Da divisão do trabalho social. Abril Cultural, São Paulo

Fernández VR, Brandão CA (2010) Escalas y políticas del desarrollo regional. Davilla y Miño, Buenos Aires

Habermas J (1981) The theory of communicative action. Lifeworld and system: a critique of funcionalist reason (vol 2). Beacon Press

Harvey D (1982) O trabalho, o capital e o conflito de classes em torno do ambiente construído nas sociedades capitalistas avançadas. In Espaço & Debates. São Paulo, n° 6, Jun/Sept, pp 6–35

Harvey D (2005) A produção capitalista do espaço. Anablume, São Paulo

Hazan VM (2003) O papel dos ícones da contemporaneidade na revitalização dos grandes centros urbanos. In: Arquitextos. Available from: www.vitruvius.com.br/revistas/browse/arquitextos. Accessed 18 June 2006

Heller A (2004) O Cotidiano e a História. Paz e Terra, São Paulo

Irazábal C (2008) Ordinary place/extraordinary events: democracy, citizenship and public space in Latin America. Routledge, New York

Katz R (1984) Empowerment and synergy: expanding the community's healing resources. In: Rappaport J, Hess R (eds) Studies in empowerment: steps toward understanding and action. Hayworth Press, New York

Kotler P, Haider D, Rein I (1996) Marketing Público. Makron Books, São Paulo

Kripendorf J (1989) Sociologia do Turismo: para uma nova compreensão do lazer e das viagens. Civilização Brasileira, Rio de Janeiro

Lefebvre H (1991) O direito à cidade. Moraes, São Paulo

Lynch K (1999) A imagem da cidade (2ª ed). Martins Fontes, São Paulo

Mauss M (1904–1905) Essai sur les variations saisonnières des sociétés eskimo. Étude de morphologie sociales. l'Année Sociologique (tome IX)

Macedo SS (1999) Quadro do Paisagismo no Brasil. EDUSP/Coleção Quapá, São Paulo

Macedo SS, Sakata FG (2002) Parques Urbanos no Brasil. Edusp, Imesp, São Paulo

Magalhães LMS (2004) Funções e Estrutura da Cobertura Arbórea Urbana. EDUR, Rio de Janeiro

Magnoli MMEM (1982) Espaços livres e urbanização: uma introdução a aspectos da paisagem metropolitana. Faculdade de Arquitetura e Urbanismo, USP, São Paulo

Miraftab F (2009) Insurgent planning: situating radical planning in the global south. Plan Theory 8:32–50

Morin E (1990) Cultura de massas no século XX—neurose. Forense Universitária, Rio de Janeiro

Mauss M (1979) Seasonal variations of the eskimo. A Study in Social Morphology. Oxon, Routledge

Moura DV (2010) Justiça ambiental: um instrumento de cidadania. In Qualit@s Revista Eletrônica, Vol 9, No 1

Nusdeo AMO (2006) Justiça ambiental. In: Dicionário de Justiça Ambiental. Escola Superior do Ministério Público da União. Available from: http://escola.mpu.mp.br

Ouriques HR (1998) Turismo em Florianópolis: uma crítica à "indústria pós moderna". UFSC, Florianópolis

Ouriques HR (2005) A produção do turismo: fetichismo e dependência. Alínea, Campinas

Reis NG (2006) Notas sobre urbanização dispersa e novas formas de tecido urbano. Via das Artes, São Paulo

Ribeiro ACT (2006) A cidade neoliberal: crise societária e caminhos da ação. Observatorio Social de América Latina 21:23–32

Robba F, Macedo SS (2002) Praças Brasileiras. Coleção Quapá. EDUSP, São Paulo

Rodrigues AM (1996) A produção e o consumo do espaço para o turismo: a problemática ambiental. In: Yázigi E, Carlos AFA, Cruz RCA (orgs) Turismo: espaço, paisagem e cultura. Editora Hucitec, São Paulo, pp 55–62

Rouanet PS, Freitag B (1980) Habermas. In: Rouanet SP, Freitag B (orgs) Habermas: Sociologia. Ática, São Paulo, pp 9–23

Ruschmann D (1997) Turismo e planejamento sustentável. Papirus Editora, Campinas, SP

Sanchez F (1999) Políticas urbanas em renovação: uma leitura dos modelos emergentes. Revista Brasileira de estudos Urbanos e Regionais, Campinas, n. 1, pp 115–132

Santos M (1996) A natureza do espaço: Técnica e Tempo, Razão e Emoção. Hucitec, São Paulo

Secchi B (2014) La città dei ricchi e la città dei poveri. Editori Laterza, Bari

Serpa AP (2013) O espaço público na cidade contemporânea. Contexto, São Paulo

Simmel G (1903) The sociology of conflict. Am J Soc 9:490–525. Available from: www.brocku.ca/MeadProject/Simmel/Simmel_1904a.html. Accessed: 15 may 2014

Soja EW (2010) Seeking spatial justice. University of Minnesota Press, Minneapolis

Souza RF, Capanema Alvares L (2012) A lógica da especulação. O Globo. Rio de Janeiro, pp 07–07

Swyngedouw E (1997) Neither global nor local: 'glocalization' and the politics of scale. In: Cox (ed) Spaces of globalization: reasserting the power of the local. Guilford Press, New York, pp 137–166

Swyngedouw E (2010) Globalización o glocalización? Redes, territorios y reescalonamientos. In: Fernández VR, Brandão CA. Escalas y políticas del desarrollo regional. Davilla y Miño, Buenos Aires

Szolucha A (2017) Real democracy in the occupy movement: no stable ground. Routledge Studies in Radical History and Politics. London, Routleddge

Vainer CB (2002) As escalas do poder e o poder das escalas: o que pode o poder local? In Planejamento e Território: ensaios sobre a desigualdade. Cadernos IPPUR/UFRJ, Rio de Janeiro, ano XVI, n. 01, Jan–Jul. pp 13–32

Vernant JP (1990) Mito e Pensamento entre os gregos. Paz e Terra, Rio de Janeiro

Author Biographies

Lucia Capanema Alvares holds a degree in Architecture and Urban Planning from the Federal University of Minas Gerais (1988), a master's degree in City and Regional Planning—Memphis State University (1992), a Ph.D. in Regional Planning—University of Illinois at Urbana Champaign (1999), and has a post-doc in Urban and Regional Planning at the Institute for Urban and Regional Planning and Research, IPPUR-UFRJ (2011). Currently an associate professor at the Graduate Program in Architecture and Urban Planning of the Fluminense Federal University, she has co-authored the book *A Construção do Turismo: Megaeventos e outras estratégias de venda das cidades* (2014), alongside authoring numerous chapters and papers both nationally and internationally.

Jorge Luiz Barbosa has a Master's degree in Geography (UFRJ), a Ph.D. in Human Geography from the University of São Paulo, and a post-doc in Human Geography from the University of Barcelona (Spain). Associate Professor at the Department of Geography at the Fluminense Federal University and Director of the Favelas Observatory of Rio de Janeiro, he is the author and organizer of several books, chapters and papers, in particular: *Favelas: Alegria e Dor da Cidade* (2005); *O Novo carioca* (2012); *Paisagens crepusculares da ficção científica: elegia das utopias urbanas do modernismo* (2013); *Solos Culturais* (2013).

Part I
About People

Chapter 2
The Power of the Body in Public Space: The Urban as a Deprivation of the Right to the City

Ana Fani Alessandri Carlos

Abstract This chapter is based on the hypothesis that space production is a central element to understand the modern world, both from the viewpoint of the cumulative process of capital realization and of the reproduction of social life, insofar as production of space is the condition, medium, and product of social reproduction in its totality. The transformations of the city today are marked by the contradiction between what is necessary to the reproduction of capital and what are the needs/desires of a society that makes the city a place of conflicts, since urban praxis continually restores the inequality resulting from the process of valuation that creates the city as segregation. In Brazil today, as in various parts of the world, we live a time of demonstrations in streets and squares (as a reaffirmation of the public space). They have been unfolding in struggles for the city fueled by the need to appropriate urban space for the accomplishment of another life (which is basically urban) where the deprivation lived by a significant part of society is overcome. Manifestations will be understood as the form with which the residues present in daily life struggle against that which imposes itself as hegemonic and is opposed to the realization of urban life.

Keywords Right to the city · Body · Urban space · Public space

2.1 Introduction

The topic explored in this paper is imposed by today's reality and reflects the need to understand the contradictions of urban space, typically experienced in the form of conflict, and the tensions generated in everyday life by a process of unequal urbanization. The body provides a starting point to reflect on the protests that swept through Brazil in 2013 and that reached their peak in the 'Days of June,' leading to the occupation of streets and avenues in many Brazilian cities by a sizeable portion

---

A. F. A. Carlos (✉)
Department of Geography, University of São Paulo, São Paulo, Brazil
e-mail: anafanic@usp.br

© Springer International Publishing AG, part of Springer Nature 2018
L. Capanema Alvares and J. L. Barbosa (eds.), *Urban Public Spaces*,
The Urban Book Series, https://doi.org/10.1007/978-3-319-74253-3_2

of society. By questioning the present urban reality, these actions indicated the need, albeit still in incipient form, for a project to build 'another society'. No such project is possible, though, without first understanding the foundations of the present society. This is our task.

The argument developed here sets out from the hypothesis that the production of space is central to comprehending the modern world—both from the viewpoint of the process of capital accumulation and the state's investment in creating the bases needed for reproduction of capitalist social relations, and from the viewpoint of producing an urban life. This is why the conflicts in cities take the form of a struggle for space, as an exercise of citizenship, revealing a fractured practice, and not just a discourse.

We live in a constantly changing society that points to the continual metamorphosis of urban space and, consequently, to the transformations of urban life in its global character—of profoundly unequal sociospatial practices marked by segregation. Ultimately, we can be said to live in a terrorist society—one defined not by the weapons in the hands of guerrillas, though, but by the redefining of the components of a standardized, naturalized life, reduced to the world of commodities with their signs and language. A society also defined by the oppression stemming from new forms of accumulation, now under the sway of the financial world and sustained by the state. This reality is further entrenched by the loss of the urban reference points that mark and sustain life, the field where identity is constructed. This loss coincides with the construction of individualism based around a urbanity itself centered on mass hedonism, as Horkheimer (1976) highlighted, where every citizen fights for him or herself, as Lipovetsky (1991) wrote, or where every citizen is someone else's bottle of Coca-Cola, as Paquot (1990) ironically asserted.

The construction of this new individualism, which contributes to an ever-deepening atomization of the social world, is created and developed at the heart of the consumer society, pursued from a new perspective: the promotion of a hedonism that legitimizes the most intimate physical pleasures and satisfactions.

Mass culture plays a fundamental role in this process, reinforcing the social pressures placed on individuals and imposing models of collective imitation, crushing the human spirit. Today, instead of building conventions, customs and beliefs, the focus is on cultivating emptiness and abstract identity. Rather than an identity created practically by human activities, fluid images of a programmed social world apparently devoid of subjects are imposed on society as a whole, a place where people recognize each other in terms of their market demands.

2.2 In the First Place, the Body

Humans relate to space through their bodies and this mediation is necessary for us to relate to the world and to others—a relation with the spacetimes defined in everyday life. In this way, the body moves through different scales, linking them together. First the house (where subjects start to build their family relations and

2 The Power of the Body in Public Space … 29

early references); then the streets, where they begin to relate with others, establishing webs of identity. Next the neighborhood, which becomes increasingly important as a relational space containing various spacetimes mediated by social exchange (of all kinds). Finally, interconnecting these diverse levels, the body becomes immersed in a multifaceted and multiple city, filled with simultaneous activities and images that seduce and orient us. A juxtaposition of life moments and spatial scales is delineated. Our relations become spatially ever more expansive, connecting us to wider spaces associated with continuous and discontinuous time lines. This set of relations involves and concretizes the individual as a real presence, initially through embodiment[1] in the spacetimes of life. The scale of everyday life is achieved concretely, therefore, through spatiotemporal relations. In other words, the way in which my life unfolds reveals a spatial dimension—physics tells us that each body occupies a location in space—which poses us the question of how the realization of life can be premised on this condition. From this basis, it can be discerned that all our relations occur in locations in space, marked by specific times. The city establishes a presence as a place for appropriating life through the body and all its senses.

Our existence is embodied because we act through the body. It affords us access to the world, which for Perec (1974) is the vital and immediate link perceived by society as a source and support of every culture.[2] Taking the body as a starting point sheds light on the city's materiality. This is because social relations assume a real existence in the form of a concrete spatial existence. In other words, social relations occur in a determined place without which they would be unable to become concrete, and take place in a fixed or determined time that sets the duration of the activity. Space and time thus emerge as inseparable dimensions through human action, revealing an activity realized as a mode of appropriation. A social and historical product emergent over the course of the civilization process—as a moment in the process of the constitution of the humanity of humankind, which envisages an objective world that only exists and has meaning on the basis of and through the subject—that appropriates places for living out human life. Along these lines, the city's meaning is attributed through use, i.e., through modes of appropriation aimed at producing human life (and all that this implies). As a place, the city is reproduced as a reference point and, in this sense, a locus for the constitution of an identity that sustains memory, revealing the human condition.

---

[1] "The place of the body marks the boundary between self and other in a social as much as physical sense and involves the construction of a 'personal space' in addition to a literally defined physiological space" (Smith 2000: 145).

[2] "[…] extension, the external, what is external to us, what we move about in the midst of, our ambient milieu, the space around us […]. Not so much those infinite spaces, but spaces that are much closer to hand, in principle anyway: towns, for example, or the countryside, or the corridors of the Paris Métro, or a public park […] We live in space, in these spaces, these towns, this countryside, these corridors, these parks. That seems obvious to us. […] In short, spaces have multiplied, been broken up and have diversified. There are spaces today of every kind and every size, for every use and every function. To live is to pass from one space to another, while doing your very best not to bump yourself" (Perec 1974: 13–14).

The use of places for living life through the body corresponds to the human activity of producing a real and concrete world, restricting and imprinting 'traces' of civilization with its historical components. Based on the body, therefore, but surpassing the body and the materiality of space, it encompasses culture, as well as a form of awareness of the activities carried out. Consequently, the city, as social practice, is a spacetime of the activity that establishes human life in its objectivity/subjectivity, seeing it not as a simple field of experience, but as a social product, a place for human life, a condition for reproduction, involving two distinct levels: the individual (revealed most fully in the act of dwelling) and the collective (the realization of society) as history. By focusing on the practice in its multiple aspects, therefore, thought flows toward the concrete and real urban practice with all the contradictions this implies.

For Bernard (1995), it is pointless to justify a reflection on the body, since life itself imposes it on a daily basis: it is through the body that we feel, desire, act, create, and express ourselves. Hence, the body performs a social mediating function (Bernard 1995: 7). But rather than develop an ontology of the embodiment of our existence as a kind of ultimate refuge of our individuality, I wish to foreground the body's social dimension within a dialectic of passivity and the consequent subversion that the body unleashes through the appropriation of public space. Passivity here is associated with the private appropriation of the wealth generated by society, which sets limits on the free access to the spacetimes of everyday life, submitting subjects to representations that they themselves sustain in order to legitimize this inequality. That is, the way in which the body traverses the spacetimes in which everyday life unfolds, includes, at its core, the potential to reject them as they are spacetimes permeated by standardized forms of access, which are the outcome of the many divisions that mark life in differentiated spaces subject to the coercion exerted by the private ownership of urban land. The body, then, is open to lived experiences at the heart of a practice that is sociospatial in nature, suggesting an analysis that runs counter to its justification as sexual exploitation or the mere display of commodities (as demonstrated by the advertising billboards that dominate the contemporary urban landscape, masterfully analyzed by Drummond (2001) in his poem "Eu, etiqueta" (*I, label*)).

The body is thus an expression of the social relations founded on a subordination/subversion dialectic.

2.3 Public Space

An analysis of the body entails an analysis of the relation between private space (the house and family) and public spaces, including the central role played by the encounter in the constitution of an identity and a collective history within the public sphere. This relation demarcates the inside and the outside—places inhabited by

Hestia and Hermes,[3] respectively—but, above all, it is through this inside/outside dialectic that the meaning of the city and relational life itself is realized. This relation thus highlights and contains the meaning attributed to the city through the historical process of civilization.

At the beginning of the Iliad (Homer 2002: 59), as a plague swept through the Greek army besieging the city of Troy, an assembly was held. Homer writes: "For nine days the god's arrows fell on the army; but on the tenth, Achilles [...] called the people to assemble." The gathering is a means of collective decision-making, allowing everyone's voice to be heard in the construction of a common destiny. In this particular case, decision focused on the military strategies and the planned sequence of battle. But what the Greeks did more generally was to create an 'exercise of participation,' as a meeting of everyone in a debate to define a future strategy of action, held in a space with the symbolic spatial meaning of the *agora*, though the meeting actually took place near their anchored ships rather than a precise and enclosed place in the polis. Here, the spatial representation realizes an action. So wherever men gathered, public space existed as an ever-present possibility, even when the city had yet to assume the materiality with which it is now associated.

Among the Greeks of the sixth and fifth centuries B.C., therefore, public space became associated with the idea of belonging to a space and a community Jaeger (2003). That was a spacetime in which everyone could make decisions about their common future, in which everyone participated. Public space becomes an active meeting place, a location for gathering and close proximity between members of a given society, without which discourse and action, as a moment for making joint decisions, would be impossible. It is this centrality that marks and delineates life, giving it meaning. Public space is from then on the place for social exchanges of all kinds, including those involving the spoken word, the discourse that emphasizes and defines collective action as conflict and struggle, identity and difference. It has become the space of demonstration constituted as a form of political activity and inseparable, as such, from the situations producing it (Carlos 2011). It is also a place for trading goods, the dialogue that such exchange imposes, and its rules. Public spaces bring together different people without predefined motives, united through the simple fact of existing.

Today the relations observed in the city's public spaces are marked by an urban crisis primarily caused by the transformation of the city into a business space, geared toward economic reproduction rather than the social needs that punctuate urban life and make its realization explicit. This process has been accompanied by the very evident authoritarian presence of the State and its powers of surveillance. But also by a multitude of small actions that resist by indicating the potential of public space to function as a venue for whatever differs from and challenges the norm.

---

[3]Gods from the Greek Pantheon, Hestia represents the hearth, located inside the house, and thus private space, while Hermes represents the outside, public space.

2.4 The Twenty-First Century Urban World as a Source of Deprivation

The contemporary global crisis reveals the difficulties involved in ensuring the process of accumulation. Somewhat contradictorily, capital is still reproduced, yet the crisis cannot be reduced to an economic crisis, nor is capitalism ultimately an economic phenomenon. At its social base, capitalism consists of a set of relations that delimit and define the plane on which human life unfolds, subjecting the latter to it. Capitalism proposes alliances and recreates new relations between the public and private sectors. Today's crisis requires a new relationship between the state (at its various levels of domination) and space, since political power is exercised through space as a form of control. Accordingly, public policies are implemented to direct the means for removing the obstacles hindering accumulation in various ways: by opening up new areas of investment, which are now becoming central to the production of urban space; through changes to city's planning regulations that standardize the use of space, setting guidelines for urban master plans, and channeling and ranking investments in the city; by bailing out banks and financial institutions; and, last but not least, through cuts in social spending. This relation makes explicit the convergence of the political and economic aspects of society, demanding ever more specifically targeted policies. Having precipitated the current global crisis, the financial market now appeals to the state for assistance, reinforcing the latter's role at the same time as the market prevents it from effectively becoming the manager of a private company. Political power is reproduced under these conditions, constantly intervening in the reproduction of space to ensure the implementation of strategies of capital accumulation. These strategies, in turn, reestablish the foundations of capital: the creation of inequality controlled by the creation of private property and social wealth, which guides the process of valorizing value.

At a spatial level, as part of the urban crisis and the implosion of sociocultural orientations, the metropolis separates and divides citizens in line with the forms of appropriation established by the private ownership of urban land. Property, as both the basis and outcome of the process of producing space under capitalism, drives the tendency for the means of appropriation to be subject to the world of commodities—and, consequently, for the content of sociospatial practice to be reduced to inequality of access. These processes hint at a new spatiotemporal order: the production of an amnesic space—which is built without practical reference points by a society dominated by accumulation—in direct relation to the ephemeral time of velocity (devoid of history). Transformed into abstractions, space and time outline a new way of life in urban centers, cities where a clearly defined boundary separates the house from the street, reducing and degrading the use and meaning of public space, erasing neighborhood life (where everyone once recognized everyone else, since this was the space where life was lived), and turning the city into an anonymous, functional and institutionalized realm (the contours of a new urbanity).

Consequently, urban praxis sheds light on the contradictions of capitalism, whose reproduction presumes and generates inequality at its very foundation, under constantly renewed forms of valorization that create the city as segregated space. At this point in time, the constant process of urban renewals involves the destruction of places, which confront individuals as alien objects and as independent powers; time in which alienation extends itself to all moments and spaces of life. That is an impoverished life, marked by different forms of appropriation, subsumed under the logic of wealth distribution. Taking the form of private ownership of urban land, this logic restricts and standardizes access to the city as the spacetime in which urban life is realized. Trapped in an everyday world split into separate, functional, organized sectors, activities are structured and divided into the areas of work, of private life, and of leisure. These are separations of citizens from the urban spacetimes, consequently leading individuals to relate to the city as though it were an alien force. Here modern life appears in all its ambiguity: an individual's home may keep him or her connected to the entire world via a computer network and television, which enables an ever-expanding spatial amplitude (providing the sensation that spaces and times have been 'tamed'), while, in reality, the mediation of technology separates individuals from each other. With the speed of contacts and the efficiency of communication, digital technology creates the feeling of incessant communication, concealing the real predominance of nonyi-communication. Individualism is built on a help-yourself society[4] in which the race for the new (illustrated by the queues forming outside Apple stores whenever a new gadget is released) is a thin disguise for producing more of the same. The immersion of culture and leisure in the 'world of commodities,' embellished with brands and images of success, differentiates people as a justification for class privileges.

In this 'technological environment' under constant renovation, the individual operates in an ever-shrinking concrete and practical space: the use of venues for public meetings has been reduced to the use of closed, private environments (a housing unit, for example). While communication is allowed, the mediation of social relations by the new technologies, quickly absorbed into our everyday lives, leads to alienation. This everyday life tends to be invaded by a regulatory system on all levels, therefore, imposing models of behavior and values that stimulate consumption, control life, formalize and frame social relations, reducing them to abstract forms and thus dissipating spatial awareness. This is due to the fact that, in our society, the only thing that acquires any real autonomy is exchange value, with all relations submitted to its logic through the regulatory and organizing actions of the state, founded on the contractual form (legal deeds) and on private property (as a concrete abstraction). Due to the real and concrete existence of the private ownership of urban land, the latter defines the limits and boundaries imposed on the use of space, within the total sum of wealth and according to the new forms of labor exploitation. As exchange values permeate social relations, they turn life into a

---

[4]The service sector eliminates jobs by transferring tasks to the client: automated teller machines, check-in terminals at airports, convenience stores, bakeries, gas stations, and so on.

source of deprivation of rights. Looking at the extension of commodification, we can see the privatization of the world—privatization led by the major companies listed on global stock markets.

This phenomenon points to transformations in the meaning of public space within a fragmented and divided city in tune with the unknown and the violent. Dominated by the actions of political authorities, urban morphology and urban life are shaped and justified on a drawing board, which design space as an empty abstraction, as geometric and visual ideas that will guide planning initiatives. The increase in the interchangeability of space is achieved through forms of coercion called norms. These affect not only the urban surface, but also the paths taken by city dwellers. In this process, the role of each inhabitant in the places of the metropolis is redefined by the limitations imposed on the use of space—which reduces and confines creative possibilities and imposes on everyday life the coercions of technical rationality and of interchangeability as if they were requirements, through forced planned solutions. Hence, these limitations penetrate everyday life, destabilizing it. What is in evidence here is the contradiction between the social production of space (realized by society as a whole) and its private appropriation (subsumed under the social existence of the private ownership of wealth) in which the exchange value of space prevails over its use value.

2.5 Urban Demonstrations Posing a Challenge to the Analysis

Brazil, as various other parts of the world, lives currently in a time of mass protests in streets, squares, and parks (as a reaffirmation of public space), which develop into struggles for the city driven by the need to appropriate urban space as a means to realize another life (which is essentially urban). In this situation, we can glimpse the need to 'change life' through the questioning of 'this life'.

In June 2013, demonstrations grew in strength and visibility in the media due to their size, duration, and intensity, with the initial issue being public transport: fare prices, the quality of services, and inefficiency. A paradigmatic example, however, was the case of Istanbul, where the construction of a real estate development in a public area prompted a huge number of people to take to the streets. In Brazil and Turkey alike, these bodies have taken over space, including the public sphere, by calling attention to the subject and his or her destiny. Taken together, these and other struggles, occurring in different spaces and times around the world, point to an urban crisis, requiring researchers to engage in a collective effort to understand the phenomenon, transcending, without excluding, political discourse.

The present crisis is revealed, therefore, through its eminently social dimension. It signals the production of an urban world in which access to the city, as the place of urban life, is subsumed under exchange value and political strategies. The urban world is now constituted as a business realm, created and guided by alliances between the public and private spheres, contrary to the interests of society as a whole. One of the dramatic consequences of this process is segregation in the heart of a society that posits private property as an unquestionable mainstay of social structure, mediating and shaping all relations between individuals (through various contractual forms) and between them and the space of life (through the private appropriation of urban land). In São Paulo, what used to appear under the topic of mobility, suggesting an analysis of the right to come and go, has revealed, however, an overbuilt metropolis that separates living and workplaces, driving out significant parts of society from central urban areas, a prime target for real estate speculation, to be relocated on the urban periphery. By limiting access to housing, the existence of private property determines all other forms of access to urban space, indicating a society constituted through an inequality of rights.

Consciously or otherwise, people mobilize to oppose this reality. Occupying the streets shows their 'unease' with life in an alien city, at the same time as the action evidences the core meaning of public spaces as central places for urban life, conceived and planned as places for cars and circulation. As the use of streets has been subverted, people now show the outrage and discontent felt with urban life and the way in which the city is built to segregate and to offer precarious levels of social inclusion. The struggle comes out questioning mobility and, along this path, constructs a discourse in support of pragmatic and urgent measures to solve the crisis provoked by the bodies that have taken over the streets and the city.

These demonstrations are the form taken by the residual opposition to the hegemonic. They take place in a diffuse and dispersed way in central areas or 'crossroads' in the metropolis to maximize their visibility. Just as diffusely, they raise questions, signaling the demand for a right that, in reality, is a demand for another life in another kind of urban world. Interpreting the multitude of campaign issues enables us to venture a hypothesis: these various issues can be united through the various facets and planes involved in the realization of the idea of the 'right to the city' formulated by Lefebvre (1968).

The relationship between the inhabitant and the city is permeated by modes of appropriation and use that involve a multitude of possibilities. The sphere of everyday life underlines the intertwining of scales and times: what happens in the work place and out of it, the production of broader relations, linking to relations that occur at home, during leisure hours, in private life, maintaining the dynamism of the relations between need and desire; actions that elude the 'established power' or rebel against it and against hegemonic trends (found latent in urban life). Hence, the struggle for space emerges in this context, indicating a radical need, in the words of Heller (1983), as a struggle for life.[5] But not just any life. Praxis, Marx argues, involves the work of the negative, the revolution that transforms the world. Here I refer to the concrete construction of alternatives to neoliberalism, achieved by reconnecting social force and the political sphere. There is no common future if the

---

[5]It is not just a struggle for property, despite including a need to be relocated.

target does not include a profound critique of capitalism as a model of civilization and the role of the state in this conception.

Fillieule and Trattakowsky (2008: 11) highlight the fact that uprisings typically involve a relation of spatial and temporal immediacy with their cause and objective, frequently unfolding in the same place as the denounced injustice or near the residence of its perpetrators, often implying violence. However, these demonstrations are not limited to the immediate only. They also express deeper changes founded on the construction of a group identity and presume organizations with a collective strategy. Certainly, demonstrations on urgent issues continue to take place, but today in Brazil we can witness a connection between the two kinds of protest, united around the project of the right to the city.

What the demonstrations have gradually exposed is the inadequacy of those discourses claiming a reduction in the percentage of the population living below the poverty line, through a reduction in the number earning up to three minimum wages. These data, however, reveals a new problem surfacing in the urbanization of contemporary Brazil: the increase in income translates as the inclusion of the low-income population into the everyday world, immersed in the world and logic of the market place, including the consumption of space through access to home loans. The federal government program *Minha Casa Minha Vida* ('My House My Life' during the years Lula and Dilma) associated with this income bracket addressed a need for the real estate market to continue to expand. At the same time that it revealed the extent to which the social base needed to expand the accumulative process as a moment in the reproduction of space on the periphery of Brazilian metropolises, by focusing on the construction of gated communities for a population earning between three and five minimum salaries. In effect, therefore, this process involved an expansion of the commodities world, attaining a population previously excluded from it and now included in precarious form, consuming the signs of wealth and submitting itself to everyday life as a capitalist program (that is, as a spacetime of accumulation) through the inevitable submission to commodification. These are social relations mediated by market values, signs, representations and so forth. In this situation, inequality is renewed: the contradictory form of inclusion in a society that continually excludes is achieved through a change in status from a peripheral population to a space-consuming population.

Another kind of demonstration, one which took place virtually during the same period, highlights this process: the phenomenon known as the *rolezinho*.[6] As a completely new form of demonstration, it has become part of public actions in a different way, highlighting the power of this world of commodities, a public expression of the social relations imposed by its influence. It points to a segmentation of human activities wiped out by the process of homogenization that 'pasteurizes' people and, in this sense, makes them identical. It sheds light on the universal status of the consumer, experienced by citizens as part of their submission

---

[6]In this context, *rolezinho* can be understood as a group outing of youths from outlying neighborhoods to 'hang out' in public spaces, particularly shopping malls, in more central districts.

to consumption, leaving people to differentiate themselves in the world of fashion, segmented by the income stratification imposed by the hierarchy of consumer brands. In this situation, the commodity emerges as an autonomous figure imbued with its own life independent of humans. In the modern world, this situation has reached its limit. The commodity has become autonomous, generalized vis-à-vis the subject, determining the relations between people (since the reproduction of social relations encompasses society and space as a whole) and guiding their behavior.

At the level of social behavior, the *rolezinho* is one way in which the commodity produces celebritization in our society, accompanied by the trivialization of life and the emptying of social relations. It renews the ways in which our fascination for goods is manifested, the defeat of the human being, who shifts humanity's fulfillment from the dream of attaining creative freedom to the possession of consumer goods. At the level of the spaces where this desire is realized, the invasion of shopping malls—with their luminous and aseptic interiors—replaces the appropriation of public spaces as venues for young people to meet, while their forms of struggle are replaced by the display of consumer objects: they are youth gatherings immersed in a sea of advertising imagery. The *rolezinho* reveals alienation within/from consumer society, as well as the ways in which commodity symbolism invades their dreams, establishing the possession of such symbols as personal fulfillment—bearers of a happiness that attracts fans. The *rolezinho* expresses the commodity fetish in modern guise.

Simultaneously, and contradictorily, the *rolezinhos* also contain a subversive element. By occupying spaces that do not belong to them, the young people challenge the hierarchized forms of access operating in the malls with their specific rules and targeted customers, shaped by a class society. These demonstrations reveal to society that, contrary to their social representation, metropolitan shopping malls are not public spaces but in fact private areas with specific rules and private security guards. Despite their apparent submission to the symbols of consumerism and the dazzle of new products, the *rolezinhos* aim to consume space unproductively and, though incompletely, satisfy desires immersed in the signs of merchandise.

The Brazilian demonstrations, combining various issues in different places, have highlighted:

(a) The gentrification processes frequently observed in urban spaces and responsible for driving out the poor, forcing them to live in ever more distant peripheries, as an outcome of the strategic transformation of the city into a source of business—a situation exacerbated by public policies that create the infrastructure and urban policies (master plans, new zoning laws, increase in building highs, etc.) necessary for doing business;
(b) The way in which the real estate sector, the transportation companies, and the major construction firms build alliances to their own advantage;
(c) The way in which public policies channel public funds toward particular land uses in selected areas of the city, creating infrastructure and incentives for private enterprise, exacerbating segregation in urban space;

(d) The segregation experienced in everyday life, which initially presents itself as differentiation, be it in the access to housing (as the clearest expression of the commodification of urban spaces) or to urban transportation (as limits on the access to urban activities), meaning the separation of the citizens from established centralities;

(e) The deterioration, curtailment, and persistent reduction of public spaces, leading to a narrowing of the public sphere.

Thus, a society that faces differentiation as an expression of inequality, materialized as a separation/apartheid that shapes social relations and the ways in which each citizen appropriates space. A segregation emerges in contradiction with the encounter—the deepest meaning of urban practice—and as a form of deprivation which, in this aspect, comes as the negative of the city.

As a gateway to understanding life conditions in urban space, urban segregation surfaces either in the discourse of exclusion, which suggests policies of inclusion (the need to include everyone in the commodities market), or as a poverty trademark, which demands policies for its eradication. But policies for eradicating poverty and the negative effects derived from it (e.g., hunger, lack of access to education, stripping away human dignity) cannot be achieved without a project for society. The radicalism of the term 'eradication' is reduced to rhetoric and fails to insist on the need to radically transform the system responsible for producing what is intended to be eradicated, to transform the very foundations of present-day society.

Hence, beyond the strict limits of indicators associated with our patterns of consumption and consumer status, what is revealed is the status of the non-subject, the status of the stigmatized ones: poverty comes associated with violence, with ugliness and with what seems incompatible with the globalized scenario constructed in urban spaces. This discourse justifies planning strategies that eliminate and sanitize all signs of whatever the capitalist aesthetic deems backward and out of date. Reduced to indicators of consumption and access to goods, the situation in which the subject is deprived of his or her human condition as a producer of space is concealed. Moreover, the transformation of city spaces into commodities (as an extension of the private ownership of urban land) indicates urbanism as a means to think and guide actions in the planning sphere. Ideological in nature, this class-based planning is implemented contrary to the well-being of a significant part of society that lacks rights and is unable to protest (present, for example, in the debates on new ways to discriminate against demonstrators and to increase their punishment).

It is about the dispossession of people's humanity, reducing human beings to the conditions for mere survival, reproducing their animalistic state—in other words, catering for their basic needs alone: eating, drinking, and sleeping (the initial and natural state of human life). It is about reducing humans to their extreme limits, beyond which they cannot stay alive and make history. In this alienated state, the subject faces a life devoid of meaning (the meaning of realizing the human through the construction of an object capable of epitomizing all human activities).

Today, urban renewal policies—which promote the opening of major avenues, constructing immense scars in the urban fabric, dividing social groups, creating new leisure areas, clearing land for new office towers or middle-class gated communities —destroy neighborhoods, wiping out reference points that sustain life and driving out those judged to be incompatible with change, namely those unable to pay for the rising value of urban spaces. This policy model that separates and isolates is backed by a discourse that reduces citizens to the status of workers, generating urban policies that turn the city into a home/work commute. A significant example is the fact that the mayor of São Paulo, responding to the demonstrations for better public transport, increased the number of lanes for exclusive use by buses throughout the city, as a means of solving the social crisis, merely providing a negligible and temporary decrease in the journey time for bus users. That was an ideological form of understanding the space and time of social practice. In the discourse of inclusion, the subject is treated as a consumer of products, including urban infrastructure. In reality, the new initiatives are part and parcel of the commodification of the world, signaling strategies for reproducing urban space that reorient social practice, subjecting all life to it.

2.6 The Exteriority of Space Generates New Forms of Alienation in Urban Society

The process of accumulation requires two elements. On one hand, there is the demand to produce space as a commodity, constituting the movement toward commodification of the world. In this context, the urban fabric is torn apart, separating and restricting actions and activities in space. Social relations are also subject to this logic. On the other hand, there is the need to broaden the consumer base, which today reaches the base of the social pyramid, in which the divided subject (who experiences space in fragments) is constantly reduced to the status of consumer. As such, the subject's project is to increase his or her quality of life as a way to access a new social status through the possession of consumer goods. This possession reflects the components of capitalist citizenship—a reduction of the subject to the status of a participating member of the consumer world, reduced to the purely economic realm, dominated and controlled by the media, which constantly produces new social behaviors. Urban practice, in turn, replaces life as a source of deprivation, pointing to new forms of alienation in which segregation reflects property in its fullest sense—'private' and, in this case, abstract. It hovers over society and governs uses, explicitly restricting the appropriation of time and space, proposing the emptying of neighborhood streets, downgrading street parties, which either dwindle in size or are transformed into spectacles. In this logic, alien traditions like Halloween parties are imposed along with their symbolism.

Relations between people are defined by a world where the ephemeral is imposed as a 'way of life' and reference points become obsolete along with history.

Domestic life, invaded by the timing of production society, reflects a transformation of the subject into a spectator. Activities shrink to the domain of private life and to the simulations of social life provided through culture and sports, for example. In public space, the experience of the city as innumerable fragments has reduced the possibilities for interweaving activities that punctuate life and are capable of enabling/renewing everyday events. Shopping malls are presented as a public space, a place that brings people together in the modern world, gaining 'centrality' in urban life in the wake of the real and symbolic emptying of public spaces.

The 'spectacle-making' (of space) and 'celebritization' (of the individual) mark this impoverishment, revealing new components of urbanity. The globalized world camouflages frustrations. The examples are notorious: Reality shows encourage and engage in voyeurism, simulating audience participation in the decisions over who stays in and who gets out; Facebook, meanwhile, stimulates the 'celebritization' of completely normal individuals, attaching an aura of glamour and importance to the posting of mundane scenes shared by a group of 'followers'—an appropriate way of describing a social relationship marked by vacuity.

In both cases, a reformulation of the terms of alienation can be identified, involving the degradation of the human in various forms. In this process, metropolitan life leads to the development of an abstract identity that transforms everyday life, imposing the signs of a manipulative model, organizing social relations oriented by the consumption of these signs and the spectacle. The practical existence of abstraction occurs in a defined and real moment: in everyday life, in urban spaces, promoted by the separation between use and exchange. By depriving people of the rights that establish and shape social relations, placing society in the subaltern condition of mechanical reproducer, the conditions of deprivation increase. This practice which denies any realization of the essence of being human results from the fragmentation of the social process as a whole. Deprived of this totality, the individual loses sight of it, and the segregated sociospatial practice constantly re-imposes the rejection of the human in the city.

2.7 From Deprivation to the Right to the City

Immersed in a cloud of images, trapped by shapes, bound by discourse and subject to ideology, the human being today has a poor understanding of his or her relations with society. Instead of dominating these relations, people are dominated by them, manipulated by economic and political forces. The street demonstrations that have erupted in various metropolises allow for a dialectical approach to this situation, introducing democratic practices. They appear as spacetimes of resistance, therefore, places of hope, since they emerge from the need to change real life, permeated by possibilities that tend to reject it. As such, they amount to contradictions and conflicts in the heart of reality that lead to the surfacing of problems posed by virtualities. This is how the work of the negative operates: from the need to fulfill/free humankind by ending exploitation and oppression.

2 The Power of the Body in Public Space ...

Crucially, the struggle for 'another possible world' is under way, along with the need to identify a path toward building this radicalism, informed by a deep understanding of our contemporary reality. However, another possible world depends on its capacity for subversion, on its rejection of the established order and the values of present society, refusing the logic of accepting capitalism and its dehumanizing logic.[7] At stake is a project that breaks with the dominant rationalism, enabling practical demands to be advanced instead. In such an approach, the theoretical plane is connected to the plane of reality, is connected to praxis as sociospatial practice. Here theory refers to the realization of human life: virtuality, unlike necessity, is the dialectic of the possible and the impossible.[8]

Social movements, as well as demonstrations, in different ways and with different structures, signal an awareness of the extreme deprivation suffered by human beings, not their condition as consumers of goods and services.

Hope is not a social state, a state of well-being or consumption, or even a question of the privileges already enjoyed by affluent minorities. Hope only exists as the possible, what can be, what is yet to be, but is announced in the social conditions that human beings have been able to build thus far, through the efforts of everyone and not just the few. This possible only exists if and when mediated by a critical social awareness, by critical knowledge, by a critique that continuously reassesses truths, their limitations, their stumbling blocks (Martins 2010). As such, the desire to change one's life requires the satisfaction of a radical need,[9] something that supersedes capitalism, involving a profound and devastating critique of political power.

The notion of 'the right to the city,' as formulated by Lefebvre (1968), creates a new intelligibility, shedding light on a project for society: (a) as an outcome of the radical critique of planning and its production of a form of knowledge about the city that reduces urban issues to the question of spatial management, aiming at restoring the coherence of the growth process (based on technical knowledge that utilizes strategic planning coordinated by the state, justifying its policy); and (b) as a movement of praxis, in everyday life. The 'right to the city' built from a rejection of the upside-down world with its divisions, abstract identities, passivity, its constitution of life as an imitation of a model of happiness built on the possession of goods, its segregation founded on private property, the importance attributed to institutions and the market, its repressive power, the vanishing of the particular and the singular, the process that produces time as ephemeral and space as an amnesic production, the reduction of everyday space to the homogeneous, destroying spontaneity and desire.

An idea advanced by the French dramatist Artaud (1984) contains a message that never ages and may still pose a challenge today: "And everything that has not been born can still be brought to life if we are not satisfied to remain mere recording organisms."

---

[7]These movements are negative work in action, but this status is only realized in the world as a whole; this is the universality necessary for overcoming the fragmentary nature of the struggles.

[8]As asserted by Henri Lefebvre in various works.

[9]As Heller (1983) argues.

References

Artaud A (1984) O teatro e seu duplo. Max Limonad, São Paulo

Bernard M (1995) Le corps. Seuil, Paris

Carlos SFA (2011) A representação arcaica do espaço e o espaço público para além da esfera pública e seu sentido atual. In: A condição espacial. Contexto, São Paulo, pp 125–140

de Andrade CD (2001) Antologia poética. Record, São Paulo

Fillieule O, Trattakowsky D (2008) La manifestation. Presse de la Fondation de Sciences Po, Paris

Heller A (1983) A filosofia radical. Brasilense, São Paulo

HOMERO (2002) Ilíada. Ediouro, Rio de Janeiro

Horkheimer M (1976) Eclipse da razão. Labor do Brasil, Rio de Janeiro

Jaeger W (2003) Paideia: a formação do homem grego. Martins Fontes, São Paulo

Lefebvre H (1968) Le droit à la ville. Anthropos, Paris

Lipovetsky G (1991) Espace privé, espace public à l'âge postmoderne. In: Baudrillard J et al. Citoyenneté et urbanité. Esprit, Paris, pp 105–122

Martins JS (2010) A sociabilidade do homem simples. Contexto, São Paulo

Pacquot T (1990) Homo urbanus. Félin, Paris

Perec G (1974) Espèces d'espaces. Galilée, Paris

Smith N (2000) Contornos de uma política espacializada: veículos dos sem-teto e a produção da escala geográfica. In: Arantes AA (ed) O espaço da diferença. Papirus, São Paulo

Author Biography

Ana Fani Alessandri Carlos is a Full Professor in the Department of Geography of the University of São Paulo, where she received her undergraduate degree, a master's (1980), a doctorate (1987) and the habilitation (2000) in Human Geography. She also undertook postdoctoral positions at University of Paris VII in 1989 and University of Paris I in 1994. Among her most important books are: *Espaço-tempo na metrópole* (Honorable Mention at Jabuti Awards in Social Sciences in 2002); *O espaço Urbano—novos escritos sobre a cidade* (2005); *A condição especial* (2011). She is also a member of "La somme et le rest" network, based in Paris and a number of research groups in Brazil, having received numerous distinctions, including the Prêmio de Geografia Crítica, Universidade de Barcelona in 2013 and the Prêmio da Associação Nacional de Pós-graduação em Geografia, ANPEGE, 2015.

Chapter 3
Reinventing Public Spaces: Politics of Oneself and Politics with Many Others

Jorge Luiz Barbosa and Ilaina Damasceno Pereira

Abstract Public space is constituted by social subjects in the creation of themselves and in the political action of their presentation. It is, above all, ways of affirming and recognizing differences in the construction of the city. In this sense, politics with many others become a movement of incorporating conflict as inherent in the plurality of human meanings and purposes of life in society. Public space assumes the expression of multiple potentialities and acts of self-presentation situated in the space-time of their existences. Being as self, living, feeling and being in the world are related to the material and symbolic socio-spatial conditions of men and women in their distinct visibility experiences. Therefore, the analysis of city appropriations carried out by diverse social groups—with their socio-political belongings agendas—make the right to difference a trademark of space reinvention. This chapter departs from Foucault's aesthetic of existence as the mediation to understand the subject's daily practices and actions regarding living in the city. Then, it addresses life in common through the debate on visibility, constitution and maintenance of spaces of collective manifestations, which Arendt calls spaces of appearance.

Keywords Difference · Self-creation · Aesthetic of existence
Spaces of appearance · Space reinvention

J. L. Barbosa (✉)
Programa de Pós Graduação em Geografia, Universidade Federal Fluminense,
Niterói, Rio de Janeiro, Brazil
e-mail: posgeo@vm.uff.br

I. D. Pereira
Afro-Brazilian Studies Center, Rio de Janeiro State University, Rio de Janeiro, Brazil

© Springer International Publishing AG, part of Springer Nature 2018
L. Capanema Alvares and J. L. Barbosa (eds.), *Urban Public Spaces*,
The Urban Book Series, https://doi.org/10.1007/978-3-319-74253-3_3

3.1 Introduction

Public space is constituted by the social subjects inventing themselves and acting in the world. A politic of oneself is generated while experience of the relations between autonomous and collective subjects, whose act of living in the city shows the extent and depth of creative processes of disclosure in the public scene. In this sense, the specificity that shelters the creation of political subjects shapes the action with others, in which it is possible to recognize our alterity and multiplicity in the construction of the city. Therefore, it is a politics with many others, a movement that includes conflict as something inherent to the many human meanings and purposes of living in society.

Public space, as conceptualized here, is a set of multiple powers and acts of self-disclosure spatially situated that becomes real when social subjects seek political recognition (Barbosa 2013). These are ways of living, experiencing, being and self-disclosing related to material and symbolical socio-spatial conditions of men and women in their diverse urban experiences. So, political action gains the meaning of living in society, exactly because subjects affirm their own differences in the possibility of the other's differences. We believe this recognition path demands the right to the existence of individuals and of collective groups, waving as their struggling banner the "we" of the differences in being and the unity for guaranteeing shared common rights.

The constitution of this public sphere of self-creation with others is decisive to fight the corporative and private domination order that turned the city into machines of inequality reproduction. It is in the counter-hegemonic movements against the "city owners" that we can confront, on a daily basis, the uniformity imposed on urban reproduction, creating ways of living as we conduct experiments on the relations with others and on the tensions that are essential to affirm human plurality as a reference for social relations change.

We advocate that creative ways of connecting with others and the world are expressed through political action, as subjects show who they are to one another not only in everyday life but also in exceptional and extemporaneous events of proposition and rupture of hegemonic orders. These situations of political expression give visibility to the subjects and the established relations between them, presenting ethical references such as friendship, cordiality and solidarity in the ways they act and appear.

Creation and action offer to men and women possibilities of fulfilling their roles as public subjects in spaces of encounter and conflict between the different in unequal positions. These interactions allow a glimpse into a wide landscape of possibilities for multiple others and for the city transformation.

The debate herein will depart from the aesthetic of existence (Foucault 2010, 2011) as the mediation to understand the subject's daily practices and actions regarding living in the city. Then, we will address life in common through the debate on visibility, constitution and maintenance of spaces of collective manifestations, which Arendt called spaces of appearance (Arendt 2000a, b). Finally, we

3.2 Politics of Oneself: The Aesthetic of Existence

The subject shapes his or her life through the practices that guide his or her conduct in the midst of strategic games of power relations (Foucault 1995, 2004). The situated constitution of men and women is elaborated in daily life and in multiple and changing existential styles, which simultaneously evade, juxtapose, speak and at the limit, oppose hegemonic strategies of socio-political domination.

Style of existence is a collection of daily attitudes of men and women regarding themselves, others and the world; sensible acts through which they establish relations of care with themselves and others. Expressions of solidarity, friendship and lovingness are among the acts of care that make us part of others. The importance of acting with others resides in the fact that it is a continuous elaboration, in which the subject creates him or her and invents sociabilities capable of questioning the social conventions that mostly prevent the constitution of a more life-appreciative world (Foucault 2010, 2011).

The style of existence allows the subject the elaboration of ways to express his or her lifestyle. In essence, it is a way to conduct him or her in society. The style constitutes itself as confrontation to the forms of normalization and is a revolutionary achievement, a search for existential alternatives to free the subjects from social imperatives of subordination.

Therefore, style is the ethos and field of action of the aesthetic of existence. Schmid (2002) highlights the necessity to distinguish style of existence from aesthetic of existence, considering them in the constitution process of oneself as the technique and the result, respectively; the proceedings through which individuals elaborate themselves aesthetically and the temporary form of the existential experiment. Conceptually, a possible distinction would fall between the ethos, a group of practices guiding the conduct, and the ethics, as praxis and consideration of a life conduct.

Schmid (2002) points out that the central aspect of ethics—as the art of living— proposed by Foucault are the styles of existence, a multiple subject constituted by experiencing the world and taking care of him or her as a self-contemplation driven by the encounter with others. This ethics is present in the power relations terrain in order to update techniques and practices that prevent stages of social subordination, including the power relations that act upon the bodies.

Style and aesthetic of existence are respectively ephemeral practices and forms socially and politically constructed by the subjects seeking to free themselves from dominant norms. As such, they present themselves as life forces to confront disciplinary powers and biopolitics. According to Foucault (1999, p. 297) these control processes are ways to intervene on the subjects bodies, "one is a technology in which the body is individualized as an organism endowed with capacities, while the other is a technology in which bodies are replaced by general biological processes".

The style of existence realizes itself in the transition from a passive and normalized life to an active one and is therefore a freedom practice. The subject invents visibility practices and icons as a political attitude that does not elaborate universal codes of conduct, but gains shape in the processes, correlations and variations that are necessary for his or her recognition in the public sphere.

> Every Saturday afternoon in a neighborhood at the periphery of Rio de Janeiro, young black people perform under a viaduct, marking their urban spatiality with dances, music and graffiti. The unexpected gestures of their bodies challenges the functionality imposed to the space. The viaduct is a space of celebration where young blacks can be black and demand their right to celebrate, to be joyful and to dream, just as much as they need education, healthcare and decent housing.[1]

These public recognitions are creations of the self, made possible by a collective effort to being in the city; therefore it is impossible to separate the subject's relation with him or her and with others. This is not only because subjects define, through their social relation, who is the other and which bonds they want to establish, but also because style creation indicates recognizable inventions in the others and in diverse quotidian contexts.

The aesthetic forms expressed by the colour of the clothes, by hairstyles or manners, are choices that constitute a dispute of imaginaries on the subjects' sense of themselves. The choices on seeming and being are enlisted within a political disclosure of oneself, therefore affecting the desired city that will be shared.

The subject's aesthetic in the public space is a field of multiple actions and practices of lasting or ephemeral encounters. It is a spatial way of manifesting the tension with the urban quotidian standards—consumable and consumed—imposed on daily life. Public space, in contemporary society, is an ephemeral experience, since it is open to conflict, as especially constituted by different subjects in unequal positions of power.

The aesthetic of existence can be translated as the way in which the subject conducts his or her own life, the result of actions and style creations. Thus, it is the interaction between spatial and temporal circumscribed practices, as part of individual narratives that give the different possibility to be seen in the city. The aesthetic of existence is a life power, resulting from subject creations that oppose a city governed by private propriety and controlled by commercial consumption.

To create aesthetics in discursive and practical styles is to confront hegemonic norms that suppress the multiple others and portray them as a threat to communal life. Eliminating alterity is not only taking people lives, but also "expos[ing] people to death, to increase the risk of death, or simply the political death, rejection, expulsion etc". (Foucault 1999, p. 306). On the other hand, when subjects act in an

---

[1]Notes on *Charme* and Hip-Hop dance parties that have taken place, for at least 16 years, under a viaduct in Madureira (a neighborhood of Rio de Janeiro), and gather young blacks from favelas and peripheries to celebrate their differences in the city.

3 Reinventing Public Spaces: Politics of Oneself and Politics …

Fig. 3.1 Invisible bodies in Rio. *Source* Observatório de Favelas

oriented way to transform their feeling experiences, they fight the restriction to differences and open the debate on the reasons why some subjects are silenced, ignored or even exterminated (Fig. 3.1).

> Largo da Carioca, Rio de Janeiro downtown. Young black people from different favelas are drawing body shapes of young people killed by the police on the floor. There were no memories or sorrows on the streets, but the silence of 60.000 homicides per year in Brazil, most of them of black youngsters. Passersby don't understand the bodies that calmly fill the shapes drawn on the floor. In the silence of that afternoon they were expressing the desire of a youth marked to live.[2]

The highlighted issue was not only the denouncing of homicide rates and the demand for a humanized public security policy, but especially to show a crucial attitudinal change regarding the aesthetic of young black male bodies. The performance exposed the physical and symbolic violence against curly hair, dark skin,

---

[2]The campaign Youth marked to live (*Juventude Marcada para Viver*) held in Rio de Janeiro by youngsters of the Escola de Comunicação Crítica do Observatório de Favelas, in December 2014, had 400 people drawing body shapes of youngsters who were killed in the position police's reports showed, and then laying down to fill the void of life printed on the floor. The intention was to raise awareness and mobilize people about the need to support the demand on the State Government to sign a protocol holding the state accountable for the implementation of measures to guarantee citizen's rights and the reduction of police violence.

sinuous gestures and fast walking people, all characteristics of young blacks upon whom city authorities impose discretionary discourses and acts based on a lethal radicalism and their visions of life hierarchies.

The fight for visibility happens in individual actions, when youngsters assert themselves in their differences, or in group activism, in which collectives come together to demand plurality. In both cases, as subjects assert themselves, they seek to transform the city defined by disciplinary prescriptions and biopolitics of capital reproduction. The city, in these challenges and initiatives towards change is a multiplicity of spatialities, encounters and conflicts between many subjects, allowing the self-assertion of men and women.

> In the Bom Jardim Cultural Center - created in the homonymous neighborhood with the objective of offering time and spaces for the youth – groups of youngsters got organized to denounce the high violence rates and to share their differences. Youngsters associated with hip-hop practices, basketball and musical instrument manufacturing (tambores de Umbanda) etc. can meet and showcase their cultural practices to each other in festivals. Demonstrations are organized in order to put the different on the street and expose the physical and symbolic violence they endure. Participants from each and every group can be distinguished by their clothes, types of hair, insignias and gestures. The communion shows multiple youths, manifesting their right to be young without erasing differences,[3] and to have their lives respected.

The periphery youths often seen as a homogeneous group whom the main necessity is to enter the labour market, disclosure as such the diversity of their cultural practices. These are related to the diversity of space experiences that consequently expose what type of violence they endure. Hip-hop groups, basketball teams and youngsters from *terreiros de Umbanda*—along with many others—have very different trajectories and, as a consequence, certainly have different demands. The politics of oneself is a way to express life in place, what could not be reduced to a single way of being.

The styles forged in the everyday life of a periphery neighbourhood can be seen in the internal specificities of a collective when we consider each individual life or compare groups whose differences expose particular experiences in the city. In both cases, we have styles seeking temporary aesthetic forms, adjusting to the circumstances as a way to escape from being captured by hegemonic norms.

The aesthetics of existence, when seen through group activism, confirms what Duarte and César (2014, p. 410) call "present political collectives". For the authors, they do not seek tolerance and the affirmation of a single identity as capable of equalizing interests and desires. These collectives demand the denaturalization of what is considered normal and respectable. The authors analysed the Slut March (*Marcha das Vadias*) as follows:

---

[3]Bom Jardim neighborhood has the higher rate of lethal violence against the youth in Fortaleza, the capital of Ceará. The Bom Jardim Cultural Center was created to be a place where classes are offered to the youth, offering possibilities for them to enter the labor market, and a place for cultural activities. Among those activities we can highlight the annual march against lethal violence.

3 Reinventing Public Spaces: Politics of Oneself and Politics …

Curitiba, Paraná. Whose march? The Slut March. But this is cursing! Yes! So it is with tramp, whore, bitch or 'chippie'. If women are oppressed and defined by a sexist and patriarchal society, they can also redefine and be whatever they want: beautiful, prudish and home staying (ugh!), but also a slut, a fighter, a protester.[4]

When fixed social identities—that are abstractions—are challenged, they can create fissures where subjects can invent new relations with themselves and others and with the world (Duarte and César 2012). It is precisely in this movement that it is possible to confront and overcome consumerist individualism and move towards an autonomous individuality, but ensured in an alterity-based sociability and in the creation of styles of being in the city.

The styles of existence expose how subjects constitute themselves daily through conflicts and agreements that seek a life more creative, active and full of possibilities. These are expressive inventions of the right to the difference in the city through multiple experiences challenging the hegemonic models of being.

The aesthetic conduction of life has histories, memories, narratives and experiences in spaces and times politicized by the physical and symbolical presence of subjects that repeal oppressive norms and perverse naturalizations established in the city. These ways of acting are politics of oneself, but they do not exist without the presence of others, acknowledged different, in their unequal positions. That is, in the presence of the many others who question us about our actions in the world and their effects over life.

3.3 Politics with Many Others: Self-disclosure and Space of Appearance

Public space requires the presence of those who are different, and thus defines the subject as being with the other; in the public space, we reveal our identities through discourse and carry out the new through action. The presence of others is crucial to validate events, and at the same time is unpredictable because actions can provoke unexpected reactions and new actions, creating an atmosphere of human negotiations, constituted and maintained in the city (Arendt 2000a). These established relations between mankind only exist with difference and distinction: the first defined by human plurality while the second poses the subject's necessity to differentiate him or her from others through words and actions instead of only remaining different.

The desire of men and women to differentiate themselves characterizes the polis. While a political community, the polis seeks to guarantee the longevity of human accomplishments, in actions and discourses, through the constitution of a concrete physiognomy as the *place of memories* that we call "city" (Arendt 2000a).

---

[4]https://jornalistaslivres.org/2016/07/marcha-das-vadias-por-um-mundo-de-respeito-todas-as-mulheres/.

The city as an expression of memory is thus a crystallized public space that can recognize the actions of others as constituents of the inhabited world and can guarantee the continuity of action. Therefore, the city is not a receptacle; rather, its condition is to house public spaces as a permanent power made effective when subjects interact, conforming their political lives. The city provides the necessary requirements to implement public space and to fully manifest the action: a tangible space where subjects see and listen to each other, constituting reality as appearance; and representing their own world, common to all which can, by uniting and separating humankind, prevent action from being forgotten as it ensures the other's testimony (Arendt 2000a).

The city, par excellence, is the space for encounters between the different and for the constitution of distinction, thus bringing an obligation to collectivity from its inception; because the action can be divided into two parts: beginning and realizing, an individual effort and a collective effort, respectively. Subjects can consent on actions and projects, can be indifferent, or can question and problematize the proposals. To take part (or not) in the city planning/management decision-making processes affects daily life because it also defines choices about ways of being in the city. Therefore, the city is simultaneously prior and posterior to the relations established between human beings since only common experience—assured by the polis—renders it viable; yet, the reality of common experience is ensured by the city. City and polis have an uninterrupted cyclic relation once they are both requisite and condition of one another.

In this sense, we can say that *polis* is not the city as a physical formation; rather, it is the citizens that conform it. *Polis* is the community organization that results from acting and speaking as a group and its space lies between people living together, as they so desire (Arendt 2000a). It is, therefore, the relation that men and women establish with each other in the world, and that only exists when some present themselves to others through action and words, existing only when human plurality, with all of its constituent diversity, is mobilized towards the distinction that humankind seeks to establish between each of us. In this sense, *polis* is a radical project of democracy and, obviously, of the city as the space of everyday life in permanent realization.

Possessing the quality of a community that acts and speaks as one, the *polis* constitutes itself as a space of visibility. This space of appearance, where people appear to one another, does not exist continually and, even though everyone has the ability to act and speak, the minority does not live in it and no one can be permanently in it (Arendt 2000b). This space of self-appearance with others exists where subjects decide to be together. Since it stems from action and discourse, it will never lose its virtual nature, and contrary to fabricated spaces, as the city built by urban planning, the space of appearance dissipates when action ceases. In this sense, the political space is prior to any formal constitution of the public space; only through the political space the latter realizes itself (Arendt 2000a).

The space of appearance is constituted by a process of experimentation and creation that allows replacing the granted citizenship for a *vita activa* citizenship, of which the main characteristic is the embodiment of politics as expressed by the subject's aesthetics (Barbosa 2012). There are multiple creative action possibilities towards the political relations that constitute the public sphere; the fact that new inventions have an ephemeral existence or can be permanently reinvented is the reason why there are multiple spaces of appearance—as many as there are expectations and propositions of the active subjects in dispute.

The power of being together and the possibilities created by men and women, when they mark their differences through actions and narratives, promotes the city modernization once they politically add motion to the crystallized actions. Demonstrations, marches or even celebrations, can propel the forms produced by human work by questioning social relations and giving visibility to many others. No square, street or building is a public space per se. It is necessary to animate these spaces with political life in its daily manifestation in order to achieve that condition.

> The Black Awareness Day celebration took place on a Saturday afternoon In 2011, Maracatus and afoxés,[5] terreiros de umbanda[6] and hip-hop groups presented themselves at the Ferreira Square. During the performance of Acabaca afoxé, what called attention was the fact that the majority of members were white. When questioning one of them about their participation in the event, he told me that what mattered was to promote black cultural practices to all people regardless of their color, race or ethnicity. Then, the maracatu Iracema Nation held courtship, composed mainly of children and adolescents. The king and queen were a lord and a lady in their fifties. Instead of the king and queen being laureates, as usual, they crowned two members of the black movement. [...] After the maracatu parade and coronation, the afoxé Filhos de Oyá and members of the Umbanda Spirit Association of São Miguel arrived in the square. This association had tried to organize a march through the streets of the Great Bom Jardim neighborhood earlier that day in order to minimize prejudice and persecution against the terreiros de umbanda but it was canceled because the head of one of the venues was sick. In order to manifest themselves, the religious practitioners went instead to downtown, along with the afoxé group, in a bus provided by City Hall. The group Sons of Oyá arrived at the square singing songs led by a man in Iansã's (The Lady of winds and showers) robes[7] (Fig. 3.2).

When subjects share squares, they qualify these spaces as public spaces, especially when they politically exercise their appearance ability through action and narrative. This act is not only a moment of visibility that provides political power to social relations in the city, it is also a human construction, in which men and women transform themselves and the relations that unites and divides them (Damasceno Pereira 2015). The interaction cannot eliminate differences or conflicts between collectives; rather, it informs human plurality and invites each person to transform him or her in order to politically constitute the self.

We appear by the action that confirms the original and singular fact of our appearance in the world and by the narrative that prevents it from being forgotten (Arendt 2000a). Action and narrative manifest the latent self of agents whose existences are enhanced by their revealing actions and words; therefore, appearing is a deliberate attitude of confronting the world as it is presented. The public space reality is the appearance and visibility in the sense of affirming that "to be" and "to appear" are one, which means that only what does appear does exist.

---

[5]African-descendant rithms and dances.

[6]Venues of African religious manifestations.

[7]Notes about the celebration of Black Awareness Day in Fortaleza-CE, in 2011.

Fig. 3.2 Ferreira Square: Afoxé Filhos de Oya. *Source* Ilaina Damasceno

The space of appearance needs *spectators* to be effectively realized, since we depend on being acknowledged by the other to believe in the way we choose to appear. The spectator shall acknowledge as a phenomenon in the world what appears and, in this case, visibility and acknowledgement become equals (Arendt 2000b). When subjects choose their way of being inserted in the city public space, through the exhibition of their ethical and aesthetic choices, through their physical being or through breaking the modus operandi of spaces of democratic public sphere participation, the insubordination to authority, laws, institutions and mainly to common sense that makes them invisible to differences, projects an image which visibility forces spectators to acknowledge the legitimate existence of alterity and therefore to recognize individuals in their differences.

The space of appearance is constituted by the choices subjects make in order to single out themselves, but this distinction has to be acknowledged by the spectators, since they define if what affects them physically is real or not; as such, they hold the key to human affairs. In this sphere, individuals left in "self-disclosure"[8] collide, in the simple being here consistent with existing; representations of alterity mean individuals seeking singularity through their "self-presentation" (Arendt 2000b).

---

[8]According to the author, all living beings have the self-disclosure capacity, simply because they are in the world. Self-disclosure only discloses the characteristics that living beings already have, and not those that are the result of their affirmation trough politics.

If the public space is the expression of the difference-distinction relation among people whose actions affirm their existence, then we cannot see it in a consensual way. There are tensions, combinations and conversations that explicit the *polis* continuous reconstruction. It is in these links that the relation between distinction and common is established and where tensions within the appropriation and usage of the city appear.

Self-disclosure is a matter of how we want to appear to others, "an active and sensible choice" (Arendt 2000b, p. 29). But appearance is also linked to plurality, since it demands others to see and that is what guarantees the perceptible sensorial reality: "nothing that is, insofar as it appears, exists in the singular" (Arendt 2000b, p. 17). The space of appearance could be defined as continuous conflicts between hegemonic and counter-hegemonic projects. Conflicts between the different that act in self-disclosure and between them and the spectators' representations present in the city.

Self-disclosure reveals a plurality of others. Women, homosexuals, prostitutes, transvestites, blacks, lesbians, rappers, funk lovers, etc., whose self-experiences and experiences within the city confront established models and present new relations with themselves, with others and the public space. Plurality, far from being a quantity without meaning, is a ontological category spatially and temporally situated, since the subject's actions and creations refer to the highs and lows, gains and losses, strengths and flexibilities, all human ways of being in the cities (Damasceno Pereira 2015).

In this perspective, the *politics with many others* is a collection of inter-subjective relations established in confrontations and encounters that constitute the public space. A Web of interactions that arrange the aesthetic creation of individuals, materialized in the public space in demonstrations and parades that foster the embodiment of difference. This is how cities are expressions of the political emergence, where creation and action of oneself occur in the encounter with the different that is fighting for recognition in the world.

3.4 From Public Space to Public Spaces: Actions and Creations

When the *politics of oneself* and the *politics of many others* come together, the political embodiment occurs, because they highlight the possibility of each person becoming a leader in caring for the world, having as main issue the effort to transform his or her existence into a political life engendered by the interactions between the subjects and by their relation with the city as ways to define the horizon of their social existence. The claim to the right to life shows up as a claim to the right to the city, since the city offers a field of possibilities to create free ways of being, as it stops the past and projects into the future innovative experiences shared in the present.

The city is a set of materialized social relations capable of directing the subject's actions. Therefore, to create ways for a free existence is to pursuit aesthetic experiences as political attitudes, in which the subjects invest their visibility and inform the *urbe* as a space composed of multiple others. The city is where conflicts between submission and transgression are manifested, through ambiguous forms that negotiate and question the established boundaries of space appropriation, by creating new usages or original ways to appear in restrictive spaces. These actions transform the actors and, above all, affect the web of human relations, when they present possibilities of accomplishing the new regarding themselves, the others and the space-time aspect of the urban experience (Damasceno Pereira 2015).

Instead of being self-centred—the typical attitude of a consumer of material and symbolic goods and spaces—the social subject shows his or her worldliness through actions that affirm the aesthetic difference. This manifests the relations he or she takes part in and externalizes his or her permanent prospect, expressing it as a process and as an outcome. The acts and creations of men and women display multiple ways of being in the world as they reveal the appropriations and possible uses of the city.

As the public space contains virtuality, it is the condition to transform everyday life. In it, the subjects constitute the aesthetic that distinguish them and express their human plurality. Rhythms, gestures and attitudes in relation to themselves and others are styles of existence created to enhance visibility. Through them, subjects can appear and communicate the existence of those who were drawn out of the picture, of those whose sensible experiences are ignored and made invisible.

In the public space, social, economic and cultural issues engender the subject's sensible experience. In this perspective, the urban issue loses the exclusively technical aspect of efficiency and creates a path for understanding the complexity of life. Public space assumes the role of a complex Web of intent, desire and action, allowing the subject to create aesthetics of existence through styles (narratives and practices) that enable a different thinking in order to build the real and the possible as utopia that make the city a common human work.

As a place of creation and action marked by the complexity of subjects and the relations between them, public space is the result of human actions, and is also a project. Objects are filled with intentions and promote or prevent men and women to be equal in their differences. As such, they convey crystalized actions, but also communicate prospects through the subject's creative efforts of confronting the urban order based on inequalities. In other words, it is the possibility of creating the reverse city.

The city is a space of political discussion about life, where debates are drawn from the perceived and experienced reality of everyday life. Aesthetic experiences are invented to transform the city into a field of disputes of imaginaries among subjects in order to construct styles in frenetic dynamics, which moments of conflict reveal the very shape given to existences.

The city offers events that reveal, exhibit and transform the subjects' practices which subsidize the analyses of who we are, and that produce material for experiments that allow exceeding our existence conditions. If the city is a social experience of the correlations between norms, power and conducts, then it is not only "where" the existence happens, but it is the subject's space of action, speech and practice, oriented and submitted to processes of submission, or taking a transformative approach to create new forms of living through questioning and overturning the established.

Public space constitutes itself as a measure of the political relations between social subjects in their historic conditions of existence. It is the action recording that ensures the presence of the other not only as a witness, but also as an active alterity

3 Reinventing Public Spaces: Politics of Oneself and Politics ...

that confirms or denies alternative projects for the city and society. We can state that the inhabited city is a political work, as the inter-subjective constitution of each person demands the presence and participation of others in the community life.

3.5 Final Considerations

Politics of oneself and with many others are the choices subjects make to appear for each other in the world. They are propositions about life that make life itself a political object and politics that make the way we live its main object by emphasizing on the desires, expectations and prospects that can transform the city, when the possibilities are created for many others to appear and have their sensible experiences acknowledged as ways of being in the space.

The public space constituted by transgressive actions indicates conflicts between different sensible regimes, elucidating dominant behaviours and inventive efforts that make the experience in the city a field open to the transformation of the ways to live it. In order to think about politically active and creative subjects, it is necessary to understand experiences in the city as actions seeking new ways of living, because actions and creations can politicize life when they question the established norms and propose other sensible experiences of the world (Damasceno Pereira 2015).

For Barbosa (2013), the city must be thought and lived as a form of human association that seeks common good through the established relations between social subjects, in which others are incorporated as active subjects; a space for experiments that can create sociability and where conflicts are crucial for the emergence of new sensible experiences of friendship, kindness and courtesy. The existence of public space allows each individual to be a creative power.

Public space becomes an arena where contradictions reveal the political aspect of life in the city. If we analyse the subject's actions outside the standards established by the ordered and hierarchical space—the ones considered deviants, divergent, combative or troubled—we can conclude that the daily experience in the urban space generates ethical and political behaviour, through which life can be understood as the horizon of a sociability dispute.

Subjects in their movements towards recognition create ethics and aesthetics in different space-times of existence, as they produce visibility of him or her with others. They are ways to appear that affirm the differences through collective involvement and physical action that disrupt and break the hegemonic ways of being. The importance of the body in the public space, according to Duarte (2012), is another relation between politics and life, since to acknowledge the body is not an instrument to achieve a purpose, but it is the exercise of "another politics", in which life itself is a political act.

Politics of oneself and politics with many others are possibilities of other types of relations between the different, indicating the world as a place to be constructed and modified. Both are practices capable of installing new experiences through which subjects reject and take ownership of the elements dispersed in the social, economic and symbolic relations. In this sense, the conflict between established models and inventive creations emerges, in a dispute between restraining representations that face opposition and liberating presentations of experiences.

References

Arendt H (2000a) A condição humana. Forense Universitária, Rio de Janeiro
Arendt H (2000b) A vida do espírito: o pensar, o querer, o julgar. Relume Dumará, Rio de Janeiro
Barbosa JL (2012) Cidade e Território: desafio da reinvenção da política do espaço público. In: Silva JS, Barbosa JL, Faustini MV (eds) O novo carioca. Mórula Editorial, Rio de Janeiro, pp 69–73
Barbosa JL (2013) Paisagens crepusculares da ficção científica: a elegia das utopias urbanas do modernismo. Editora da UFF, Niterói
Damasceno Pereira I (2015) Performances estilísticas da umbanda na apropriação do espaço público em Fortaleza Ceará. Tese de Doutorado apresentada ao Programa de Pós-graduação em Geografia da Universidade Federal Fluminense. Niterói
Duarte A (2012) Singularização e subjetivação: Arendt, Foucault e os novos agentes políticos do presente. Princípios: Revista de Filosofia 19(32):9–34
Duarte AM, César MRA (2014) Michel Foucault e as lutas políticas do presente: para além do sujeito identitário de direitos. Psicologia em Estudo, Maringá 19(3):401–414
Duarte AM, César MRA (2012) Estética da existência como política da vida em comum: Foucault e o conceito de comunidades plurais. O que nos faz pensar, Rio de Janeiro 31:175–195
Foucault M (1995) O sujeito e o poder. In: Rabinow P, Dreyfus H (eds) Michel Foucault: Uma Trajetória filosófica- muito além do estruturalismo e da hermenêutica. Rio de Janeiro, Forense Universitária, 1995, p. 231–249
Foucault M (1999) Em Defesa da Sociedade: curso no Collège de France (1975–1976). Martins Fontes, São Paulo
Foucault M (2004) Ditos e Escritos V: ética, sexualidade, política. Forense Universitária, Rio de janeiro
Foucault M (2010) Governo de si e dos outros: curso no Collège de France (1982–1983). São Paulo, Editora WMF Martins Fontes
Foucault M (2011) A coragem da verdade: curso no Collège de France (1983–1984). São Paulo, Editora WMF Martins Fontes
Schmid W (2002) En busca de un nuevo arte de vivir: la pregunta por el fundamento y la nueva fundamentación ética en Foucault. Pré-textos, Valencia

Author Biographies

Jorge Luiz Barbosa has a Master's degree in Geography (UFRJ), a Ph.D. in Human Geography from the University of São Paulo, and a post-doc in Human Geography from the University of Barcelona (Spain). Associate Professor at the Department of Geography at the Fluminense Federal University and Director of the Favelas Observatory of Rio de Janeiro, he is the author and organizer of several books, chapters and papers, in particular: *Favelas: Alegria e Dor da Cidade* (2005); *O Novo carioca* (2012); *Paisagens crepusculares da ficção científica: elegia das utopias urbanas do modernismo* (2013); *Solos Culturais* (2013).

Ilaina Damasceno Pereira has a master's degree in Geography from the Federal University of Ceará and a doctorate in Geography from the Fluminense Federal University. She is currently a tenured Professor at the College of Education and a member of the Afro-Brazilian Studies Center at the Rio de Janeiro State University.

Chapter 4
A Cornered Democracy: The Echoes of the 2013 Demonstrations in Rio de Janeiro and the Architecture of a Crisis

Lia Beatriz Teixeira Torraca

Abstract One way to understand the complexities of Rio de Janeiro and the current political crisis in Brazil is to observe the 2013 demonstrations. The protest movements exposed a divided city, its contrasts and its contradictions, projecting a Cornered Democracy—the language of the division between the democratic asphalt and the permanent state of exception imposed on the slum. The Cornered Democracy expresses the aesthetics of violence. When analysing the protest movements that took over the streets in 2013, it is possible to empirically investigate how the current crisis was developed, how the traditional media acted through a political technique of reality construction, and how this behaviour promoted division and polarization, reducing democratic possibilities. If in 2016 we witnessed the "self-destruction" of the country, it is necessary to investigate the fire, the arsonists and the importance of embers, instead of trying to erase them.

Keywords Protest movements · Democracy · Reality construction
Slums · Police violence

4.1 Introduction

One way to understand the current political crisis in Brazil is to analyse the 2013 demonstrations. To understand the complexities of Rio de Janeiro, we need to back in time a lot more, precisely, to the government of Mayor Pereira Passos. He was responsible for the first urbanistic reform of Rio de Janeiro, in the beginning of the twentieth century, when the city was still Brazil's capital. The refurbishment aimed at the Europeanization of Rio de Janeiro, promoting the destruction of tenements, which caused the displacement of poor, black and north-eastern people to the hills of Rio de Janeiro. It was the beginning of the slums in the city. It was the first step to construct a territorial and a social division in Rio de Janeiro.

L. B. T. Torraca (✉)
Federal University of Rio de Janeiro, Rio de Janeiro, Brazil
e-mail: liatorraca@icloud.com

© Springer International Publishing AG, part of Springer Nature 2018
L. Capanema Alvares and J. L. Barbosa (eds.), *Urban Public Spaces*,
The Urban Book Series, https://doi.org/10.1007/978-3-319-74253-3_4

The second decisive moment for the city was the transfer of the country's capital to Brasília, shifting Rio's protagonism to the new capital. Since its inauguration on 21 April 1960, Rio de Janeiro began to face severe consequences of this geopolitical change, intensified by the civil-military coup d'Etat in 1964. A coup d'Etat that subjected Brazil to 21 years of military dictatorship and which presents its consequences to the present day, especially regarding some decisions that kept alive the legacies of those *lead years*. This essay tries to show how these two moments have intertwined in building a divided city and how their consequences showed up in the 2013 riots.

Although we have evolved in several aspects after the end of this dictatorship period, particularly during the two mandates of President Luiz Inácio Lula da Silva (2003–2010), many distortions remained latent, of which the main examples can be observed in Rio de Janeiro. For some years, it appeared as if the public policies that guaranteed the reduction of social inequality and, consequently, the reduction of violence, had also created a guarantee that the country had matured its democracy. But the city, in its inter-scalar division, kept the spoils of the dictatorship, both by maintaining a militarized police, and by measures that imposed on the slums of Rio de Janeiro configuring what Agamben calls a Permanent State of Exception (Agamben 2004), projected in the Units of Pacification Police (UPP). The pacification project implemented by the Rio de Janeiro's government, in 2008, was part of the city preparation for the mega-events to come, as the 2013 FIFA Confederations Cup, 2014 World Football Cup and 2016 Rio Summer Olympics and Paralympics Games approached. The project allegedly intended to retake the territories dominated by the drug traffic or by the militia, which isolated several communities from the state action. The UPPs were drawn after "The Police of Proximity" principles which, according to the Security Department, were based on the idea of establishing a partnership between the people and the public security institutions and thus fuelling the intention of doing more than just community policing. However, the security project implemented by the State Governor with the support of the city of Rio de Janeiro government ended up revealing how distanced we were from the paths of a *re-democratization*.

We would only clearly realize the social cleavages in 2013, precisely on the eve of the 2013 FIFA Confederations Cup, when Brazilian streets were set on fire by protests called by the Free Pass Movement (MPL), against the increase of twenty cents in bus fares. The dissatisfaction exposed by the 2013 demonstrations was a big surprise then; after all, we were not suffering the oppression of a dictatorship, nor were we facing the effects of a global or domestic economic crisis. On the contrary, we seemed to live an auspicious moment, a season of low inflation and low unemployment rates. However, discussions going on in the virtual space hit the public space and the voices of the streets demonstrated that we were facing more issues than we could perceive. The expression "more than twenty cents", came to symbolically represent the 2013 rallies and manifested there were much more than the increase of twenty cents to them. The shout in Rio de Janeiro echoed our divisions and our idiosyncrasies. A shout convulsed the streets and shook the hegemony of the Brazilian mainstream media that had always controlled the construction of our reality. The extent to which the dissatisfaction manifested during the protests translated reality raised a question about our understanding of the polyphony of the streets. The challenge is to identify and analyse how many more "cents" the heterogeneity of protesters took to the streets.

The 2013 cry also generated harsh state reactions and the population had to experience the expansion of a state of exception that was previously limited to the slums of Rio de Janeiro. The social division lived daily by the inhabitants of the city made itself present in the riots, what exposed the distance between the democracy of the asphalt (i.e. formal neighbourhoods) and the bare life of the slum (i.e. non-urbanized and informally occupied land). One distance that has been potentiated by the interference of the hegemonic media.

What we call a Cornered Democracy is the projection of a divided city. The concept intends to explain some aspects of the contemporary democracy, as we can see in Rio de Janeiro's cleavage and its reflections. The Cornered Democracy, as we conceptualize it, is presented as a language of this divided space, in between the democratic asphalt and the permanent state of exception imposed on the slum, realized in the (dis)order of the oligarchic projects that (dis)arrange the public space. The Cornered Democracy reflects an aesthetic inherited from the military dictatorship, in which the police institution mirrors the militarized face of the contemporary state. A democracy of privileges for those who live in the asphalt, and its absence for those who suffer in the slums.

The Cornered Democracy mirrors the age of the Democratic Anthropophagy (Torraca 2016), a phenomenon that is intrinsically linked to the contemporary democracy and to the consumer society. A process that reflects self-consumption and feeds the circularity of violence in which we are immersed, absorbed by fear and hate. This is the aesthetics of violence, it is the projection of inequality and of the division between slum and asphalt—our social division—in the specific case of Rio de Janeiro. However, in this same anthropophagic process emerges an innovative aesthetics of the city—an aesthetic of resistance. A resistance that emerged in the virtual spaces was transferred to the public spaces. A resistance constructed by rescuing the public space and re-signifying it, as the Occupy Movements have demonstrated.

The volume, the intensity of voices and the visibility of issues made believe that the Brazilian government would promote the reforms demanded during the riots, particularly the political reform. The results of the 2014 polls for Brazilian Presidency, Congress representatives and State Governors, however, showed how far we were from responding to the demands that convulsed the country in 2013. Not only did we keep most of the political actors on the National Congress, one of the places where this crisis was forged and that was responsible for maintaining the same political format with its distortions, but we also voted to the right wing, setting the stage to worsening differences, divisions and inequalities. The first steps in the construction of a crisis scenario were then clear. Facing now a scenario of political, economical and social collapse in the country, it is imperious to reflect on the construction of this crisis, which necessarily involves the investigation of the Brazilian media role, especially during the year 2013.

Instead of forgetting the 2013 demonstrations and moving on, we need to explore those events because they have the potential to show how the traditional media operates through a political technique for constructing not only reality but also a crisis. This technology has become visible through the performance of a new media, which began to organize events through social media and stream live images of the demonstrations. This alternative media was able to break the circularity of violence, fed back by the traditional media that, alone, has always constructed a reality according to its own interests.

During the 2013 rallies, it was possible to watch a dispute over the construction of reality between this new media and the traditional media. This dispute decentralized mass communication, which has always been concentrated in the hands of mainstream media groups—managed by only five families in Brazil—and had the potential to strengthen Brazilian democracy. However, it was also in 2013 that the mainstream media was able to reconnect itself to the circularity of violence, retaking its hegemony in the construction of reality through an anti-corruption discourse, establishing political polarization—the embryonic crisis. From this observation, we can understand the political and economic collapse as a result of the re-signified role of the traditional media in reframing Brazilian democracy and its influence to construct a divided society. Looking back at the 2013 riots, it is possible to understand how the current crisis was forged, how the traditional media acted using a political technique for constructing reality, and how this behaviour promotes divisions and polarizations, reducing the democratic possibilities. If we now witness the "self-destruction" of Brazil, it is necessary to investigate the fire, the arsonists and the importance of embers, instead of trying to erase them.

4.2 The Echoes of the 2013 Demonstrations

The Brazilian scenario in the 2013 beginnings denoted a reality distant to collapse and did not indicate that the country would be caught in the wave of protests that erupted around the world. However, dissatisfaction, previously restricted to the virtual universe, came to occupy public spaces, revealing a diverse reality than that printed on the newspapers headlines until then.

The voices of the streets exposed numerous discontentment, summarized in the phrase "more than twenty cents", and intensified in the cry "we want schools and hospitals FIFA standards", which was later re-signified by the mainstream media in a crusade against corruption. It is incontestable that "more than twenty cents" caught our streets on fire. It is certain that these "cents" call for a deep discussion about urban mobility, and about public policies that promote social welfare through quality hospitals and education, and are capable of facing inequality, as one way to face the violence problem.

For those attentive and aware of the political and social scenario, it was possible to envision that the demonstrations did not erupt unexpectedly, neither did the police violence, as that was not a specific response to the protests, especially in Rio de Janeiro's case, considering the polemic public security policy deployed by the State Government, particularly the occupation and pacification projects. Although the feeling of living under a state of exception is the reality of the poor population living in Rio slums, the discussion on territorial, social and legal division, subsistent between slum and asphalt, emerged with all its intensity since the state reactions during the 2013 riots.

The demonstrations reflected a divided city, between lead bullets (for the slums) and rubber bullets (for the asphalt), amidst fragmented senses of a hijacked democracy, between the "permanent state of exception" (Agamben 2004) and the "oligarchic rule of law" (Rancière 2014), producing and reproducing violence uninterruptedly to attend exclusively to private interests, forged in a discourse in favour of the welfare of all.

The empathy drawn to the protest movements was also divided between the slum and the asphalt as can be noticed in a comparison between the adhesion to the demonstrations staged by the "asphalt" and the spontaneous demonstrations of the slums that were bulldozed by the bloody lead bullets. The commotion with the victims of violent police actions, which, at first, provoked solidarity, brought sizeable groups of the population answering the calls to join the riots, whereas the same reaction was never true in face of the countless demonstrations called by poor community residents to protest against the same—or worse—police violence, the violence that actually KILLS! Slums riots count only with the solidarity of other members of the communities, some activists, members of non-governmental organizations and human rights movements, and a few political parties.

The 2013 demonstrations promoted the visibility of aspects of the "war against violence" once masked, such as those concerning the State of Rio de Janeiro public security policy through the Pacifying Police Units, which legitimized violence. The pacification project potentiated the territorial division between slum and asphalt, between the democratic space and the absence of law, projected in the police presence, at sovereign wills' disposal (Agamben 2010). The Pacifying Police Units brought the militarization to daily life that had been invisible to the terrified eyes of the asphalt world; they saw in the security project presented by the media-state partnership the solution to the "endemic violence", and therefore a promise to resolve the public (in)security crisis.

The pacifying discourse promoted another form of submission, setting the narrative of citizenship throughout the rescued territories. Its project promoted a new territorial and social setting through the removal of the visible traits of the white presence: a wall built on the limits between the Red Line Highway and the Maré community allegedly meant to serve as an acoustic protection for the inhabitants, as state authorities declared. In reality, a pacification through walls constructed to limit the inclusion of *The Other* (the black inhabitant of the slums) in venturous territories, and to hide the exclusion of *The Other* (the white highway user) in the bare slum territory. A project thought out to isolate the different, to deny the difference. Those walls of silence are nothing less than instruments of control, isolation, containment and real estate protection, such as the numerous protection gates in luxurious buildings spread around the city, intended to avoid the risk of exposure to

Fig. 4.1 "Pacification war" in Rio's favelas. *Source* Observatório de Favelas

the other and to ensure the boundaries of social division, under the pretext of security. These latter divisions ended up becoming a right to security. The fences intended to protect the façades of capitalist icons against the acts of "vandalism" during the 2013 riots, also reproduced the same techniques of division, the same methods of isolation imposed on Rio's slums.

The pacification project was the only alternative to face violence, as authorities have declared. However, the "pacification war" (Fig. 4.1) had already expressed the contradiction in its own denomination, and as pointed out by Hannah Arendt in her book On Violence, "peace is the continuation of war by other means" (Arendt 1985, p. 8).

From this perspective, the only choice left to the "pacified" population is to resist. A resistance that seeks the survival of subjectivity, vulnerable and available to the discourse of fear and (in)security. Much more than sticking to the discussion on the state model to which we are submitted, the era is of Resistance. Democracy needs conflict to survive.

Inserted in this reality, anyone would consciously or unconsciously struggle, as Bauman notes, trying to reach "meaning and identity", pulling efforts together within the dynamics of the "liquid-modern" city (Bauman 2007, pp. 86–87).

Public spaces have been demarcated as spaces of exclusion, instead of being shared as constructions of relationships based on our own differences. In between visible and invisible walls, the institutionalized racism serves as a barrier for the attempts to build a unique Rio de Janeiro; instead, the city follows a tendency to raise walls that set a permanent state of exception and demarcate the collective memory with the shadows of walls that remain dividing society, fragmenting life, whether in Gaza, Berlin or Rio de Janeiro.

The division between slum and asphalt also relates to the colonial power of oligarchic structures which, in their turn, relate to the history of police institutions in Brazil. A culture of colonization that can be seen in the alienation of a consumer society, preventing the construction of a subjectivity of the economically colonized; a society in which the roots of prejudice are reproduced in the subterranean are invisible to scattered eyes and are concentrated on the spectacle of empty bodies controlled by terror.

4.3 A Cornered Democracy

When thousands of Brazilians took over the streets in 2013 to express their dissatisfactions, they did not expect to experience on the democratic asphalt the extent of exceptions perpetuated on the slum. The "voices of the streets" faced an apparently disproportionate reaction of the state. But that reaction was actually compatible to the model that had been systematically adopted by the asphalt in a one-way only road. Due to the demonstrations, the asphalt felt its proximity to the "establishment, through the state of exception, of a legal and civil war that allows the physical elimination not only of political opponents, but also of entire categories of citizens who, for whatever reason, do not seem integrated into the political system" (Agamben 2004, p. 13). A state of exception paradigm, not as a concept which excludes the law, but as biopolitics realization, which exposes the paradoxical relationship between contemporary democracy as rule, and its exception as the legal form of what cannot have a legal form. A state subject to the domain and control of an order that structures its logic on the will of the sovereign; an oligarchic and totalitarian will that seemed restricted to the slums, and, with the demonstrations, broke into the democratic asphalt. A democracy cornered by inequalities of a city divided between slum and asphalt.

As in the context of the "war on terror" declared by the USA, the state of Rio de Janeiro also elected its enemies: a category of bare life citizens. On a case built by the media, the figure of Amarildo, a bricklayer assistant, resident of the Rocinha slum, who disappeared under the state custody, on 14 July 2013, stood out as a symbol of that category in a war against drug trafficking and against the "vandals" of the asphalt. Amarildo projected Agamben's *homo sacer* (Agamben 2010), the countless lives available to the will of the sovereign and in name of his security, his projects and commitments. He symbolized the victims of the violence of a state that had chosen to remain militarized, countering the democratic ideal. The disappearance of Amarildo coincided with the period in which public opinion began to question the violent police repression against demonstrators during the riots and thus his figure starred the collective mourning of a deadened society. A society robotised and hypnotized that cannot see or touch the *other* that does not sympathize with the pain of the *other*, just pities the similar *other*.

Amarildo's case is also emblematic because it represents the trend of expansion of Democratic States' executive powers, under which torture, surveillance, summary executions and people disappearances establish a state of political exception. In these cases, the permanence of such exceptional practices as contemporary techniques of government empties the sense of temporarily from the concept. According to the declaration of The Citizenship and Human Rights Protection Committee of the State Senate of Rio de Janeiro,[1] Amarildo represented the thousands missing in the state. The data compiled by the Public Security Institute of Rio de Janeiro indicates there were 5,934 disappeared persons in 2012 alone, and a total of 50,389 people who disappeared between the years 2003–2012. In slums with UPPs, there was a 72.7% growth in disappearance cases within the first year of the project's implementation.

The Pacifying Police Units are examples of these techniques of government, although they do not admit themselves as practical features of a state of exception; rather, they publicize themselves as containment mechanisms of violence to ensure the population safety, and therefore, the success of the mega-events.[2] Reality, however, is far from the political discourse focused on the promotion of society's welfare or on inclusion and the combating of inequalities. The latent violence observed in the relations between people in the pacified communities and the pacifying police is a symptom of a state that still restrains acts of resistance, evoking the linkage of these distortions to the incompleteness of Brazilian democracy, as it maintains a militarized police.

The choice to continue with a militarized state after the end of the dictatorship shows a logic that implies the admittance of distortions and the application of force as a security strategy, which ends up causing more violence with episodes such as those witnessed during the 2013 riots, or the countless cases of torture, disappearance and murder by the police. The militarized peace is guaranteed through tanks, armed vehicles and fusils, although the authorities' statements refer to non-lethal weapons used by peacekeeping forces. The militarized reality captured by the resident's lenses contradicts the peace discourse.

If, in the USA it is the war on terror that justifies the exceptional measures, in Rio de Janeiro the war on drugs has legitimized exceptional measures in the spaces used to the absence of law, which Agamben defines as empty spaces (Agamben 2004)—potentially spaces of bare life (Agamben 2010). During the demonstrations, it was as if those anomic spaces had their borders dilated, as if the suspicious or threatening standard behaviours were expanded.

The war against drug trafficking brought surveillance into the slum and private spaces, and, alike the US war on terror, the control has been established through the

---

[1]Information available on pages 48 a 50 of The Citizenship and Human Rights Protection Committee of the State Senate of Rio de Janeiro Report: <http://ddh.org.br/wp-content/uploads/2014/01/relatorio2013cddh.pdf>

[2]See first note.

4 A Cornered Democracy: The Echoes of the 2013 Demonstrations …

dissemination of a war idea, which ultimately undermines the resistance. The slum survivors are so impregnated with violence that many do not even get to realize the great trap of the state with its peace discourse through war, disguised as a "war against drug trafficking", "that annihilates the black youth, poor and slummed" as denounced by State deputy Marcelo Freixo.[3] Rio would not be doomed to this situation should the demilitarization be part of the national policy agenda. In Brazil, the police has represented an auxiliary to the armed forces, hence its name "military police"; demilitarization would be a way of disarticulating the destructive structure of a militarized state and its destabilizing wars that feed the circularity of violence, but the only legislative initiative on demilitarization so far has been the amendment project 51/2013, presenting proposals to separate the police and the armed forces, still pending before the House of Representatives.

The Cornered Democracy is presented as a language of these divided public spaces between the democratic asphalt and this permanent state of exception imposed on the slum, mirroring the (dis)order of the oligarchic projects. The Cornered Democracy reflects an aesthetic inherited from the military dictatorship, in which the police institution reflects the militarized face of the contemporary state. The police institution in Rio de Janeiro is, to say the least, polemic in the exercise of its duties, which are easily subject to the state interests.

The Cornered Democracy mirrors a state that causes criminality, violence and the marginalization of the "slum". It is a cruel inversion that labels the community citizens as criminals, violent and marginals. The state itself is the main responsible for criminalizing, ravishing and marginalizing citizens. It is the state who promotes a systematic destruction of the identity of the slum resident who has been subjugated to the sovereign interests. This is what Labica calls an organizational violence that promotes complete social dehumanization (Labica 2009).

The permanent threat speech is orchestrated in a "totalitarian" manner, as Zizek warns, "in which evil is transformed into a mythic threat with which the community establishes a temporary truce and against which must maintain a constant state of emergency" (Zizek 2008, p. 26). The community is thus subsumed to the policy of fear—the post-politic biopolitics. For Zizek, what we call democracy these days is the tyranny that takes on new disguises (Zizek 2008, pp. 27–30). As part of a new digital democracy, a "cyberdemocracy" which avoids a centralized state control, while it covers up a series of gaps and uncomfortable tensions,[4] despite the communication amplitude and the self-organizing capacity. This comes as a paradox that reinforces the image of what would be a typical case of the democratic anthropophagy era.

---

[3]See first note.

[4]Zizek refers to the notion of "atonal" world—*monde atone* (Zizek 2008, p. 42), elaborated by Alain Badiou, "in which lack the intervention of a Master-Signifier to impose meaningful order onto the confused multiplicity of reality" (Zizek 2008, p. 42).

Despite the intrinsic difficulties in the very form of democratic regimes, Bobbio reminds us that

> democracy is certainly the most perfect among the ways that men were able to imagine and, at least in part, to perform; but precisely because it is the most perfect it is also the most difficult. [...] democracy is the most desirable regime, but also the most difficult to make work and the easier to ruin: it sets out the task of conciliating two contrasting things, which are freedom and power. (Bobbio 2013, p. 35)

4.4 The Age of the Democratic Anthropophagy

The "twenty cents" may be useful to think about the democratic anthropophagy (Torraca 2016) as the term intends to explain phenomena that are intrinsically linked to the contemporary democracies and to the consumer society. It is a term meant to highlight self-consumption, as it feeds the circularity of violence in which we are immersed. The era of democratic anthropophagy is marked by the aesthetics of violence which, in the specific case of Rio de Janeiro public spaces, is the face of inequality, of the division between slum and asphalt, of violence as a Spectacle of the Real. It is the "law of the cannibal", to which the famous Brazilian modernist author Oswald de Andrade made reference in his Cannibalist Manifesto; it is the life "through a somnambulistic law", because "we never admitted the birth of the logic among us" (de Andrade 1928).

The era of democratic anthropophagy is the reflection of this way of integrating the individual in a society that is mediated by consumption. We consume objects, images, information, and even the *Other*. Existing as a subject depends on one's existence as a consumer, even if it means the annihilation of one's identity. The projection of the democratic anthropophagy comes as the subversion of what was once political into material goods designed to be avidly consumed, anaesthetizing the pain of life. It is the self-consumption of democracy in the process of constructing reality. It is the use of this construction as truth, as the only reality, opening space for dealing with democracy destruction within the legal system.

Interesting enough, the Occupy movements re-signified consumption and social relations through the occupations of public spaces. The crisis in Greece, for example, as Douzinas explains (Douzinas 2013), has led to a reorganization of the priorities in the daily lives of countless people, as it also happened with the use and re-appropriation of public spaces. The consumption of goods was replaced by the exchange of help and affection, the sharing of needs and difficulties and the dialogue about the use of public spaces. This political reactivation represented a way to construct a space of acquaintanceship, with all and for all, without divisions, walls or exclusions.

The division designed by the exclusion of the public space is responsible for labelling what is a crime, who is the threat. Actions tolerated in the asphalt receive a name, while the same action will be named a crime or a criminal offense if it is practiced in the slum. The city division is reproduced in the narrative disseminated by the mainstream media: vandals × peaceful, looter × orderly, invaders × occupants. This division is imposed on the differentiation between graffiti and "pichação",[5] between culture and apology to crime, between music and noise, between disorder and crime, between permission and prohibition, between silence and freedom.

By criminalizing culture and destroying identities, the state regains control and legitimizes repression, exile, and human displacement, aggravating the division of the city, the polarization of society. The greater the oppression, the more it increases the possibility of a violent reaction, because the tendency of social explosion tends to be proportional to the imposed oppression. The aesthetics that emerges from the slums demonstrates how politics has been synonymous to unfulfilled promises, and shows how the military occupation of slums has deepened gentrification processes, annihilating memories, crystallizing inequalities and perpetuating the dichotomy between slum and asphalt.

Despite the discourse of social ascension of the slum population, disseminated by both the state and the mainstream media, the reality still is our social debt to this population, their daily massacre, oppression, control and division. The slum resident voices continuously refuse the agenda of demands created for an envisioned "new middle class", which would correspond to an envisioned citizenship supported by the supposed increase in income, and therefore with unprecedented purchasing power as "new consumers". The democratic belonging ideal was hit by an anthropophagic dilemma between consuming or be consumed.

Resistance seems to come with the perception that everything is consumed, even one's humanity, as dictated by the aesthetics of the (dis)order. The reality of the slum does not hide how people are transformed into trash after forced evictions that break family and friendship ties, destroy the residents' self-esteem and suppress community histories. The state legalizes the extermination of identities through expropriations. The pacification war spreads the rests of a silenced democracy in between its walls and tanks where peace has not arrived in the form of education, health and sanitation, but at rifle point—a militarized peace.

As a form of resistance, public spaces occupations represent the political reactivation of a society consumed in time and in its own space in a search for the sense of democracy. It is the rescuing of political practice against consumerist kidnapping of lives and dreams. It is the resistance to the occupations promoted by the state and its pacification project—the war on occupations.

The artistic events and activities in slums present themselves as a resistance to the circularity of violence imposed by the state, obstructing, blocking and prohibiting communication. The prohibition of funk music, for example, goes beyond a negation of leisure, and it reaches the resistance of the oppressed, their most spontaneous demonstration, asphyxiating their survival, their culture, their history.

---

[5]We can say that graffiti is the urban art, the asphalt art, and "pichação" is the art that comes from the slum. Graffiti is tolerated by the public authorities while "pichação" is prohibited and imputed to conduct as a criminal offense, denominated as vandalism.

Funk music mirrors the rearranged city, "reterritorialized" between militia and drug trafficking, between the crime and the possibility of identity construction, and mainly, founding new ways of integrating informal trade due to its ability to generate capital.

The same happens with urban art, which presents itself as a medium of resistance, as a possibility for the oppressed to express their histories as consequences of the social fragmentation experienced in public spaces, whereas the city is a space where signs are exposed, urban art represents the subversive aesthetic of freedom as a political element, the fragmentation of the discourse and the relationship with the symbols of the city. Urban art, as a new political language, subverts the vandalism discourse. If there is a way for slum and asphalt to dialogue, it is the graffiti/pichação dialogue. That explains why the vandalism discourse is used to keep them separate, especially due to their political power, transgressing public spaces in the form of resistance to oppression. State attempts to criminalize the graffiti/pichação, enlisting it as a crime against property[6] is, thus, not surprising.

4.5 The Spectacle of the Real and the Dispute of Reality Construction

In the era of the Democratic Anthropophagy, the crisis is transformed in spectacle by the mainstream media. During the demonstrations of 2013, the symbolic violence of the oligopolistic media found in the alternative media a reaction to the exclusive construction of reality. A new media appeared in contrast to the narrative of peace through war, of militarization of life and, mainly, of the attempt to transform the activist in an enemy, a Manichean logic according to which the "good, peaceful and lethargic" always wins the "evil, vandal and threatening" (Fig. 4.2).

The alternative media was responsible for making the spectator see how the traditional media constructs reality as truth, becoming a new form of resistance, capable of breaking the hegemony of a unique glance, of a unison voice, of a uniform view of the facts. A resistance à la Oswald de Andrade: "Down with the reversible world, and against objectified ideas. 'Cadaverized'. The stop of thinking that is dynamic. The individual as a victim of the system. Source of classical injustices. Of romantic injustices. And the forgetting of interior conquests" (de Andrade 1928).

Perhaps, the greatest revolution regarding the 2013 riots was caused by the digital media and its dispute with the mainstream media over the power to construct reality, raising questions on the legitimacy of the media, and on the formulation of information which is digested in news and credited as truth. A power that had seemed unshakeable, given the symbolism and the strength of the great media oligopoly, until contradicted by media activists, through the images released *online*

---

[6]See Brazilian Penal Code, articles 163 and 305.

4 A Cornered Democracy: The Echoes of the 2013 Demonstrations … 69

Fig. 4.2 2013 riots within a Cornered Democracy. *Source* Ana Carolina Fernandes

during the riots. If, to traditional media, the start of the demonstrations was only a disturbance to traffic caused by a group of rioters, being confronted with the social upheaval achieved by protesters was quite astonishing. After the surprise, however, it immediately transformed protesters in vandals and enemies of the state and the society.

The rejection of the spectators to the mainstream media coverage during the demonstrations exposed, much more than the effects of the lost credibility, the difficulties of the Brazilian democratization process and the construction of its memory. Identities do not transform themselves overnight, and they are continually renewed and fed by social memories as present events, not as something that is already past (Luhmann 2005). A possible truth is, thus, subject to the future identities as they will be shaped by social memories.

When established by violence, the power relations that link state and communication networks behave as a catalyst of a technology according to which language can cunningly manipulate the public opinion, transformed into mere published opinion, bringing demonstrations of disbelief and revolt with the revelation of contradictions. We need to bear in mind that information can be transformed into weapon in the mainstream media language. The vandalism speech disseminated by the mainstream media was a projection of violence, which insisted on criminalizing poverty and those who dared to protest. While traditional media underestimated the rioting voices, the alternative media transmitted online the violent police action against the movements. That ended up inciting outrage of part of the population and caused increasing adhesion to demonstrations. Hence, when the vandalism narrative was contradicted by the alternative media the circularity of violence was temporarily broken.

However, if the digital connections were able to (re)join victims of the same oppression in a single fight for dignity, they were unable to prevent a reconnection to the circularity of violence. The unison cry against corruption during the 2013 riots was responsible for opening a space for traditional media to recover its control in the exercise of reality building. From then on, it has created and managed a public crisis for its own benefit. In a country where roughly half of the population has access to the internet, the traditional media power is enormous, and the open TV programming gains relevance as an oppressive instrument. On the contrary, it could as well have acted as an empowerment channel to the spectator.

As the vast majority of Brazilians remains informed through the traditional media, which holds the monopoly of the reality construction, it becomes mandatory to reflect on its relationship with democracy. The mainstream media has managed to transform the original meaning of the riots from a cry for rights into a "war against corruption". This resignification reveals how the reality is constructed to satisfy a specific political motivation. When the traditional media moves away from presenting the reality of the facts to construct reality with political goals, it opens a path to the destruction of democracy through the construction of a crisis.

Activists did not allow the intervention of the mainstream media in the movements, since there were no established leaderships to deal with, but specially because protesters rejected any top-down intervention. Nevertheless, the traditional media was able to re-signify the "much more than twenty cents" in an anti-corruption discourse. Surreptitiously, the mainstream media linked the urban cry for rights to corruption and to trial the criminal prosecution 470,[7] re-establishing the bridge with its "audience"; through the appropriation of an urban-based narrative, it managed to influence the opinion against federal government and congressmen. The same manoeuvre was articulated in the Amarildo's case, transformed into a symbolic victim of the endemic corruption that contaminates politics and institutions, and allows the state of exception (Agamben 2004) to be perpetuated in the everyday lives of community residents. When the vandal discourse began to lose momentum, and could no longer make media headlines, it gave way to the anti-corruption crusade. Brazil then witnessed the construction of a political and economic crisis within the same narrative: a war against corruption.

It is important to recall that the power of the mainstream media had already been successfully tested in Rio de Janeiro when it instrumentalized the slums peace process. The need for violence to achieve peace, violence serving as an instrument to build peace, as an authoritarian and unilateral construction and reproduction of the "truths" was introjected onto both asphalt and community residents. Reality then came to be a spectacle broadcasted by the mainstream media, since it was the exclusive owner of the right to spread fear or (in)security, up to the arrival of an alternative media that destabilized this mediation between society and state.

---

[7]The criminal prosecution 470 (Ação Penal 470), judged in the Brazilian Supreme Court, was known as "mensalão petista". It was a corruption case involving politicians of several parties that received money to vote according the federal government interests.

4.6 Conclusion

The protests in 2013 show us the walls—visible and invisible—that divide the public spaces of Rio de Janeiro, between the lead bullets that bleed the slums and rubber bullets that frightened the democratic asphalt. The protests revealed some concealed aspects about the public security policy of Rio de Janeiro, which mission was to bring pacification through the "war on drugs", imposing, since 2008, a militarized life to the population that lives in the slums. It is the wreckage of democracy; those are reflections of the architecture of violence that draws the shadows of political deconstruction that projects itself in the deepened division of a split society and in the construction of a crisis.

If in 2016 we witnessed the Brazilian political, economic and social self-destruction, there is a need to account for what was lost in the path we forged during and since 2013. The streets cried their disbelief in the political system as a catalyst of the society's needs and interests, what ended up creating a vacuum of representation, especially regarding politics as a mediator of social conflicts. Worse yet, that disbelief together with a lack of control, forged the negation of the 2013 riots. The antidemocratic and extremely risky behaviour developed in later movements reflected the heterogeneity within the arsonists, especially expressed in social networks posts that continuously call for a dictatorship revival, in claims that associate security to military presence.

Nevertheless, 2013 let us rediscover public spaces as a new form of resistance: the occupations; they symbolized the politic reactivation of a society consumed in its time and its own space. The occupations are a pursuit of the sense of democracy, are the rescue of political practice against the kidnapping of lives and dreams.

We live the aftermath of the 2013 torched public spaces. The political and social crises, together with the uncontrolled violence of the state towards society, are reflections of those fires. To turn those results off is to silence democracy. To turn the fire off is to erase Galli Mathias' definition of law as it appears in de Andrade: "the guarantee of the exercise of possibility" (de Andrade 1928).

Denying the importance of the 2013 demonstrations is encouraging social demobilization; the same social demobilization that allowed the mainstream media to retake control of building reality by itself, and to disseminate speeches able to legitimize anti-terrorism laws. Turning our backs on 2013 is getting caught and entangled by the media-judiciary construction of a crisis.

If in 2013 we sought to transform the territories, to share public spaces, and to knock down all the walls, in 2016 we lived the recrudescence of the old division. Territories were hopelessly catching fire with violence. A violence that burned, destroyed, and rebuilt the walls and the illegalities in spaces void of colour. While during the dictatorship years the enemy was communism, in democratic times the enemy is the vandal, the protester, the activist, the invader, the poor, the drug dealer. At this point in time, the threat is political, and the enemy is a political party. This political and economic destruction is a consequence of the resignification of the media role in Brazilian democracy, is the projection of the democratic anthropophagy. Once again we see our public spaces empty. Those are the echoes of a Cornered Democracy.

References

Agamben G (2004) Estado de Exceção. Homo Sacer, II, 2nd edn. Boitempo, São Paulo
Agamben G (2010) Homo Sacer: o poder soberano e a vida nua I, 2nd edn. Editora UFMG, Minas Gerais
Arendt H (1985) Da Violência. Editora Universidade de Brasília, Brasília
Bauman Z (2007) Vida Líquida. Zahar, Rio de Janeiro
Bobbio N (2013) Qual Democracia? 2nd edn. Edições Loyola Jesuítas, São Paulo
de Andrade O (1928) Manifesto Antropófago. Revista de Antropofagia, São Paulo
Douzinas C (2013) Philosophy and resistance in the crisis. Polity Press, Londres
Labica G (2009) Democracia e Revolução, 1st edn. Editora Expressão Popular, São Paulo
Luhmann N (2005) A Realidade dos Meios de Comunicação. Paulus, São Paulo
Rancière J (2014) O Ódio à Democracia, 1st edn. Boitempo Editorial, São Paulo
Torraca LBT (2016) Democracia Encurralada. Os reflexos das manifestações de 2013 no Rio de Janeiro, 1st edn. Lumen Juris, Rio de Janeiro
Zizek S (2008) Violence. Picador, New York

Author Biography

Lia Beatriz Teixeira Torraca has a Bachelor's degree in Law (1992), a master's degree in Law (2015), and is currently working on her doctorate degree in Law with an emphasis in Human Rights, Society and Art at the Graduate Program in Law of the Federal University of Rio de Janeiro, where she is also the media coordinator. She is an assistant editor for Mares Editors, Brazil, member of the research group Movie and Law at the Federal University of Rio de Janeiro, of the Latin American Network for Research in Systems Theories, Law and Policy and the Network for Latin American Democratic Constitutionalism, and has authored the book *Cornered Democracy: the aftermath of the 2013 manifestations in Rio de Janeiro*, published by Lumen Juris Editors, 2016.

Chapter 5
Leisure and Work in Contemporary Urban-Metropolitan Space: Perspectives, Tendencies, and Utopias

Ângelo Serpa

Abstract The starting point for the discussion proposed in this chapter is the premise that the production of leisure spaces is inseparable and dialectically related to the production of work spaces in contemporary cities and metropolises. It is also based on the assumption that capital-work/work-leisure relationships have undergone relevant modifications in recent decades, which should be considered in the analysis of the proposed theme. The aim is to characterize the economic, political, social, and cultural transformations of capital-work/work-leisure relationships in the contemporary world, starting from the consolidation of industrial society and the modern era, and moving on to present a specific case study of working-class neighborhoods in Salvador and Feira de Santana, about the work and leisure of micro-entrepreneurs, the proprietors of micro-businesses, and consumers in neighborhoods in the study, indicating and problematizing these transformations in a spatial-temporal context. Based on the concepts of "creative idleness" and "telework", the discussion is widened to dwell how on the changes in capital-work/work-leisure relationships may impact on daily life in cities and metropolises and on the consequences for the use and appropriation of urban public spaces, based on the trends presented here, deepening a prospective vision of these impacts in an urban and metropolitan context.

Keywords Leisure · Work · Entrepreneurship · Creative idleness
City · Metropolis

An earlier version of this paper was published by Mercator (Fortaleza) vol. 14, Fortaleza, Dec. 2015.

Â. Serpa (✉)
Department of Geography, Institute of Geosciences,
Federal University of Bahia, Salvador, Brazil
e-mail: angserpa@ufba.br

© Springer International Publishing AG, part of Springer Nature 2018   73
L. Capanema Alvares and J. L. Barbosa (eds.), *Urban Public Spaces*,
The Urban Book Series, https://doi.org/10.1007/978-3-319-74253-3_5

5.1 Introduction

To speak of leisure spaces in the production of metropolises means discussing the socio-spatial relationships encompassed by the phenomenon, linking it to its dialectic and inseparable pair: work spaces in the contemporary metropolitan context. In other words, problematizing leisure also implies thinking about work, especially the multiple spaces and times involved in both activities. I begin with the assumption that capital-work/work-leisure relationships have been subjected to important modifications in recent decades that need to be considered in the analysis of the proposed theme.

Based on the thinking of David Harvey, Hannah Arendt, and Richard Sennett, initially we seek to characterize the economic, political, social, and cultural transformations of capital-work/work-leisure relationships in the contemporary world, starting from the consolidation of industrial society and the modern era. Secondly, based mainly on the concepts of "creative idleness" and "telework", as conceived by Domenico de Masi, the discussion is amplified to reflect on how changes in capital-work/work-leisure relationships can impact on daily life in cities and metropolises, deepening the prospective vision of these impacts in urban and metropolitan contexts, after which we present a specific case study of working-class neighborhoods in Salvador and Feira de Santana which concern the work and leisure of micro-entrepreneurs, small business owners, and consumers, showing and problematizing these transformations in a specific space-time context. Finally, in the final considerations, the discussions undertaken throughout the text are resumed, while at the same time reflecting, albeit briefly, on the implications of the commercialization of leisure on the meanings of contemporary public space—on the scale of the city and the neighborhood—especially as an experience of sociability.

As an introduction, I will begin with the issue of work and automation. Labor and capital are inseparable in the capitalist mode of production, but the work of social reproduction was not (or was marginally) incorporated as productive work in the dialectic of the means of production. That is, housekeeping and caring for children or oneself are not considered productive work. This is the logic of the means of production, and even with what we call the flexible accumulation of capitalism in its current phase, this maxim still holds.

If the logic of productive work in core countries, and later in peripheral countries, tends toward automation and flexibility, increased precariousness, and short term, the reproductive work in the private sphere ambit, that of the family and the individual, is long term. So, what would the world be like with less productive work (freed by automation) and more time for labor, for reproductive work?

It is clear that there are also consequences for the dialectic of leisure and work in the form that it is known today. Leisure is reproduction, work is production, but what would leisure and work be like when dialectically related in the sphere of reproduction? For example, in The Fall of Public Man (Sennett 1998), Richard Sennett shows how children's games prepare future adults for social rules, to control their emotions and self-distancing, and to negotiate their emotions in the public sphere. That is, playfulness is a precondition for cooperation between human beings, for social existence. The contradiction is that nowadays playfulness has been captured by the mode of production logic; leisure has become a possibility of seizing gains, although in the urban-metropolitan cracks and crevices the ludic and art can help subvert relationships from their current established forms (Serpa 2007).

5.2 On Capital-Work/Work-Leisure Relationships in the Contemporary World

In a lecture given at the XIII SIMPURB, in Rio de Janeiro, David Harvey stated that when capital is doing very well, in general, people are doing very badly, emphasizing that this fissure between capital's well-being and people's well-being grows continually faster in both quantitative and qualitative terms. Referring to Marx's concept of alienation, Harvey asks himself "what the relationship is between the professional life and quality of life" and "how far will people go without saying that they cannot live this way" (Harvey 2014, p. 55).

Harvey refers to a survey on professional satisfaction in the USA that revealed that 70% of the population "have an aversion to or are absolutely indifferent to the work they carry out", believing "that they live in workplaces with totally unimportant jobs, that they do not take pride in, which are unsatisfying and that they consider tedious" (Harvey 2014, p. 55). In this context, the author raises a particularly pertinent question for the discussion proposed herein: "Why, in a society that has created every type of timesaving technology to most of us, in fact, have less time to think and relax?" (*op. cit.* p. 55).

5.2.1 Work and Leisure in the Modern Era: Industrial Society

According to several authors, the functional (and radical) separation between work and leisure—in both temporal and spatial terms—goes back to the dawn of industrial society. Evidently, this had consequences for the city, which

> in turn, also specializes itself: developing industrial zones, where production takes place; residential neighborhoods, to rest in; commercial neighborhoods, to shop in; zones for leisure, places for fun, etc. This is the functional city, so dear to Corbusier (...) a synchronized factory requires a synchronized city (...) the city is congested neighborhood after neighborhood, due to the displacement of all its inhabitants at the same time; this is one of the greatest wastes of industrial society. (De Masi 2000, p. 57)

Hannah Arendt states that the danger of automation in industrial society is "less the much deplored mechanization and artificialization of natural life", but the unprecedented intensification of society's vital process of reproduction, since the rhythm of the machines "intensify the natural rhythms of life enormously", undermining the durability of the human world (Arendt 2000, pp. 144–145). Her reasoning is based on the distinction between labor and work. The former, concentrated "exclusively on life and its maintenance, is so oblivious of the world that it might as well not exist", which products—the result of the metabolism of humans with nature—"do not stay in the world long enough to become a part of it" (*op. cit.*, p. 130), while the latter "fabricates the endless variety of things whose sum total constitutes human artifice. They are mostly, but not exclusively, durable objects for use" (*op. cit.*, p. 149) and "the things of the world [that] have the function of stabilizing human life" (p. 150).

Arendt criticizes Marx for not making this distinction between labor and work, between *animal laborans* and *homo faber*, a criticism that she extends to other social thinkers of the so-called modern era. However, for her, the distinction between productive and unproductive (or reproductive) work has, even today, "albeit in a prejudicial manner", "the most fundamental distinction between work and labor":

> The modern age in general and Karl Marx in particular, overwhelmed, as it were, by the unprecedented actual productivity of Western mankind, had an almost irresistible tendency to look upon all labor as work and to speak of the *animal laborans* in terms much more fitting for *homo faber*, hoping all the time that only one more step was needed to eliminate labor and necessity altogether. No doubt the actual historical development that brought labor out of hiding and into the public realm, where it could be organized and "divided", constituted a powerful argument in the development of these theories. (…) Unlike the productivity of work, which adds new objects to the human artifice, the productivity of labor power produces objects only incidentally and is primarily concerned with the means of its own reproduction (…) never "produces" anything but "life". (Arendt 2000, pp. 98–99)

From this perspective, labor and consumption are only "two stages of the same process, imposed upon man by the necessities of life", leveling "all human activities to the common denominator of securing the necessities of life and providing for their abundance" (Arendt 2000, p. 139). Following the Arendtian reasoning, we reach the classical opposition between work and leisure, typical of the modern era and industrial society:

> The (…) trend to reduce all serious activities to the status of making a living is manifest in present-day labor theories, which almost unanimously define labor as the opposite of play. As a result, all serious activities, irrespective of their fruits, are called labor, and every activity which is not necessary either for the life of the individual or for the vital process of society is classified as leisure (…) From the standpoint of "making a living", any activity unconnected with labor becomes a "hobby". (Arendt 2000, pp. 139–140)

In other words, the work equated with labor corresponds to need, and leisure to liberty, since "it is indeed remarkable to see how plausible it is for modern thinking to consider leisure to be a source of freedom". (Arendt 2000, p. 139). Arendt finds the role of the hobby in modern society surprising and hypothesizes that this is at the root of experience in work-leisure theories: In Marx's utopian society, free from work, "all activities would be performed in a way which very closely resembles the manner of hobby activities" (*op. cit.*, p. 140). However, Marx's utopia, in which free time would emancipate men from need, making *animal laborans* productive is fallacious, as this free time "is never spent on anything but consumption, and the more time left to him, the greedier and more craving his appetites" (*op. cit.*, p. 146).

5 Leisure and Work in Contemporary Urban-Metropolitan Space ...

The fact that these appetites become more sophisticated, so that consumption is no longer restricted to necessities but, on the contrary, concentrates mainly on the superfluities of life, does not change the character of this society, but harbors the grave danger that eventually no object in the world will be safe from consumption and annihilation through consumption". (Arendt 2000, p. 146)

5.2.2 Recent Changes to the World of Work

For Sennett (2006), automation has had deep influences on the bureaucratic pyramid of public and private institutions, especially in core countries, drastically reducing its base from the end of the twentieth century. Thus, in both manual and intellectual work, thanks to innovative technologies, organizations can disseminate routine tasks more efficiently: "It is not just that it has become possible to simply reduce the size of the workforce, in addition management can reduce the functional layers of the base—an institutional army in which the soldiers are circuits" (Sennett 2006, p. 46). This especially hinders the inclusion of the masses in the workplace, leaving out "the most vulnerable elements of society, those who want to work but do not have specialized skills" (*op. cit.*).

Sennett defends the idea that at the end of the twentieth century, the capitalist mode of production turned some decisive pages: Power shifted from management to the shareholders of large companies, and investment banking services effectively became international; investors took on the active position of judges, building up or breaking up entire companies; a focus on short-term rather than long-term results; the "delayering of institutions", with the delegation of certain functions to third parties in other businesses; attracting or disposing of employees as the company moves from one task to another; shortening the organization's operational time with an increased focus on immediate and smaller tasks (Sennett 2006, pp. 41–51). Sennett also points to three main deficits for companies, as a consequence of these institutional transformations: "a low level of institutional loyalty, a reduction of the informal confidence among workers and a weakening of institutional knowledge" (*op. cit.*, p. 62).

The result of these processes is the crumbling of work identities in a context of constantly reinvented institutions: "Most corporate restructuring processes have (…) the character of a self-consuming passion in action, especially in the quest for prospective synergies in the processes of company mergers" (Sennett 2006, p. 131). This is the same self-consuming passion that causes the consumer to look for the stimulus of difference in increasingly homogenous products, like a "tourist travelling from one cloned city to another, visiting the same shops, where they buy the same products. However, the point is that they have travelled: for the consumer the stimulus is in the process of movement itself" (*op. cit.*, p. 137). This is also how workers, objects, and places become disposable, as the constant search for new stimuli brings renunciation and disposal to no longer being experienced as losses.

In the working world of the new capitalism, lifetime employment has gradually disappeared, along with careers dedicated to a single institution. Temporary work has increased and is the fastest growing sector of the workforce in countries such as the USA and Great Britain, currently accounting for

[Eight percent] of the American workforce. If we add people employed on short-term contracts to avoid expenses with benefits, in the retail trade, restaurants and other jobs in the service sector, the percentage would be around one fifth of the workforce. (Sennett 2006, p. 51)

Sennett takes the view, particularly interesting for the discussion proposed herein, that these transformations alter the character of the individuals submitted to them, asking how long-term objectives can be sought in a short-term society and how narratives of identity and life history can be developed in a society composed of episodes and fragments. For the author, "on the contrary, the conditions of the new economy feed experiences adrift in time, from place to place, from job to job", corroding the "character qualities linking humans to each other" (Sennett 2007, p. 27). The motto "there is no long term" is the most tangible sign of the new forms of organizing time, especially working time in contemporary times (*op. cit.*, p. 21).

On the other hand, to escape from the instability of temporary and short-term employment, many workers set themselves up as individual entrepreneurs, particularly in the tertiary sector, with micro, small and medium enterprises. Unlike the logic of large companies and institutions, many of these enterprises are only local in scope or are family businesses. This occurs in core countries like Britain and the USA—where most companies have less than three thousand employees and some offer artisanal services, such as small-scale construction companies (Sennett 2006, p. 47)—but also in peripheral countries like Brazil, where entrepreneurship is being adopted on a large scale by low-income classes, as will be briefly analyzed in Sect. 5.4 of this chapter.

5.3 Telework and Creative Leisure: The Amplification of Free Time

In his book "Creative Idleness", De Masi takes issue with a particular fact, found, according to him, frequently in Brazil, but sometimes in Italy as well, where he has seen in hotels and business centers "young men, who to earn their daily bread, spend the whole day inside an elevator, pressing the buttons that match the floor where clients want to get out." In view of this, he asks himself the reason for "belittling the life and intelligence of a youth to this point, keeping him closed up (…) eight hours a day in an elevator, to carry out idiotic and useless work", would it not be better for society in general to "give him the same amount of money, asking him in return to continue studying" (De Masi 2000, p. 265).

For De Masi, post-industrial society, unlike rural or industrial society, is characterized by "a progressive delegation of work to electronic devices and an increasingly imbalanced relationship between the time dedicated to work and free time" (*op. cit.*, p. 101). According to this logic, employees currently do in ten hours what they could accomplish in half the time, but "even if the working day was reduced by half (...) they would not create any hiring requirements for new staff. For this, it would be necessary to reduce the working day to three hours", and this reduction "should soon be followed by a week made up of a maximum of three working days, and every month would have, at the most, three weeks work." Even so, he believes that overtime would not be resolved, as people would stay at work many hours more than the regular working day, as they "are no longer used to staying at home, having time for themselves. (...) it's only in the long term that they will begin to appreciate free time and learn to value it" (*op. cit.*, p. 164).

In accordance with the tendencies pointed out by Harvey and Sennett, De Masi also believes that a large part of the new jobs generated in the USA, Japan, and some European countries are jobs with reduced shifts, "of poor quality and poorly paid, most of which are done by immigrants" (*op. cit.*, p. 100). However, De Masi differentiates this type of employment from part-time jobs, which, in his opinion, may "be the only form of work distribution that will be accepted by companies" (*op. cit.*). In the early 2000s, this was already taking place in countries like Holland, England, and the USA, where part-time jobs accounted for 36, 22, and 20% of the workforce, respectively. Even assuming that some people are overloaded at work due to badly distributed time and tasks, the author believes that "for the majority, work has reduced, so that many people can limit themselves to working five or, at the most, six hours a day" (*op. cit.*, p. 160).

Another argument used by De Masi to maintain that we generally work double the time required is the research done on telework, "work that is not carried out in offices but one's own residence" (*op. cit.*, p. 163). This research "shows that tasks that require eight to ten hours to accomplish at the company, can be accomplished, comfortably, in half the time: four to five hours at the most" (*op. cit.*). It is based on these ideas that the author proposes the introduction of telework and the "extremely short week", not only to radically change the organization of work, but also of life, as "people would have to plan a three or four-day weekend, instead of only two days, to recover their relationships with their wives and children and participate in civil life" (*op. cit.*, p. 166). According to De Masi, "for the first time, (...) since the times of Taylor, changing the organization of work could mean 'changing the organization of a whole existence'" (*op. cit.*, p. 167), despite the fact that to do this would require "a re-education for free time" (*op. cit.*). To summarize:

> Now it is possible to produce more and more goods and services with less and less human work. This means that nowadays for a 20-year-old young person, work only represents a seventh of all the time they are going to live (...) once executive tasks have been delegated to machines, for most people only the performance of intellectual, flexible, creative and entrepreneurial activities will be left: flow into study and games. (...) in other words, in the past years it was work that colonized free time. In the years to come free time will colonize work. (De Masi 2000, p. 298)

Still according to De Masi, the present society should take on reeducation for free time, which is also an education for idleness and creativity. In this light, individuals should be taught "the pleasure of living together, of introspection, of play and beauty" (*op. cit.*, p. 313), the habit "of domestic activities and the autonomous production of many things that until now we have bought readymade" (*op. cit.*), the careful choice of places "to rest, to be entertained and to have fun" (*op. cit.*), educating young people not just for the meanderings of the world of work but also for the "meanderings of various possible leisure options" (*op. cit.*). Reeducation for leisure, creativity, solidarity, and living together would thus be a need of post-industrial society, in which "most people do not know how to entertain themselves or even how to rest. This was understood when there was time" (*op. cit.*, p. 314).

In contrast to the "universe of precision that coincides with industrial society", a universe that is "a rigid, programmed, linear, mathematized universe, in which the affluent abundance of standardized products is the product of creative work by a restricted elite of engineers and the mechanical work of an endless mass of executors" (*op. cit.*, p. 295), post-industrial society, one of creative idleness and telework, is a universe of approximation, "a reflective, mature, conscious, complex approximation, which proceeds from scientific consciousness and precision, covering them and overcoming them" (*op. cit.*, p. 297). This new society of approximation would, for De Masi, have advantages not only for companies and government offices, but also for the workers, due to the "autonomy of times and methods, the coincidence between the home and the workplace, the reduction in costs and the tiredness caused by commuting", among others (*op. cit.*, p. 206).

Although controversial and considered utopian by his critics, it is worth reflecting prospectively about De Masi's proposals and their consequences for life in cities and the production of work and leisure spaces in cities and metropolises. On the one hand, telework opens up the possibility to "carry out activities without leaving home, saving the time that was spent on daily displacements between home and the office" (De Masi 2000, p. 155), and, on the other hand, "the requirements of specialized studies, work and culture increasingly impose changes from one city, country or continent to another" (*op. cit.*). Obviously, this has impacts on the organization of urban and metropolitan space as on this scale micro-displacements are reduced, while "displacements of a greater distance and duration multiply" (*op. cit.*).

We agree with De Masi that, if taken as true, his assertions would inevitably lead to an overhaul not only of cities (and metropolises), but also of nations, churches, and companies that should equip themselves "for a collective life in which leisure and a growing number of attributes predominate, which should be carried out not for who works but for who rests and has fun" (De Masi 2000, p. 305). Of course, this would affect public spaces, but also affect holidays and journeys, infrastructure and touristic flows, as well as maritime leisure resorts and the strategies of the tourism real estate market.

The dichotomy between the armies of tourists and holiday makers who are guided by a "consumer culture" would also change, the "millions of people who consider everything that is not invasive, noisy, full of confusion and haste 'funereal'" and those, much less numerous, who conceive of their vacations and their free time as " a culture of rest, reading and privacy" and consider "a hell everything that is not silence, order, calm, beautiful and clean" (*op. cit.*, p. 307). Perhaps the scales tilt to the second group, in the medium or long term, with the reeducation for free time and creative idleness, or, in the worse of hypotheses, a short-term deepening of the fissures and the segmentation/standardization of leisure spaces in contemporary cities and metropolises. "Meanwhile, traffic jams on the highways, railways and airports" and overcrowded hotel chains would get even bigger, indicating obvious signs of accelerated degradation (*op. cit.*, p. 308).

On the scale of nation-states, the changes guided by the phenomenon of workless development will also affect governments and employment generation policies in the medium and long term, although this has not been the case until now:

> Persecuted and threatened by an omnivorous technology, that devours at the same speed both the tasks attributed to laborers and employees or executives, instead of reducing working hours and the numbers of posts, governments reduce the fees and taxes to be paid by employers, incentivize foreign investment in their own countries, exhume once again the gangrenous forms of protectionism and incentivize contractual flexibility. (De Masi 2000, p. 100)

With the drastic reduction in working hours, there would also be advantageous changes in the spatial organization of employment for society as a whole, as work could "even be spread to isolated, depressed or peripheral zones" (*op. cit.*, p. 208). There would also be "more work available for hitherto excluded groups, such as people with disabilities and the elderly", and it would be possible to "free up overpopulated areas and, above all, reduce traffic and pollution, as well as road and street maintenance" (*op. cit.*). Among the possible disadvantages would be infrastructure costs (with cables, for example), the need to control the tariffs for information and communication services and the "possible emergence of poorly protected areas of work, and information technology work not declared to the tax authorities, which is much harder to control than traditional forms" (*op. cit.*).

Finally, there is a final question in response to those who consider De Masi's proposals utopian or unrealistic. How would "value" be generated in this new society of creative idleness, guided by free time and no longer by work time? To this question, the author replies that:

> I deny (...) that creativity and innovation can germinate in organizations that are still administered with times, methods and command systems conceived one hundred years ago, not to innovate or create but to execute. That is all. (...) And who is it that pays? Citizens who are always working more. (...) This does not mean that they are going to stay home with their feet up, but it means that they will not have to kill themselves working anymore (...) In this new model of society (...) the winners, apart from the individual are science, art – therefore with an ulterior production of wealth – and the quality of life. (...) Where boring, tiring and dangerous operations are performed by machines and the wealth they produce is distributed by a principle of solidarity, and not competitiveness. (De Masi 2000, pp. 309–310)

5.4 Popular Entrepreneurship in Bahia: No Time for Leisure

Before embarking on an analysis of the relationship between work and leisure in the universe known as "social class C" in Brazil, and particularly in working-class neighborhoods of two cities in the state of Bahia, we briefly present the basics of our research project, "Popular entrepreneurship and social mobility in different urban and regional contexts", and the first results of the two case studies carried out so far: in the neighborhood of Tomba, Feira de Santana, and in the neighborhood of Paripe, Salvador.

In this research project, we depart from a new phenomenon that has manifest itself in the working-class neighborhoods of Brazilian cities, which have an increasing number of residents with higher incomes and in the process of relative "social ascension." These areas have become more complex and self-sufficient, with the multiplication of subcenters (and their diversification). The neighborhoods of Tomba, in Feira de Santana, and Paripe, in Salvador, were selected for the 2014–2015 survey based on the following criteria: the SEBRAE[1] classification of "entrepreneurial neighborhoods", their density of trade, services, and entrepreneurs, the diversity of commercial and service establishments, population density, and the presence of cultural facilities.

Once the case studies were defined, all commercial and service establishments located in the two popular neighborhoods were catalogued and mapped. Two questionnaire models were developed for consumers and entrepreneurs in order to delineate their profile through non-probabilistic sampling by saturation (sample size delineated when responses become redundant). In the neighborhood of Tomba in Feira de Santana, 240 questionnaires were applied to consumers and 18 were applied to entrepreneurs; the Paripe survey resulted in 209 consumers' questionnaires and 17 entrepreneurs' questionnaires. The application of questionnaires was carried out in the most significant commercial and service centers in both neighborhoods, in the locations with the highest concentration and flow of consumers and entrepreneurs.[2]

Following the enterprises characterization and the consumers and entrepreneurs profiling, qualitative interviews were conducted with the sampled entrepreneurs who answered the questionnaires during the first research phase, choosing the most representative cases regarding their entrepreneurship trajectories and the types of enterprises surveyed in both neighborhoods (resulting in ten cases in Tomba and seven in Paripe), in order to characterize them according to their position and condition in the social structure, with an emphasis on their trajectories and their capital (social, cultural, and economic, as in Bourdieu 2007 [1979]).

These interviews permitted to comprehend that the interviewees' ascension in the social structure implies the indebtedness and impoverishment of the social

---

[1]Brazilian Support Service to Micro and Small Enterprises

[2]The classification of trade and services enterprises was based on the methodology developed by SEBRAE/DIEESE (2013), in conjunction with Complementary Law No. 128, dated December 19, 2008 (Brasil 2008). SEBRAE classifies the companies according to the number of employees into four categories: micro (up to 9), small (from 10 to 49), medium (from 50 to 99), and large company (100 or more). The federal law 128 establishes the figure of the individual micro-entrepreneur (MEI): the person who has an annual gross revenue of up to R \$36,000.00. In both Tomba and Paripe, most enterprises were characterized as micro-enterprises or those interviewed are individual micro-entrepreneurs.

capital available to them. The schooling/cultural capital remains almost unchanged; to continue in school requires a huge effort on the part of those who are willing to do so. There are strong indications that this ascension takes place more from the insertion in consumption than from an increase in the years of schooling or participation in cultural events or manifestations. On the other hand, it is also apparent that insertion through consumption can interfere in the life of social relations in the poorer neighborhoods analyzed, with the impoverishment of the social capital of entrepreneurs (and consumers), in their upward trajectories in the social structure of the cities and the regions where they operate, therefore with implications for the social structure of the neighborhoods as a whole.

In the national context, it is also known that working-class neighborhoods—usually heavily populated and covering a big territory—concentrate a large part of the small businesses in Brazilian cities. Although it has not conducted actual statistical research, SEBRAE carried out a business by neighborhood survey in order to create a Business Guide; according to it and in the case of Salvador, the more entrepreneurial neighborhoods are ranked as Brotas, Cabula, Cajazeiras, Itapuã, Itapagipe, Liberdade, Pau Miúdo, Pau da Lima, Paripe, and Pernambués (Sebrae 2013).

According to the Brazilian Franchising Association, the growth of small businesses in the decade 2000–2010 is related to the ascension of more individuals to class C, who use their own resources or bank loans to start new businesses (Borges 2013, pp. 1–3). In addition, SEBRAE has developed mobile collective task forces on "individual entrepreneurship" in low-income neighborhoods in cities of Bahia, such as Feira de Santana, where the task force reached the Feira 9 and Morada das Árvores neighborhoods (www.ba.agenciasebrae.com.br/).

In this briefly considered context, let us take up the question posed by Harvey for that particular universe: Why do most of us actually have less time to think and relax, in a society in which technology increasingly liberates more free time for leisure, as De Masi has argued? In the first place, most of the interviewees expressed their desire to expand business, diversifying their activities or opening branches in other neighborhoods or downtown, or even in other cities in their region. The objective was always to grow and expand the undertaking, which naturally ruled out leisure and fun in the short and medium term in the daily lives of these agents.

The interviews give insights that permit the entrepreneurs' trajectories to be situated in time and space, allowing the understanding that the interviewees' ascension in the social structure implies, as mentioned above, the impoverishment of the social capital available to them, a fact which is evidenced by their restricted leisure time and by the lack of time for friends or to frequent cultural facilities. Despite belonging to different generations/age-groups and urban–regional contexts, in practice, the interviewees restricted their leisure to activities with their families and resting at home.

When time permitted, their preference was to frequent shopping malls, church services, and mass with their families; they rarely went to the beach or a social club on weekends. A few declared some interest in cultural activities such as cinema, theater, or concerts. The most extreme cases stated that leisure was resting at home to "recharge your batteries" after the long workdays they faced in their daily lives, as demonstrated below by some extracts selected from the interviews:

> Look, here in Paripe I don't [go out], I start at noon and leave at six PM, I don't have time. In Stella Maris [the neighborhood where the interviewee lives], I go to the beach, I really like the sea. But, I confess that today, if you ask me "what do you do outside of work?", I go home, put my dog on my lap, switch on the television and travel in whatever is on the television, to empty my mind because it gets really overloaded. (Márcia Virgínia Medra dos Vasconcelos, owner of a shop selling baby clothes and products in the Paripe neighborhood, Salvador).

> Nowadays I don't have time, we don't have weekends, we don't have time off, we don't have public holidays, we can't arrange to meet up with the family, because usually we are tired and we have to rest, any time we can rest is a priority. Nowadays time to rest has become a priority because we don't have a normal routine for resting, you have to open up at 7:00 in the morning and you don't know when closing time will be, you work on holidays, and you work all day Saturday and Sunday until 13:00 or 14:00. I say that because I don't work on Sundays but my husband does, he leaves home at 4:30 in the morning to catch the trade and stays until 14:00 while it's busy, so I lose that leisure time, I don't have any leisure (Joseany Santos, the owner of a packaging shop in the Tomba neighborhood, Feira de Santana).

> … just soccer and some events here at the square. In my free time I rest. Here, it goes from 7 in the morning until 7 at night; sometimes I close the workshop but I still stay here working (Orlando dos Santos Silva, owner of a bicycle repair shop in the Tomba neighborhood, Feira de Santana).

> Usually I stay home on weekends, when we go out it's quite quick. Usually it's home, when we don't visit a relative it's just home. Paripe we don't really… (You don't go to the beach here?) No, usually when we go to the beach it's further away. (But do you go to the beach?) Yes, we do. (What about other places, even out of Paripe?) Yes, as we have a little girl we go to the zoo, the movies, the shopping mall, the food court… (Leandro Santana, owner of a baby layette shop in Paripe neighborhood, in Salvador)

> In my free time, we try to go to a club here called Águas Claras to relax my mind. There aren't many leisure options in Feira de Santana. I don't know if it counts as leisure, but I like to go to church, to take part in church activities. (Joelio dos Santos Guerra, owner of a clothes shop in Tomba neighborhood, in Feira de Santana.)

The initial results of our research are consistent with Jessé Souza's arguments that the so-called class C in the working-class neighborhoods of our cities bring together "elements of a 'post-Fordist' worker's class (…) super-exploited, with no tradition of class solidarity and believing themselves to be their own bosses, with elements of a small bourgeoisie (…), in the sense of undertaking small businesses (…)" (Souza 2015, s/p). The sociologist classifies these workers as "Brazilian warriors", the title of one of his most recent books (Souza 2010):

> The life of these "warriors" is completely different. It is marked by the absence of the 'privileges of birth' that characterize the middle and upper classes. As they lack both the cultural capital so highly valued by the 'real' middle classes and the economic capital of the upper classes, they compensate for this lack with extraordinary personal effort, a doubled workday and an acceptance of every type of super-exploitation of labor. This is the typical way of life of the working classes, thus our hypothesis of work developed in the book, which denies and criticizes the concept of the 'new middle class' and attempts to build a concept of the 'new working class', a product of the new conditions of the international

division of labor and the new global dominance of financial capital. These factors mean that this new class has nothing that is 'specifically Brazilian', as countries like China, India and a large part of Southeast Asia also owe a good part of their current dynamism to the same phenomenon. (Souza 2012, s/p)

We can affirm, therefore, that in the two working-class neighborhoods analyzed in this study, both entrepreneurs and consumers bring together exactly the characteristics listed by Souza for the "new working class", a stratum "that animated the Brazilian economy in the last decade and stimulated the market for the consumption of consumer goods" (Souza 2015, s/p). This is a "very heterogeneous class, with important regional differences and ranges from small business owners to super-exploited workers with no social rights" (*op. cit.*). As highlighted here, the super-exploitation that Souza discusses also involves the free time of the workers and consumers in our research, who work many hours a day and who, in terms of schooling, did not make it to higher education; in fact, some may not have completed elementary education.

The study shows that this newly born class "C" who lives in Brazilian metropolitan peripheries is still far from reaching the "idleness" envisioned by De Masi due to a lack of time; worse yet, not only it does not engage in cultural enlightening activities, but there has been a good deal of impoverishment of the social capital of entrepreneurs. It seems like different class fractions may be situated in different stages toward the desired "creative idleness." Also, Souza's observations allude to Sennett's reflection regarding the social capital available to the different social classes, a fact that is also relevant in the context of core countries:

Here class is everything. A person from a privileged background can give him or herself the luxury of strategic confusion, which does not happen with the child of the masses. Casual opportunities may be offered to a child of privilege due to their family environment and educational networks; privilege reduces the need to draw up strategies. Wide and strong human networks allow those at the top of the scale to deal with the present; networks are a safety net that reduces the need for long-term strategic planning (…). The masses however, have a sparser network of contacts and informal support, thus remaining more dependent on institutions. (Sennett 2006, p. 76)

5.5 Final Considerations

Finally, it is worth emphasizing the main thesis defended here, that it is not possible to uncouple the discussion on spaces for leisure and reproduction in cities and metropolises from discussions regarding spaces for work and production. There is here a dialectic that makes work and leisure inseparable in the processes of the production of space on all the scales subject to this type of approach. It becomes clear that this would have consequences for social sciences research dealing with the theme of contemporary leisure spaces and the public sphere.

We also need to highlight that capital-work relationships have undergone changes in the mode of capitalist production and that it is necessary to untangle and reveal these spatial-temporal relations to have a better understanding of the production of leisure and work spaces in the modern world, reflecting on the relationship between production and the organization of space in our cities and metropolises, in light of their future tendencies and perspectives.

It has been demonstrated that the discussion on leisure and work in cities and metropolises demands a theoretical-conceptual deepening of the concept of social class, only set out here, as the different classes and fractions of classes are living the contradictions in the mode of production in diverse ways. This implies a radical dialectical approach to the production of leisure and work spaces in cities and metropolises for different social classes, avoiding the current tendency to prioritize the analysis, which is very evident in current research of leisure in geography, of spaces destined to specific social segments, without this being made explicit in the research and the results presented.

In this context, it is also necessary to fill the gaps and crevices of playfulness and play in our cities and metropolises, evidencing the action and the strategies of the different groups, classes, and fractions involved in these non-hegemonic processes of the production of space (Serpa 2007). This also requires some geographical imagination (Serpa 2008) to think prospectively about the production of leisure and work spaces in the cities and metropolises of the future, including taking into consideration utopian perspectives to dream of other possible worlds.

Finally, it is also important to think prospectively on the consequences for the use and appropriation of Urban public spaces, based on the trends presented here. If it is true that we are definitely moving to a society with more time for leisure and creative idleness, this, of course, will have immediate consequences for urban public spaces. An education for leisure and creativity, as proposed by De Masi (2000), can even foster the elaboration and implementation of new urban policies for the revaluation of these spaces, where creative leisure prevails over leisure and entertainment guided by consumption. What urban forms will serve these new functions based on creativity? How will the urban public spaces be like in this future of less work and more leisure, more creativity and less consumption?

A society based on solidarity and not on competitiveness, with more free time, can also give rise to new energies and a disposition for political action and participation, fostering the emergence of a new urban public sphere and rescuing the political sense of urban public spaces in the mid- and long terms. On the other hand, the reduction of micro-trips at the intra-urban and metropolitan scales, with more people working at home and sparing the fatigue of the daily (long) trips between home and work, can also release new energies for the requalification of nearby spaces at the neighborhood scale. As a consequence, there could be greater participation and greater citizen interest in streets, squares, neighborhoods, parks, etc., generating new activism and neighborhood movements in our cities.

Of course, this presupposes a new form of social and spatial organization of society and cities, which we are still far from achieving, although it might already be identifiable in contemporary urban space. On the other hand, these tendencies do not take place homogeneously in the different countries and regions of the world, nor are they experienced in the same way by the different social classes, as we have tried to demonstrate here. For the time being, we see, for example, popular entrepreneurs overburdened with work and no time for rest, leisure, family, etc., as evidenced in the testimonies collected in our field surveys. The future will tell us the role that urban public spaces will play and what kind of society model we are headed to, but the dialectic between work and leisure is undoubtedly essential if we are to prospectively imagine the future forms and functions of public spaces in our cities.

References

Arendt H (2000) A condição humana, 10th edn. Forense Universitária, Rio de Janeiro
Borges C (2013) Expansão da classe C impulsiona o comércio em bairros populares. Jornal A Tarde. Salvador, 28/4/2013, pp 1–3
Bourdieu, P (2007) A Distinção - crítica social do julgamento. Porto Alegre: Zouk, 2007 [1979]
De Masi (2000) Domenico. O ócio criativo, 2nd edn. Sextante, Rio de Janeiro
Harvey D (2014) SIMPURB: Conferência de Encerramento. In: Oliveira FG, Freire DG, De Jesus GM, de Oliveira LD (Org.). Geografia Urbana. Ciência e Ação Política. Consequência, Rio de Janeiro, pp 45–64
SEBRAE (2013) Serviço Brasileiro de Apoio às Micro e Pequenas Empresas; DIEESE. Departamento Intersindical de Estatística e Estudos Socioeconômicos. Anuário do trabalho na micro e pequena empresa. SEBRAE/DIEESE, Brasília, DF
Sennett R (1998) O declínio do homem público. As tiranias da intimidade. 6ª reimpressão. Companhia das Letras, São Paulo
Sennett R (2006) A cultura do novo capitalismo. Record, Rio de Janeiro, São Paulo
Sennett R (2007) A corrosão do caráter. Consequências pessoais do trabalho no novo capitalismo, 12th edn. Record, Rio de Janeiro, São Paulo
Serpa A (2007) A Cidade e o Urbano: Discutindo o Conceito de Centralidades Lúdicas. Espaço e Geografia (UnB), Brasília, vol 10, pp 265–278
Serpa A (2008) Como prever sem imaginar? O papel da imaginação na produção do conhecimento geográfico. In: Serpa A (Org.) Espaços Culturais: Vivências, imaginações e representações. Editora da Universidade Federal da Bahia - EDUFBA, Salvador, pp 59–67
Souza J (2010) Os batalhadores brasileiros: nova classe média ou nova classe trabalhadora? Editora da UFMG, Belo horizonte
Souza J (2012) Entrevista de Jessé Souza ao blog Prosa em 12.05.2012. Available in: http://oglobo.globo.com/blogs/prosa/posts/2012/05/12/entrevista-com-sociologo-jesse-souza-444686.asp. Acesso em: 17 Fev. 2015
Souza J (2015) Ralés, batalhadores e uma nova classe média. Entrevista especial com Jessé Souza. Available in: http://amaivos.uol.com.br/amaivos09/noticia/noticia.asp?cod_canal=41&cod_noticia=16935. Acesso em: 17 Fev. 2015

Author Biography

Ângelo Serpa is a Full Professor of Human Geography at the Federal University of Bahia (UFBA) and a researcher with a productivity grant from the National Council for Scientific and Technological Development (CNPq); he is also a permanent professor in the Graduate Programs in Geography and Architecture and Urbanism at UFBA, where he is the editor responsible for GeoTextos Magazine, leader of the Research Groups Espaço Livre, and Territórios da Cultura Popular. He is the author and editor of several books, among which, *O espaço público na cidade contemporânea* (Contexto, 2007), *Lugar e Mídia* (Contexto, 2011), *Territórios da Bahia* (EDUFBA, 2015), *Cidade Popular* (EDUFBA, 2007) and *Fala, Periferia!* (EDUFBA/PROEXT, 2001).

Part II
About Spaces. And People

Chapter 6
Open Public Spaces and the *Vita Activa*

Eugênio Fernandes Queiroga

Abstract Free spaces are of great importance for cities—although they are often treated poorly by public and private agents—as spaces of daily life, as places of coexistence at the most diverse scales, as preferred loci of political manifestations and many other social practices. Free spaces are also the main elements capable of providing environmental services in urban areas. The public relevance of free spaces in Brazilian capitals, metropolis, and medium-sized cities is the theme discussed in this chapter. It presents a system of concepts that allow a better understanding of the theme and that may prove useful for the production of public policies seriously interested in improving the quality of urban spaces in Brazilian cities and metropolises in special, but is not limited to the reality of this country.

Keywords Free spaces · Multifunctional spaces · Public policies
Brazil

6.1 Introduction

More than a few Brazilian researchers have acknowledged the valorization of the private sphere as evidence of a strong decline in public life, contradicting the evidence emerging today of the many potential relations between the public sphere, open public space, and the communicative use of the information environment. The arguments of US authors[1] on the matter are sometimes applied without proper consideration of the substantial differences between the (sub)urban reality of the USA and the urbanization processes found in Brazil.

---

[1]Among the most cited is always Richard Sennett. See Sennett (1977).

E. F. Queiroga (✉)
Faculty of Architecture and Urbanism, University of São Paulo (FAU-USP),
São Paulo, Brazil
e-mail: queiroga@usp.br

© Springer International Publishing AG, part of Springer Nature 2018
L. Capanema Alvares and J. L. Barbosa (eds.), *Urban Public Spaces*,
The Urban Book Series, https://doi.org/10.1007/978-3-319-74253-3_6

The advance of residential condominia and gated housing developments in contemporary urban Brazil has undoubtedly weakened traditional forms of appropriating squares and streets at the neighborhood level. So far, though, this process has not had a marked impact on leisure activities and public interaction in parks or other open spaces at either city or metropolitan levels. On the contrary, studies by the National Research Network on Landscaping and Open Space Systems (QUAPÁ-SEL)[2] reveal a strong demand for parks and shorelines adapted for public use, as well as sidewalks and spaces primarily occupied by pedestrians in traditional city centers or new central zones. To this, we can add the ever more frequent political demonstrations and rallies held in the most important public spaces in the country's medium and large cities.[3] The intense appropriation of such spaces adds a further layer of complexity to the polemics of public life in urban Brazil. The present chapter discusses various aspects of public importance concerning open spaces in these contemporary city contexts.

Public life is transforming the public sphere, yet this far from signifies its demise. In fact, we can observe a greater diversity of life *in* public, empowering the public sphere in a narrower sense (Arendt 1991) or the political public sphere to use Habermas' terminology (1989). This chapter presents a series of concepts that systematically correlate and distinguish open space, public space, and the public sphere, enabling a clearer comprehension of the topic in the contemporary setting, as well as potentially proving useful in the development of public policies genuinely interested in improving the quality of urban space in Brazil's cities and metropolitan regions. The discussion and conceptual schema presented here do not apply to Brazil alone: They also help to shed light on the contemporary urban world more generally, taking into account socio-spatial relations of production, but not limited to them.

6.2 Public Sphere, Public Spaces, and Open Spaces

Arendt (1991) associates the *vita activa* with three basic human activities: labor, work, and (political) action. Labor corresponds to the biological processes of the human body, of which the human condition is life itself. Work relates to the

---

[2]In Portuguese, *Rede Nacional de Pesquisa Quadro do Paisagismo—Sistema de Espaços Livres.* The QUAPÁ-SEL National Network includes researchers from all the country's macro-regions, representing 25 universities in total. QUAPÁ-SEL projects have already studied more than 60 cities. Among the most significant we can cite almost all the state capitals: Brasília, São Paulo, Rio de Janeiro, Belo Horizonte, Salvador, Recife, Fortaleza, Curitiba, Porto Alegre, Manaus, Belém, Goiânia, São Luís, Natal, Maceió, Vitória, Florianópolis, Campo Grande, Palmas, Rio Branco, and Macapá, as well as the metropolitan areas of Campinas, Santos, São José dos Campos, Sorocaba, Maringá and Campina Grande, and the medium-sized cities of Uberlândia, Ribeirão Preto, Uberaba, Santa Maria, Anápolis, São Carlos, and Criciúma.

[3]On June 20, 2013, alone, demonstrations were held in 388 Brazilian cities, including 22 state capitals. More than a million and a half people took to the streets to demand greater investment in public transportation (especially), health care and education.

artificialness of human existence, its condition defined by 'worldliness'. Finally, (political) action is specific to humans and is the only kind of activity entirely dependent on the presence of others. It is plural by definition, therefore, since it is the only activity directly performed among humans.

For Arendt (1991), all human activities are conditioned by the fact that humans live together in social groups, with action being the only activity inconceivable outside of society. In Ancient Rome, living was synonymous with 'being among men' while dying meant 'ceasing to be among men'.

The sphere of life corresponds to actions and thus to the public sphere, implying activities that pertain to a common world. Here, we can recall that for Arendt (1958, p. 52): 'The public realm, as the common world, gathers us together and yet prevents our falling over each other...'.

Aristotle deemed just two human activities to be political and constitutive of what he called *bios politikos*: action (praxis) and discourse (lexis), which together comprised the 'sphere of human affairs,' excluding everything that is merely necessary or useful (Arendt 1991).

For some people (citizens) to be able to dedicate themselves to the public sphere, others (slaves) had to provide them with the material conditions to do so. Nevertheless, labor still implied the participation of citizens in the sphere of family life. Hence, work and labor are activities proper to the private sphere, necessary for maintaining life. The distinction between public and private spheres has corresponded to the existence of the political and domestic spheres as separate entities ever since the emergence of city-states.

For Arendt (1991), therefore, the political actions of life in public comprise the public sphere. Seeking to historicize Arendt's categorization of the modern period, Habermas argues that:

> the theme of the modern (in contrast to the ancient) public sphere shifted from the properly political tasks of a citizenry acting in common (i.e., administration of law as regards internal affairs and military survival as regards external affairs) to the more properly civic tasks of a society engaged in critical public debate (i.e., the protection of a commercial economy). The political task of the bourgeois public sphere was the regulation of civil society. (Habermas 1989, p. 52)

Today Habermas's vision of the public sphere has widened. Since the publication of *The Theory of Communicative Action* (Habermas 1987), the inclusion of the everyday has enabled the inference of relations between the quotidian world and the public sphere. More recently, in the first decade of the twenty-first century, Habermas (2006) has proposed an important distinction between two types of public sphere: a general public sphere, denominated 'public space' by the philosopher, and a narrower public sphere, denominated the 'political public sphere' or 'political public space'.

In order to avoid confusing concepts of the public sphere with those of public space, so fundamental to the social sciences and other disciplines where space is the main object of investigation and proposal (Geography, Architecture, Urbanism, Landscaping, and Urban Planning), the following conceptual system is advocated:

- the political or narrow public sphere: in the Habermasian schema, the field of public debate (political, philosophical, scientific, and artistic);
- the general public sphere: all life *in* public in a broad sense, including demonstrations held in spaces with open public access and visibility, both publicly and privately owned, including public appropriations of virtual means of establishing public communication.[4] The general public sphere is not opposed to the political public sphere, insofar as it encompasses the latter. Indeed, it can be argued that the more intense and diverse the general public sphere, the more the political public sphere is itself empowered;
- public space: all publicly owned spaces, ranging from those intended for common use by the population, proper to the public sphere, to publicly owned properties not designed for common use, the case of diverse public assets with specialized uses (crèches, prisons, hospitals, biological reserves, ecological protection areas, and so on) as well as unused public assets[5];
- open space: all space free of buildings (at urban level) or free of urbanization (at regional level), as proposed by Magnoli (1982). Open spaces include streets, fields and forests, parks and squares, house yards and uncovered courtyards, rivers and beaches, and many other similar areas.

The discussion about open space systems should not therefore be limited to the systems formed by green areas like parks and gardens. Although every city can be said to possess a system of open spaces (SOS), this does not mean that the system concerned is sufficiently adequate in relation to the public sphere or urban mobility, or in terms of mitigating the environmental impacts caused by urbanization. Hence, the road system, the system of green areas, the system of spaces for public interaction and leisure activities, and the system of environmental conservation areas all comprise subsystems of the SOS, which also encompasses the large number of open spaces located on private properties (Queiroga 2012).

Though the above categories are interrelated with numerous ways, taking them as synonymous hinders a clear understanding of the spatial dialectics and the possibility of working proactively with correlated systems of spaces (public, public interest, open, environmental interest, and so on). The conceptual system proposed here can foster more wide-reaching analyses and proposals that go beyond sector-based and compartmentalized approaches, such as policy proposals that

---

[4]Here, it is important to distinguish between communication and information. To communicate means to 'make common,' to enable the establishment of communicative reason, a mutual understanding between subjects, and to presume dialogue rather than merely a relationship between a transmitter of information and a receiver.

[5]The Brazilian Civil Code of 2002 (Brazil 2002) identifies public assets as properties belonging to the federal government, federal states, and federal district, municipalities, autonomous bodies, and public foundations. Public assets are divided into three categories: (1) assets for common use of the population, intended to be used by the general public (streets, squares, beaches, etc.); (2) assets for special use, intended for the execution of public services (e.g., hospitals and public schools); and (3) unused publicly owned assets, or in other words properties without any established public purpose, constituting an available public asset capable of being sold off.

consider the road system solely in terms of vehicle traffic, failing to recognize streets as spaces for public interaction, or environmental conservation area systems that severely limit human uses of watersides in urban environments.[6]

Public spaces—whether open or built—may be of public interest without necessarily lending themselves to public life. This is the case of crèches, nursery schools, biological reserves, and so on. Similarly, the actions of the public sphere are not limited to spaces held under public ownership. Privately owned spaces may also exhibit public appropriations pertaining to the general public sphere, including bars, shopping malls, or empty land informally transformed into soccer pitches. Such spaces may also present a public interest not directly linked to the public sphere: Examples include the Private Natural Heritage Reserves (*Reservas Particulares do Patrimônio Natural*: RPPNs), conservation units that provide important environmental services of public interest despite being privately owned.

A theoretical-conceptual framework on the relations between spaces and public dimensions is proposed here, therefore, to enable a better approximation to the concrete reality, recognizing the temporary and the hybrid, as Milton Santos (1996) taught, and complexity as Morin (2008) emphasizes. Bi-univocal classificatory rigidity is eschewed without relinquishing theoretical-conceptual rigor.

6.3   Questions Concerning Systems of Open Public Spaces in Large and Medium Brazilian Cities

Open public spaces are publicly owned assets with varying degrees of accessibility and appropriation. The system of open public spaces forms the main subsystem of open spaces intended for the sphere of public life (general and political), particularly those assets intended for common use by the population (publicly owned properties). In contemporary Brazilian urbanization, large-scale private developments sometimes assume the role of providing formally enhanced open spaces. Access to such spaces is typically severely restricted and highly controlled, however, weakening the general sphere of public life, especially at a neighborhood level. These kinds of developments can be found not only in the country's largest metropolitan regions but also in numerous medium-sized cities.

In Brazil, urban road systems constitute the largest portion of built open public spaces. Since 1979, the legislation related to land use in Brazilian municipalities has stipulated that 35% of areas under development must be assigned to public use,

---

[6]In Brazil, watersides are identified as Permanent Preservation Areas (*Áreas de Preservação Permanentes*: APPs), which provides them with legal protection from intensive human use, including those areas located in urban environments. In practice, though, this legislation is widely ignored and illegal occupations are common. It would be better, therefore, for these areas to be effectively integrated into urban space, taking into account, of course, natural aspects, seasonal rainfall patterns, floods, the role of such areas in gene flows, and so on.

20% or more of which end up as space dedicated to the road system, leaving around 10% of such areas as 'open spaces for public use'[7] (squares, parks, and the like).[8] These legally defined percentages alone show just how large an area is consumed by road systems within the overall system of open public spaces.

São Paulo, the most heavily populated municipality in the country, containing 12 million inhabitants (IBGE 2016), possesses 7.6 million vehicles, most of them cars (5.3 million: Denatran 2015), without including figures for the wider metropolitan region.[9] The São Paulo capital possesses 41,695 hectares of open spaces accessible to the public, 47.9% of which correspond to the road system, followed by parks with 30.3%. It should be emphasized, though, that 27.4% correspond to environmental conservation units with low levels of social appropriation (state parks and municipal natural parks), while rivers and reservoirs account for 14.9% of the total. Meanwhile, effectively implemented squares make up just 1.2% of the total open spaces with public access, a rate even smaller than that dedicated to cemeteries, which corresponds to 1.3% of this total (Macedo and Queiroga 2016).

Vehicle circulation has driven the design of the vast majority of Brazil's urban road networks since the second half of the twentieth century and the automobile industry's imposition of cars onto the Brazilian culture, in particular its urban culture, as the privileged means of transportation, a symbol of social status and modernity. Despite numerous critiques and actions opposing this mindset, it remains hegemonic in the mid-2010s.

Road widening with bulldozers has been going on in the country's biggest cities ever since the 1900s, in detriment of the surrounding areas and their biophysical support capacities. Initially, avenues were designed with ample sidewalks and control of the size of neighboring buildings, shaping the urban landscape along 'European' lines. With the advent of expressways in the 1960s, though, large and medium cities began to build avenues where pedestrian walkways were replaced by grass areas. In the twenty-first century beginnings, despite the increasing awareness

---

[7]'Open spaces for public use' is the expression used in Federal Law 6.766/79 (Brazil 1979) to designate all spaces intended for public interaction and leisure. In various municipalities, these spaces are commonly referred to as 'leisure systems,' a somewhat impoverished expression of what such spaces actually comprise. This terminology probably stems from the influence of modern functionalist urbanism and its reductive simplification of urban functions to dwelling, working, recreation, and circulation.

[8]Law 9.785/99 (Brazil 1999), which revised the federal legislation on land use, allowed municipalities to stipulate the percentages to be allocated to public spaces, a neoliberal decision typical of the federal government of the period. Fortunately, the culture created by the earlier Law 6.766/79 had already taken root and the 35% level was almost always maintained, or even increased, as in the São Paulo case where 40% has to be allocated to public spaces, including 15% to open spaces for public use.

[9]The Municipality of São Paulo lies at the hub of a metropolitan region with more than 21 million inhabitants (IBGE 2016), and containing almost 12 million vehicles in circulation in 2014 (Denatran 2015).

of environmental issues, some of these roads are still being widened, removing gardens that are already residual and leaving cars, trucks, and motorbikes to dispute every inch of tarmac.[10]

It is commonplace to reduce the concept of the road to its carriageways, as though the public sidewalk was a category apart. Many property developers pay little heed to mobility along sidewalks. Tree-lined walkways of a reasonable size, allowing both abled and disabled pedestrians to circulate freely, should really be a *sine qua non* condition for Brazilian municipalities, particularly those located in the tropical zone. Unfortunately, such conditions prove to be the exception rather than the norm in the country's urban areas (Fig. 6.1).

In the 1970s, the increasing functional conflicts between vehicles and pedestrians led to the first city center streets dedicated exclusively to pedestrian use, also called *calçadões*, 'broadwalks', or 'promenades'.[11] From the pioneering 'Rua das Flores' (Flowers Street) in Curitiba, capital of Paraná, to the present day, numerous roads have been closed off to vehicles in all kinds of urban contexts from medium-sized cities to large metropolitan centers. Brazilian sidewalks are appropriated for many different uses that go beyond simple circulation and access: They provide places for commerce and even services, areas for being in public and interacting socially, spaces for holding demonstrations, all of which enhance the public sphere most of the time.

In medium and large Brazilian cities in the 2010s, debates have focused on the precarious and dangerous spaces provided to pedestrians and cyclists in contrast to the spaces dedicated to car use. But despite these concerns, the largest metropolitan areas[12] still lack integrated cycle lanes and public transport systems consonant with their scale. Solutions remain modest and palliative, although they do at least point to other paradigms of urban mobility and public appropriation of road spaces.

Squares, parks, gardens, and similar spaces form the officially recognized structure of open public space system for interaction and leisure in Brazilian cities. Since the introduction of Law 6766/79, all new urban developments in the country

---

[10]In the city of São Paulo, in 2010, congestion reached daily levels of between 70 and 230 km. The average speed on the city's expressways in these day-to-day situations of congestion is less than 10 km/h, much slower than traveling by bicycle (25 km/h). In the worst traffic jams, the average speed is equivalent to the pace of a chicken.

[11]It is worth pointing out that the 'oldest' and most famous 'promenade' in the country, the Copacabana Promenade (1970), designed by Roberto Burle Marx, does not fit the type cited above since the sidewalk is not used solely by pedestrians: In fact, it is very wide, running alongside an avenue parallel to the shore front—Avenida Atlântica—and includes various lanes for motor vehicles and a cycle lane implanted in the 1990s.

[12]In 2016, the country had two metropolitan regions with more than 12 million inhabitants (São Paulo and Rio de Janeiro) and eight metropolitan regions with a population between 3 and 6 million inhabitants: Belo Horizonte, Porto Alegre, Brasília, Fortaleza, Salvador, Recife, Curitiba, and Campinas (IBGE 2016). Officially, the metropolitan areas that include municipalities from more than one federal state, like Brasília, are denominated 'integrated economic development regions' (*regiões integradas de desenvolvimento econômico*: RIDEs), while the others are called 'metropolitan regions' (*regiões metropolitanas*: RMs).

Fig. 6.1 Maringá, a city in Paraná state planned in the 1940s, has a nationally recognized tree-lined road system. *Source* Author's personal collection, 2009

are required to set aside 'open spaces for public use'. Previous legislation on land use at the municipal level (where such legal frameworks existed) usually sets lower requirements for the allocation of open spaces for social interaction and leisure. In 1989, Federal Law 7.803 also extended the creation of Permanent Preservation Areas (APPs) to urban areas, as defined in the Forest Code[13] enforced at the time and previously 'observed' only in rural zones. As a result of the application of the Forest Code in urban regions, though slow and still partial, narrow banks alongside watercourses are no longer incorporated as elements of the leisure systems, at least in municipalities showing some degree of environmental concern in the new developments approval processes.

The dedicated leisure areas together with the fluvial APPs that are yet to be implemented provide a potential gap for functional deviations and may be occupied by favelas or even by public facilities and services. The notion that open public spaces are empty, deserted spaces that can be freely occupied is neither new nor extinct. The urban development plan for the city of São Paulo (Law 7.688/71), enforced until 1988, stipulated maximum rates of public buildings occupation in 'green areas', applied to public buildings not intended for common use by the population, such as crèches and infant schools. The São Paulo legislation enforced

---

[13]Brazil (1965). Law 4.771 instituted the new Forest Code. Brasilia: Presidência da República. Casa Civil. Available at www.planalto.gov.br/ccivil_03/leis/L4771.htm. Accessed on March 17, 2012.

in 2016 also permits partial occupation of 'open spaces' by institutional facilities such as schools, health centers, and the like.

The valorization of environmental issues and physical activities since the beginning of the present century has stimulated the creation of parks across the country as a whole. Rio Branco, the capital of Acre, for example, created proportionally more linear parks than São Paulo in the 2000s. Vitória, the capital of Espírito Santo, has implemented more parks than Campinas, the second most important metropolitan zone in São Paulo state, despite having a third of the latter's population. Even small towns around 10,000–15,000 inhabitants and located on the periphery of metropolitan regions, like Holambra and Engenheiro Coelho in the Campinas Metropolitan Region, have their own parks. Public investments for the implementation and maintenance of parks are not merely a consequence of the size of the cities or their public budgets; they are first and foremost political decisions.

A wide range of other types of open spaces exists dedicated to social interaction and leisure, enhancing the open public spaces systems in Brazil's medium and large cities: urban beaches, viewing points, courtyards, hedged areas, woods, thematic gardens (zoological, botanical, etc.), sports centers, public swimming pools, or soccer fields of varying degrees of formality. Some of these fields are professionally designed and equipped, others built by local residents themselves, revealing the importance of public interaction and leisure for the populations concerned. In some cities like Campinas and Recife (the capital of Pernambuco),[14] research has been undertaken on 'informal' soccer pitches, revealing their importance to public life, both quantitatively and qualitatively. In the case of Maceió, for example, the capital of Alagoas, information published in 2009 showed that there were more 'kickabout fields' than squares officially implemented by city council.[15]

More important than the exhaustive work of classifying specific types of public spaces is to recognize their hybrid nature within the social interaction and leisure systems in Brazilian cities. Among the most important spaces are the garden squares. Although more often officially referred to simply as squares, the large numbers of trees and plants in these spaces impede public demonstrations from being held, making them unsuitable for the political public sphere. On the other hand, there have been proposals to distinguish 'garden squares' from 'gardened squares' (Queiroga 2002): the planted areas of the latter allow them to function as squares, but there is sufficient paved ground for activities related to the political public sphere to take place.

Given that most of the country is located in the tropics, gardened squares with dense overhead vegetation provide a space well-suited to public use, enabling the population to use the area even in the noon sunlight and outside temperatures above 30 °C.

Parks and beaches are increasingly used to practice physical activities. The same applies to central strips in some park avenues, used for walking, running, and cycling.

---

[14]On Campinas, see Queiroga (2002). On Recife, see Ribeiro et al. (2000).

[15]Findings reported at the QUAPÁ-SEL Research Workshop held in Maceió in 2008.

These central strips, originally used exclusively to organize circulation, are now multifunctional since they form part of the system of interaction and leisure; a continuous stretch of sidewalk amid the grassed areas and tree-lined roads is enough for walking and running activities. Acknowledgment of this appropriation prompted the emergence of better equipped public spaces, full-blown linear parks with vehicle traffic on either side. This is the case of numerous avenues along São Paulo's valley bottom, the Jaguariúna Linear Park in São Paulo state (a project extending for more than 5 km in length that made use of preexisting central strips in main avenues), the Environmental Axis implanted on the Arthur Bernardes Avenue[16] in Curitiba, or the cycling path on the Afonso Pena Avenue in Campo Grande, capital of Mato Grosso do Sul, for example. They are 'central strip-avenue parks' at the beginning of this twenty-first century; well-equipped hybrids very different from the parkways first proposed by Olmsted back in the nineteenth century.

These and other multifunctional spaces so frequently encountered in Brazilian cities reveal an excellent strategy for exploiting available resources. Half-square, half-park, half-garden, half-avenue spaces enable public appropriations for social interaction, leisure, and physical activities. Ideally, not all of these would be needed were cities able to rely on the development of urban fabrics in which spaces better suited to public activities were predesignated, designed, implemented, and properly maintained. But given their absence, it makes sense to exploit the opportunity and readequate spaces not originally planned as parks and such.

The appropriation of squares, streets, and avenues has undergone decades of decline. This is especially true of middle- and high-income districts in medium and large cities given that vertical and/or horizontal gated condominiums built since the 1970s in Rio de Janeiro and São Paulo already contained leisure areas that diluted the demand for interaction and leisure in the nearby streets. Today a revival in the use of squares, streets, and avenues is readily observable, and the number of new appropriations is intensifying: Important streets and avenues are closed to vehicle traffic on weekends exclusively for leisure, social interaction, and physical activities,[17] bar tables sprawl across sidewalks, open spaces once 'unquestionably' dedicated to parking are now disputed by bicycles, roller skates and skateboards, parties and demonstrations held by a variety of social groups and political issues.

Art collectives and other groups are increasingly appropriating open public spaces to stage their activities. Some are rebuilding and maintaining local squares in their neighborhoods, others intervene fleetingly in different spots of the city with

---

[16]The carriageway was reduced and its central reservation converted into linear park.

[17]Some prominent examples: Brasília on Sundays closes the Eixo Rodoviário (Road Axis), a route almost 14 km length known as the 'Eixão,' the most important avenue linking the North and South 'wings' of the city; in Rio de Janeiro the same occurs on Avenida Atlântica, the avenue running alongside one of the world's most iconic urban beaches, Copacabana; in São Paulo each of the 39 district councils closes at least one main road on Sundays for leisure and social interaction, including the Avenida Paulista, perhaps the city's most symbolic roadway, where São Paulo's bank head offices and numerous industrial and commercial business organizations are located, along with cinemas, cultural centers, and the city's leading art museum.

greater visibility, looking to raise the awareness of busy passersby, while others focus their actions on squares with large numbers of visitors, 'tactical urbanism' actions, spatial practices demanding the right to the city in Lefebvre's sense (2008).

In the dense outer peripheries of large cities, where private open spaces are practically nonexistent, the main stage for social life has always been the streets. They are important spaces for everyday social interactions, as well as for cultural collectives' activities and for a wide range of different religious manifestations. In sum, the street is the main public sphere space, despite its design being centered on vehicle traffic. In the 2010s, the organized crime also stages concerts that attract big crowds of young people on weekend nights. At these events, the criminal factions impose their control and promote diverse illegal activities, including child prostitution and drug trafficking.

The inherit materiality of a space may or may not enhance the *vita activa*, but can never fully determine it. Public life can be curtailed, for example, by allowing roads to be closed off in residential districts, or by failing to invest in a good distribution of quality open spaces of diverse kinds and sizes. Expanding the political public sphere depends, among other important aspects, on upgrading the spaces of the general public sphere. By enhancing public life, conflicts become more clearly manifested and communicative reason can be established as public reason (Habermas 1987), thereby enriching the political public sphere.

While built spaces provide the ideal protective enclosure for private life, the main physical material support for public life is found in open public spaces: These are the spaces with the highest degree of accessibility, the biggest capacity to welcome diversity, plurality and the unpredictable, all characteristics of a richer public sphere. Obviously, open public spaces are not the only support available for the public sphere: The Internet and other communications media are also increasingly important elements. What can be observed here is not an opposition between real and virtual media, but the establishment of systematic relations between them, allowing the public sphere to be comprehended as a system of actions realized through a system of concrete spatial objects and virtual environments, constituting an ecosystem of cultural symbols and values.

Long before the public protests in the Brazilian Autumn/Winter of 2013 or the Arab Spring, Santos (2000) had already announced the beginning, perhaps, of what he labeled a 'popular period of history,' highlighting the importance of the 'docility' of the current technological base of information and communication (capable of being employed by people without capital) as potential tools for organizing popular social and cultural events 'towards another kind of globalization' (Santos 2000).

At the same time, not all open public spaces are suitable for the public sphere, either general or political, though this does not mean that they lack public relevance. Public spaces should not be confused with open access spaces. Only public assets for common use by the population are by nature (public ownership) properties with open public access. Even so, their use may be subject to norms and restrictions established by the responsible public authorities.

Due to their specific nature, special use assets do not provide unrestricted access, precisely in order to ensure they can meet their public social function. A multipurpose sports court in a state school, for instance, will have restricted and controlled access, giving preference to students enrolled at the school. At the same time, the sports court may be available to use by a wider public in some situations.

According to the National Conservation Units System (*Sistema Nacional de Unidades de Conservação*: SNUC), a variety of open spaces are included under the category of special use public assets. Some of them, as highly important public assets, could be severely harmed if they were appropriated by the population on a large scale, exceeding their carrying capacities. Such is the case, for example, of the Ecological Stations and Biological Reserves, and the Full Protection Units (*Unidades de Proteção Integral*: UPIs) with the highest restrictions on public access.[18] In these conservation units, public visits are prohibited save for educational purposes (and then in compliance with the conditions stipulated in their regulations and management plans); access for scientific research also depends on prior authorization and is subject to conditions and restrictions established by regulations and by the unit's administration. It is in the public interest to protect the rich and intact environmental heritage and that justifies the almost total exclusion of the population from such areas.

Multifunctional public spaces, either mixing built and open areas, or special uses and common public use, have emerged for all kinds of purposes. For example, in 1976 Campinas inaugurated the city's Cultural Conviviality Centre. The project not only met the original demand for a municipal theater, but it also included simultaneously a set of open spaces (with stands and a central stage) and covered spaces (the theater, exhibition spaces, and art galleries) under the stands, interspersed with open spaces of various sizes. This innovative project was built on a garden square that had been initially built as a Public Promenade in the nineteenth century. Because of its morphological complexity and diverse uses, mixing built and open spaces, neither the Square (an asset for common use by the population) nor the Conviviality Centre (a special use asset on the inside, but a common use area on the outside) can be characterized in isolation. A rich transgression of more rigid classifications and definitions can thus be identified as a 'hybrid', or multifunctional space (Fig. 6.2).

In planning an open spaces system, therefore, it is important to consider all open spaces, including the public assets designated for special use. This permits different public policies—regarding education, health care, culture, urban drainage, transport, etc.—to be linked to policies targeting at social interaction, leisure, and environmental conservation systems. This systematic and dialectical approach allows for a better reading and understanding of the potential offered by open spaces, avoiding the limitations of compartmentalized approaches based on specific sectors (leisure, circulation, housing, environment, hygiene, etc.).

---

[18]Brazil. Law 9.985 (Brazil 2000) [...] created the National System of Natural Conservation Units and Other Provisions. Brasilia: Presidência da República. Casa Civil. Available at www.planalto. gov.br/ccivil_03/leis/L9985.htm. Accessed 6 September 2011.

6 Open Public Spaces and the *Vita Activa*

Fig. 6.2 Aerial view of the Campinas Conviviality Centre implanted on the Imprensa Fluminense Square. *Source* Author's personal collection, 2008

Some brief examples of good public administration initiatives being conducted along these lines and at various levels in Brazil are:

- the 'A Fruit in the Yard' Program in Diadema[19] coordinated by the architect and landscape designer Raul Pereira between 1993 and 1996, responding to the scarcity of open spaces in the urban fabric of one of the country's mostly densely populated regions. This involved integrated activities with all the city's schools. Besides donating a fruit tree cutting to each student, participatory projects were also run to improve the open spaces of the schools and, with support of artistic activities, discussions were held on the quotidian environmental situation, contributing to the critical construction of youth citizenship through concrete actions;
- in Rio Branco, the capital of the Amazonian state of Acre, the State Secretariat for Social Housing promoted initiatives between 1999 and 2015 that combined housing,[20] environmental sanitation, and the implementation of adequately equipped linear parks with cleaned-up streams, cycle lanes, and intense usage by the population. These linear park projects do not fully respect the fluvial APPs as strips of land to be forested, nor do they meet National Environment Council Resolution 369/2006, which sets precise percentages for the appropriation of such areas as public leisure spaces. These parks prioritize fair public

---

[19]Diadema is located in the São Paulo Metropolitan Region.
[20]It is worth recalling the principal criticisms of these housing programs: The eviction of families from fluvial areas and the low quality of the housing developments produced.

appropriation, making use of grassed areas, walkways, cycle lanes, recreational spaces, sports practices, food kiosks, and the like, adequate night lighting and tree-lined areas that do not obstruct the view of their users, ensuring safe nocturnal use;

- members of the QUAPÁ Lab[21] proposed the creation of public fruition indices —for open spaces that are privately owned but open to public access—with the aim of equipping and upgrading a range of urban spaces capable of being developed for public utilization. The indices are in line with new urban guidelines and proposals for revision of the legislation on land use and occupation in the cities of São Paulo, Campinas, and Santos, the key metropolitan centers in São Paulo state. By 2016, this proposal had already been included in the city of São Paulo new urban legislation and was being debated in the public administrations of Campinas and Santos. It constitutes a new urban parameter that can be adopted by other Brazilian cities.

6.4 Open Space Systems: Complexities and Contradictions

A strong hybridism can be observed between open spaces that officially belong to one or another subsystem (highways, leisure, environmental conservation, and so on). Shifting away from legal stipulations and their classificatory forms of reasoning, in practice, most open urban spaces in medium and large Brazilian cities perform more than one role: Unlike built spaces, open urban spaces form a system.

The environmental issue cannot be conceived in a separate system of open spaces, less yet be reduced to legally protected areas. The different vegetation-covered spaces or just the permeable ones (mobile dunes, for instance) perform environmental roles. A grassed roundabout, a tree-lined street, or a garden roof cannot be ignored. Because such spaces present different propensities to maintain their environmental attributes, the system is highly dynamic, questioning environmentalist approaches based solely on prohibitive legislation to restrict occupations and uses. Environmentally adequate actions need to be encouraged, along with participatory processes for managing territories, avoiding the tendency to treat social and environmental issues in isolation.

The simple existence of streets in squares, parks and similar spaces, associated with soil permeability, already performs an environmental role. On the other hand, many conservation units contain areas that can be used for public leisure, as well as various APPs lend themselves to public interaction. In the urban environment of Brazilian medium and large cities, the interaction and leisure subsystems and the conservation subsystem are effectively indissociable, even though public policies in general fail to recognize it.

---

[21]Landscaping Laboratory of the Architecture and Urbanism Faculty of the University of São Paulo.

6 Open Public Spaces and the *Vita Activa*

Still according to Brazilian environmental laws, the maximum legal percentage of areas in urban APPs that can be unforested is 20%, what may be too low in various cases, notably where there is a shortage of spaces for social interaction and leisure. In these areas, a well-lit linear park would be preferable to a simple forest corridor breaking up the urban fabric. In Brazilian poor peripheries, it is unnecessary to dwell on the dangers posed by the use of dense linear forests by workers and students at night. Here, it is essential to recognize the specificities of Brazilian urbanization, its contradictions and conflicts, rather than idealize natural protection solutions found in exogenous contexts like the Anglo-Saxon American culture. Even there, the forestry protection legislation relating to watercourses in the urban environment is not usually as stringent as Brazilian law.

At the other end of the spectrum, various private appropriations of open public spaces can be observed. Some of these situations enhance public life, such as the presence of commercial activity in streets, squares, and parks, so long as they do not harm the other activities intended for such spaces (circulation, social interaction, scenery fruition, and so on). There are, however, appropriations that clearly infringe the constitutional right to come and go: This is the case of gated communities developments and the closure of streets and neighborhoods, whether occupied by medium- and high-income sectors of the population, or imposed by organized crime on low-income communities.

Open-air markets often characterize the dynamic of streets, squares, districts, and even of entire Brazilian cities: They not only comprise spaces for work, income, profit, and consumption (the domain of necessities) but also places for encounters, social interaction, culture, and public life (the domain of freedom)—the *vita activa*.

On a larger scale, informal commerce can lead to fairly substantial tax fraud, often involving the participation of officially established storeowners and organized crime. Outdoor vendors cease to roam the streets and occupy specific locations on public land instead, charging a high price for their 'sales points'. The 'fixed' presence of street vendors on public roads can hinder the circulation of pedestrians, just as newspaper stands and the like, authorized by municipal authorities, becoming obstacles to passersby on narrower sidewalks—many of them, in fact, are no more than a meter and a half wide, especially in areas developed within the first decades of the twentieth century.

Space is a continually shifting hybrid, even when its materiality persists over time. Considering urban spaces, open spaces are those that can most readily accommodate changes. This characteristic enables them to more clearly manifest aspects of the socio-spatial dialectic. Contradictions and conflicts, presence and absence, wealth and poverty, strength and weakness, violence and solidarity are all expressions continually found in open urban spaces, in particular those used more intensively by the public.

The ways in which social processes traverse open spaces systems include dynamics capable of 'privatizing' public spaces; private spaces or public properties intended for very specific uses, may as well, become strongly 'publicized'. These processes do not concern formal questions of (il)legality but the dynamics of social appropriations of such spaces over time. Lived open space is constantly transforming itself, transgressing plans initially adopted by the state and by developers. It is not merely a question of recognizing Lefebvre's critique of the action of the state and its urban planners (Lefebvre 2009). The structural relations between state, capital, and work are not fixed: They become established within a dialectical process. The future is not given.

It is important to stimulate participatory processes for designing and managing open spaces systems, so that spaces better adapted to the uses desired by the population can be generated. More than just meeting demands, the aim should be to constitute a communicative public reason (Habermas 2007) through discussion and increased awareness of the public relevance of space, the recognition of individual and social rights and of obligations concerning city and metropolitan spaces. A participatory process established in this way fosters alterity recognition, exchange of knowledge, and collective construction of new knowledge. A critical, participatory, political, and citizen-oriented pedagogy of public space is thus potentiated. Dissension and consensus are dialectically constituted in such a process, indubitably enhancing the political public sphere.

Thus, in present-day urban Brazil, the unexpected gains strength in actions that evade those planned by hegemonic actors—practices essential to the creative exercise of citizenship—in open spaces with public access, a fertile field for everyday actions and for more diverse cultural and political manifestations. Open spaces do not lend themselves merely to the functions, uses, and appropriations discussed here: They go far beyond: a 'reservoir of the imagination' (Bartalini 2010) and this assuredly is no trivial matter.

References

Arendt H (1958) The human condition. The University of Chicago Press, Chicago
Arendt H (1991) A condição humana, 5th edn. Forense Universitária, Rio de Janeiro
Bartalini V (2010) *Sistemas de espaços livres*. Interview with Lab QUAPÁ. Faculdade de Arquitetura e Urbanismo, Universidade de São Paulo
Brazil (1965) Lei nº 4.771. Institui o novo Código Florestal. Brasília: Presidência da República. Casa Civil. Available at www.planalto.gov.br/ccivil_03/leis/L4771.htm. Accessed on 17 Mar 2012
Brazil (1979) Lei nº 6.766. Dispõe sobre o Parcelamento do Solo Urbano e dá outras Providências. Brasília: Presidência da República. Casa Civil. Available at www.planalto.gov.br/ccivil_03/leis/L6766.htm. Accessed on 18 Sep 2011
Brazil (1999) Lei nº 9.785. Altera [...] as Leis [...] 6.766, de 19 de dezembro de 1979 (parcelamento do solo urbano). Brasília: Presidência da República. Casa Civil. Available at http://www.planalto.gov.br/ccivil_03/leis/L9785.htm. Accessed on 21 Sep 2011
Brazil (2000) Lei nº 9.985. Regulamenta o art. 225, § 1º, incisos I, II, III e IV da Constituição Federal, institui o Sistema Nacional de Unidades de Conservação da Natureza e dá outras Providências. Brasília: Presidência da República. Casa Civil. Available at www.planalto.gov. br/ccivil_03/leis/L9985.htm. Accessed on 6 Sep 2011
Brazil (2002) Lei nº 10.406. Institui o Código Civil. Brasília: Presidência da República. Casa Civil. Available at www.planalto.gov.br/ccivil_03/leis/2002/L10406.htm. Accessed on 18 Sep 2011

Denatran (2015) *Frota de veículos - 2015.* Available at www.denatran.gov.br/index.php/estatistica/257-frota-2015. Accessed on 16 Sep 2016
Habermas J (1987) The theory of communicative action. Beacon Press, Boston
Habermas J (1989) The structural transformation of the public sphere. An inquiry into a category of Bourgeois Society. MIT Press, Cambridge
Habermas J (2006) Entre naturalismo y religión. Paidós, Barcelona
Habermas J (2007) A inclusão do outro: estudos de teoria política, 3rd edn. Loyola, São Paulo
IBGE. (2016). *Cidades@.* Available at www.cidades.ibge.gov.br. Accessed on 18 Sep 2016
Lefèbvre H (2008) O direito à cidade, 5th edn. Centauro, São Paulo
Lefèbvre H (2009) The production of space, 2nd edn. Blackwell, Malden-MA
Macedo S, Queiroga E (2016) *Paisagem paulistana, formas, espaços livres e apropriações.* In XIII ENEPEA. Anais. Available at enepeasalvador.wixsite.com/enepea2016/copia-artigos-aceitos. Accessed on 16 Sep 2016
Magnoli M (1982) *Espaços livres e urbanização*: uma introdução a aspectos da paisagem metropolitana. Livre Docência Thesis. Faculdade de Arquitetura e Urbanismo, Universidade de São Paulo, São Paulo
Morin E (2008) O método 1: a natureza da natureza, 2nd edn. Sulina, Porto Alegre
Queiroga E (2002) *A megalópole e a praça*: o espaço entre a razão de dominação e a razão comunicativa. Ph.D. Thesis. Faculdade de Arquitetura e Urbanismo, Universidade de São Paulo, São Paulo
Queiroga E (2012) *Dimensões públicas do espaço contemporâneo*: resistências e transformações de territórios, paisagens e lugares urbanos brasileiros. Livre Docência Thesis. Faculdade de Arquitetura e Urbanismo, Universidade de São Paulo, São Paulo
Ribeiro AR et al (2000) Espaços livres do Recife. Prefeitura do Recife, Recife
Santos M (1996) A natureza do espaço: técnica e tempo, Razão e Emoção. Hucitec, São Paulo
Santos M (2000) Por uma outra globalização: do pensamento único à consciência universal. Record, Rio de Janeiro
Sennett R (1977) The fall of public man. Knopf, New York

Author Biography

Eugênio Fernandes Queiroga holds an undergraduate degree (1986), a master's degree (1994), a doctorate (2002) and a professorship (2012) in Architecture and Urbanism from the Faculty of Architecture and Urbanism of the University of São Paulo (FAU-USP). He is now an Associate Professor and Chair of the Graduate Program in Architecture and Urbanism (FAU-USP), vice-coordinator in charge of the QUAPÁ Lab of FAU-USP, of the Thematic Project on Research Space Systems in the constitution of contemporary urban form in Brazil, and of the National Research Network QUAPÁ-SEL; Chair of the Research Committee (FAU-USP, May 2014 to May 2016, and currently Vice-Chair); member of the editorial boards of the journals: Óculum Ensaios (PUC-Campinas), PARC (UNICAMP) and Landscape and Environment (USP); Member of the Editorial Board of Editora Sulina.

Chapter 7
Open Space Systems in Rio de Janeiro: The Public and Private Spheres Reflected in the Urban Landscape

Vera Regina Tângari

Abstract This chapter introduces the issues in debate by researchers, teachers, professionals and students, within the scope of the Open Spaces Systems in Rio de Janeiro-SEL/RJ of PROARQ-UFRJ Research Group. It establishes as a milestone the research that evidences the aspects of access and use of open spaces in Brazilian cities, focusing on the context of state and municipality of Rio de Janeiro and their consequences on the public sphere in terms of management, design and ownership. To this end, the following frames are proposed: the systemic relation between spaces in the public sphere and those in the private sphere, in different contexts, times, and points of view; the types and forms of use of these spaces, which are subdivided into distinct categories and types; the environmental questions and needs that guide analyzes about open spaces confronted with other social and economic demands, such as pressure for housing in Brazilian cities. It presents preliminary results of the ongoing research on the role of open spaces in the urban configuration of the municipality of Rio de Janeiro. The studies carried out and herein summarized help to understand how the observed aspects relate to socio-spatial segregation in Rio de Janeiro with the purpose of subsidizing the elaboration of socially fair and more inclusive urban planning and regulation policies.

The first and second parts of this chapter were coauthored by: Mônica Bahia Schlee, urbanist, and landscape architect at SMU/PCRJ, Ph.D. from PROARQ-FAU/UFRJ, M.Sc. in Environmental Structures from FAUUSP and M.A. in Landscape Architecture from Pennsylvania State University; Marcia Wajsenzon, architect and urbanist, Ph.D. from PROURB-FAU/UFRJ and M.Sc. in Housing and Urban Development; Rubens de Andrade, landscapist, Prof. of Art History at EBA-UFRJ, coordinator of the Hybrid Landscapes Research Group, Ph.D. from IPPUR/UFRJ and M.Sc. from PROARQ-FAU/UFRJ. The presented studies were financed by awards and research support grants provided by CNPq, CAPES and FAPERJ.

V. R. Tângari (✉)
Federal University of Rio de Janeiro, Rio de Janeiro, Brazil
e-mail: vtangari@uol.com.br

© Springer International Publishing AG, part of Springer Nature 2018
L. Capanema Alvares and J. L. Barbosa (eds.), *Urban Public Spaces*,
The Urban Book Series, https://doi.org/10.1007/978-3-319-74253-3_7

Keywords Open spaces · Rio de Janeiro · Urban landscape
Public and private spheres · Socio-spatial segregation · Classification

7.1 Introducing Concepts

The spatial and social morphology of our cities reflects the organization of Brazilian society since it is shaped by the logics, relations, and social dynamics that are expressed, directly or indirectly, in the configuration of open spaces production, both public and private, taking into account their distinctive characteristics in terms of ownership, access, form, use and appropriation.

It is virtually impossible to speak of space without speaking of time, given that this interconnection of the notions of space and time is a social construct (Santos 1997). Society creates space at a determined time and in various times, and the transformations or crystallizations of models or formats in time occur through the organization, uses and form that they reflect in space. Time passes, but the notion of a space in time does not. As Roberto Damatta argues:

> the fact is that, in order to be made concrete and be sensed as 'things,' time and space require a system of contrasts. Every society has a grammar of spaces and temporalities to be able to exist as an articulated whole, and this fundamentally depends on activities that are also organized into diverse oppositions, allowing recollections or memories different in quality, sensibility and form of organization. (DaMatta 1991, p. 41)

Demarcations and forms of organization can be discerned in social space. How is space manifested in our society? What forms does it take and what activities and exchanges happen? Relations in the urban space in different temporalities point to diverse forms of utilization.

Time, history, space, and ways of appropriation have been recurrent themes in landscape studies, whatever the different types of approach adopted. Exploring the past can reveal distinct uses and appropriations of public open spaces, helping us understand the present and its urban forms, as well as assisting in the proposal of projects designed to regenerate and manage public space.

Taking a lead from the ideas of Silva (2004), societal transformations occur through space. In the contemporary world, changes in urban space have led to the formation of landscapes that presume new forms of cultural appropriation. According to Silva, the production of public space promoted by the dominant political-economic sector exploits a lack of cultural definition in order to intervene and further its own interests where neither the landscape to be constructed nor the concerns of the local population are given much importance. Despite the prominent role played in the urban landscape, Silva argues that public urban space is relegated to dealing with questions linked to the circulation of vehicles and pedestrians, weakening its potential to foment sociability and encounters, resulting in a landscape devoid of identity.

Understanding the relationship between open space systems and the sphere of public and private life, evaluating the actions of public administration, and offering projects and initiatives aimed at fostering sustainable policies are all aims central to the research projects currently being developed by the Open Space System research group at Rio de Janeiro/SEL-RJ. These are presented here as part of a critical analysis that seeks to ensure that the management of open spaces is fully integrated into the urban planning of cities.

7.2 The Environmental Question and the Pressure for Housing

As a social product materialized in the physical environment, cities reflect the tensions and conflicts between the process of occupation and the environmental substrate. The nature of the clash between the environmental and the housing issues, exposed by the discourses and instruments that divide up and design the space of the cities, reflect the difficulty of confronting and articulating these two distinct public interests, both at a global level and in local contexts.

Over the last 50 years, Brazil as a whole has been marked by rapid urban expansion combined with an absence of structural social policies, both at the bases of the economic development model adopted in the country (Maricato 2001). According to Ferreira (2005), the unprecedented growth in the urban population was induced by an economic strategy centered on low-wage industrialization as a means to lever the country's development, seeking to provide minimum housing for the working class without spending public resources or raising labor costs.

Isolated initiatives prevailed, generating diverse forms of irregular occupation of urban space. On the other hand, the housing policies adopted at national level throughout the twentieth century prioritized a financial return on investments, thus heavily curbing the low-income population's access to the private market. As a consequence, most of the dwellings found in Brazilian cities have been produced without financing, following irregular procedures and without technical knowledge. In parallel, metropolitan peripheries gradually became consolidated as areas for housing poor workers through the widespread and frequently irregular production of urban lots (Maricato 2001; Villaça 1998).

The housing strategy adopted in Brazilian cities, especially from the start of the 1980s, sought to consolidate the land regularization of favelas and low-income housing lots, rather than developing a policy for the production of dwelling units. In the 1990s, this process was interrupted by the neoliberal ideology of the 'minimal State,' which prompted a significant reduction in sources of funding and social investments, and the adoption of programs conditioned on raising external funds. Due to the transformations experienced in Brazilian cities from the 1980s, the importance of restructuring them became clear. The 1980s and 1990s, however, were characterized by the materialization of an urban planning model based on isolated projects, with emphasis on design and spatial reorganization as an instrument of urban intervention intended to reverse the pattern of economic and social decay, boost the image of cities, and recuperate the self-esteem of their citizens.

At the same time as they benefitted from the valorization of open spaces and their potential for urban regeneration, Brazilian cities also had to confront the stigma of the standardization of landscapes and the adoption of imported models. These strategies became consolidated in the two main lines of action, regarding public open spaces, that guided the reorganization of the Brazilian urban landscape during this period: the urban redesign of central areas, or areas with the potential for centrality, and the environmental protection and recuperation of abandoned or degraded urban and peri-urban areas (Schlee 2009).

In the contemporary Brazilian setting, a new picture has emerged. A decline in migration toward the megalopolises can be observed, with this flow redirected toward medium-sized cities with thriving economies and valorized attributes. After the 1980s, the medium-sized cities began to grow more quickly than the country's metropolises.

The real estate market assigned value to new localities, inducing the fragmentation of urban territories. The gradual process of unequal urban expansion led to the fraying of the peripheral fabric of consolidated areas in both intra-urban and peri-urban contexts. The wealthier sectors of the population moved to new areas with better infrastructure, attracting the low-income social strata in search of jobs. This movement meant a diffuse expansion of the urban fabric and a generated increase in infrastructural costs: At the same time that it drove the proliferation of closed condominiums for the high-income population, these were soon joined by favelas and irregular land subdivisions, expressing in urban space the dynamic of spatial segregation characteristic of Brazilian cities in general.

In other words, part of the poorer social strata occupied the outer peripheries without infrastructure, or environmentally fragile areas not yet occupied, such as forested slopes, *restingas* and mangroves, river shores and protection zones around water sources (Schlee 2009; Reis Filho 2006). In these cases, we can highlight the gradual loss of connectivity between the new lots inserted in the urban fabric or on its outskirts and the consolidated city, combined with mono-functionality (predominantly residential use) and low density. These aspects operate contrary to the idea of the constitution of a democratic public space, a space of social participation, and tend to generate individualization, spatial segregation and high environmental costs.

In Brazilian cities, especially in the consolidated and emergent metropolises, the tensions provoked by everyday collisions between the spontaneous, the controlled (or what should be), and the induced (very often in veiled form) growth are striking. Comparing Brazil's legislation with its diverse socio-spatial realities, we can observe that these phenomena are embedded in the legal instruments that regulate urban occupation and preserve the country's natural and cultural heritage.

The socioenvironmental conflicts found in Brazilian cities arise from the ideologies, practices, and absences that orient its social organization and are strongly expressed in public open spaces. The market 'pushes' and attempts to pass off these conflicts as the consequence of the clash between low-income settlements and protected areas. But why not consider a change in paradigm in the allocation of areas of social interest? Why is the debate on allocating areas for social housing still limited to its localization in areas of interest for environmental conservation? Why not consider allocating a percentage of what the real estate sector identifies as the 'usable, developable, useful' fabric of the city to areas of social interest as part of the social return for the profit obtained? Would this not be a fairer and more sustainable form of distribution? What are the roles, functions, and potentialities of public open spaces in terms of reversing the current logic?

While public open spaces very often reiterate and reinforce the dynamics that produce and reproduce inequality in the city, their environment also demonstrate that they still possess the vitality and potential for effective urban regeneration, rooted in their articulation as a system and in their role as a structuring element in the process of planning cities so as to bring together the isolated fragments of contemporary public life. To this end, public policies need to be restructured in order for city planning to incorporate this possibility.

7.3 The Social Construction of Landscapes: A Theme and Its Issues

First of all, it is important to understand the relationship between the physical patterns of urban occupation in Brazilian cities, the modalities through which the urban fabric is expanded, the diverse configurations of the elements making up the geo-biophysical substrate, and the impacts of these conditioning factors on the landscape and on the distribution and appropriation of open spaces.

Based on previous research into the morphological, environmental, and cultural constitution of the landscape of Rio de Janeiro's railway suburbs, situated in the north zone of the city, the aim of the current research phase is to comprehend the sociohistorical process behind the construction of the suburban landscape. As part of this endeavor, we undertook a comparative study on the patterns implemented in areas of greater centrality, such as the center, south, and southwest zones, and the impacts of similar patterns implementation—with reductions and adaptations adjusted to the local socioeconomic conditions—on lower-income areas.

We recognized two prominent elements in the differentiation of the diverse parts of the city: the spatial configuration of its geo-biophysical substrate and the understanding of the historical evolution of the spatial segregation of Rio's population, which was constructed based on the analysis proposed by Abreu (1987). This analysis can be summarized as follows: the elites, previously located in the upper and lower parts of downtown and its surrounding areas, shifted southwards and southwestwards during the twentieth century, along the ocean shoreline, occupying the low-lying coastal areas; other sectors of the population settled close to the center, on the port hillsides, and in the Baixada de Inhaúma, north of the

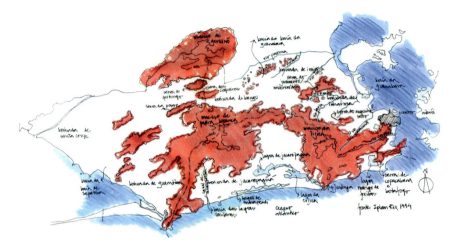

Fig. 7.1 Geo-biophysical substrate and boundaries of the municipal territory of Rio de Janeiro. Drawing by the author in 1999 based on IplanRio, 1994

center, following the main drainage routes where the railway branches, highways, and later subway lines were situated (Fig. 7.1).

Since the mid-nineteenth century, distinct territories have become configured and clearly differentiated, normally delimited by favela occupations, unofficial lots, slum tenements, and other types of spatial occupation undertaken by the population strata that were unable to find socially and financially accessible residences or available lots, when they sought to follow the movements of employment opportunities (in industry, commerce, civil construction) to new locations established by the public authorities in conjunction with the higher-income classes. In order to better understand this phenomenon, we set out from the analysis of the intra-urban space structure in Brazil, as described by Villaça (1998). The analysis proposed by Villaça, the concepts of the social construction of space, its relation to the landscape formulated by Santos (1988, 1997), and the premises underlying the capitalist production of space identified by Harvey (2005) help us comprehend processes found not just in Rio de Janeiro but in other Brazilian cities.

Taking as our starting point the questions set out above, as the basis for observation the process of landscape construction and transformation, and as method the adoption of a multi-scalar and multi-temporal approach, the primary option was to focus our analysis on the diverse systems of public and private open spaces, recognizing their social construction and their greater potential in terms of enabling collective transformation (Tângari et al. 2009). By applying the previous concepts to different case studies, the aim was to explore the systematic relationship between landscape construction, constituted by the built and unbuilt spaces, and the geo-biophysical substrate, taking into consideration the pressures exerted by capital on unbuilt public and private spaces with the potential for urbanization, and those exerted by the populations precluded of access to land, housing, transport, and employment, on unbuilt public and private spaces barred to urbanization and thus outside capital's sphere of interest. In this way, it was possible to observe the specificities and differences of each locality under study, seeking also to identify aspects of convergence at the base of the relationship between the observed patterns of occupation and the resulting landscapes.

Based on the concepts and analytic methods developed in previous research, the following elements were systemized: the conditions of the geo-biophysical substrate, the forms of land division; the two and three-dimensional relations between built and unbuilt spaces; the diverse systems of built spaces apprehended through typo-morphological studies undertaken at the level of the block and the lot; the diverse systems of unbuilt spaces, also defined as spaces without buildings or urbanization (Magnoli 2006a, b), both public and private (Tângari 1996, 1999).

A deeper examination of the suburban landscape of the city of Rio de Janeiro gave room for new lines of inquiry, which emerged from the interest in understanding the processes of the landscapes social construction in Rio de Janeiro and other cities, through the multitude of questions generated by its analysis: do the patterns of spatial occupation and the types of landscape produced recur? What diversities are there to these patterns and the types and causes involved in their constitution? How do these divergences and convergences help us understand spatial segregation, adaptation to models, job vulnerability, the fragility of substrates, the potential for transformation, and the consequent impacts on urban landscape?

7.4 Recurrence of Patterns of Spatial Occupation and the Construction of Landscape Types

In a publication about urban form and open spaces, Silvio Macedo presents us with an inquiry into the public administration of cities, the standards of landscapes quality, and the resulting open space systems:

> Despite this structural agenda, the effective constitution of landscapes is not the responsibility of the public administration and, in terms of urban space, this is a basic fact. Notwithstanding the existence of regulations and plans, there is no real certainty as to where and when transformations of the landscape will take place, nor what dimension they will take. What can be observed are market trends with investments in new constructions, apartment blocks, housing estates, shopping malls and so on, in determined locations or creating new fronts of action and myriads of small individual initiatives, reforms, the construction of small buildings and extensions, the planting of trees and gardens, the reform of commercial and residential frontages, etc. which run parallel to the abandonment and degradation of many built structures that have either become obsolete or simply been abandoned by their proprietors for diverse reasons. (Macedo 2012, pp. 291–305)

In this context, the following questions arise: what is recurrent in the relation between patterns of spatial occupation and the formulation of landscape types, irrespective of the size of the city, the size of the population, the form of administration, or the existence of the applicable planning instruments?

Based on the authors studied and described above, some of the recurrences that are reflected directly in the production of the landscape of Brazilian cities at the diverse scales are highlighted below:

- **reproduction of the urban center–periphery model**: The center–periphery relation, whether radial, linear, or poly-nucleated, is observed to be at the basis of the spatial segregation of cities and regions, with the territorial sizes of the peripheries, especially low-income areas, larger than the central areas, whose fabrics are normally dense and consolidated;
- **income concentration and the dislocation of residential areas**: Access to better jobs is limited to sectors of the population that employ and underemploy people from low-income classes in their homes and workplaces; close to zones offering employment in middle- and high-income districts, there will always be diverse forms of formal or informal low-income housing, normally in areas of environmental conservation without market value;
- **high concentration of land**: Access to land ownership and decent housing is limited to a few, and financing options are severely restricted, generating a recurrent pattern of peripheries being occupied either horizontally or vertically by poorer population, always in higher proportions than the wealthier districts, leading to urban fabric patterns undergoing distinct processes of densification and consolidation;
- **low supply of public transport**: As public transportation means are inefficient and of poor quality, and due to the need for people to commute from residence to workplace, the chosen mobility pattern at a collective level ends up being individual transportation (cars, motorbikes, bicycles), increasing the pressures on the urban fabric and stretching the commuting times of the workforce;
- **poor quality of the urban infrastructure and the public services networks**: When they exist, the urban infrastructure facilities, networks, and equipment are concentrated in sectors occupied by higher-income groups, reproducing low standards of sanitation, public health, education, and social welfare in peripheral areas and regions;
- **occupation of areas barred to urbanization**: Federal regulations (Brasil 2000) have instituted various categories of conservation units that became considered unproductive for the purposes of the real estate market. Instead, they are chosen as residential locations by the population strata otherwise unable to access land or housing, due to the combination of motives set out earlier, generating situations of social vulnerability when they settle in environment risk areas (slopes, floodlands, river and canal shores, mangroves and *restingas*).

Differences in the construction of landscapes primarily relate to the constitutional aspects of the geo-biophysical substrate, reflecting the diversity of biomes and ecosystems in which cities are located. They are also related to the historical processes of occupation, principally in terms of how the territory was formed and what was its political role, and to the cultural identity of its populations, taking into account their origins, ethnic formation, modes of production, and territorial and symbolic values (Campos et al. 2011, 2012).

7.5 Formulating a Critical Framework to Understand the Processes of Landscape Construction and Transformation

As a result of the experiences shown in an earlier publication (Tângari et al. 2012a), we came to understand that the process of landscape construction is an outcome of models of urban occupation themselves derived from various economic and cultural variables, determined by the form in which the society occupies, appropriates, and manages the territory (Santos 1997). The result of these models thus reflects the conjugation of ethical and esthetic processes, very often displaying a homogenizing effect in terms of the ideological and discursive content. These work to shape the landscape as a socioeconomic and cultural product imposed on a physical substrate with very diverse characteristics. In this context, the open spaces systems—pertaining to both the public and private spheres—reflect in a systematic, processual, and permanent manner the consequences of applying models of urban occupation without the necessary evaluation of the sociocultural and geo-biophysical characteristics of the territories involved, leading to irreversible situations of environmental damage and vulnerability.

These systems are defined by natural conditions, related to the physical substrate, and by anthropic actions, which superimpose the logic of human occupation on the logic of natural processes. This human logic, in turn, is partially dictated by official rules, defined in legal instruments regulating use and occupation, in the form of urban plans and laws, in public investments in projects and infrastructural works, and in the action of private agents responsible for producing spaces intended for the market. The logic of occupation also includes—at a huge scale in Brazil and other developing countries—informal situations where the regulation codes are established by social groups from diverse income bands, according to their own material and cultural specificities, resulting in a complex system of socio-spatial and environmental relations (Santos 1997).

In this context, the implantation of large-scale public investments in transport, energy, housing, infrastructure and industrial development, basic drivers of economic growth in developing countries like Brazil, generally affects the quality of the landscape and the physical-territorial and sociocultural environment in the regions where they take place. The urban and peri-urban systems of public and private open spaces reflect these impacts and absorb them with greater intensity, since they bring rapid transformations in the form and intensity of occupation, in both formal and informal areas of cities.

Based on these observations and those made earlier in the chapter, we can take as a starting point the urban reality and the contradictions of a process of occupation that expresses the high concentration of income and resources in some sectors and areas and the omission of public governance in others. These contradictions result in an imbalance in the supply, accessibility, and appropriation of open spaces by the population, directly affecting the quality of the physical environment and the conditions of sociability that can occur in open spaces, principally those belonging to the public sphere (Macedo et al. 2007).

The next section examines the role of urban open spaces in shaping the urban fabric and in defining centralities in the city of Rio de Janeiro, setting out a detailed classification of categories and types suitable for potential future study.

7.6 Urban Open Spaces, the Shaping and Definition of Fabrics and Centralities of Rio de Janeiro

Covering a surface area of 1,200 km^2, with a population of approximately 6.3 million inhabitants and an overall density of 53 inhab./ha in 2010, according to IBGE (2011), occupation of the municipality of Rio de Janeiro, the center of the Rio de Janeiro Metropolitan Region (RMRJ), is characterized by compact urbanization, interspersed by conservation units in the mountainous region and bordered by the Atlantic Ocean and its bays (Tângari et al. 2012b), as shown in Fig. 7.1. Its territory is made up of urban sectors with diverse levels of consolidation, distinct patterns of occupation and built density, and some regions earmarked for expansion.

The urban fabric is characterized by income concentration located in particular sectors of the city (south, southeast, southwest, and central areas), where the residential districts with a higher real estate value are situated. Middle-income groups are distributed in the north and northeastern regions, with lower incomes to the northwest and west.

Due to the historic pressure for occupation of sites with a high level of urban land valorization, in regions served by infrastructure and public investments in transport, sanitation and services, pressure grew to alter the parameters of urban legislation, especially toward investments in urban mobility in locations available for urbanization with prices accessible to the market (Cardeman 2014).

As well as revisions to the Urban Master Plan, the last approved in 2011, diverse Urban Structuration Plans have been enacted for specific urban sectors of the city, aiming to introduce urban regulatory frameworks adapted to the local characteristics of each district (Cardeman 2014). From the 1980s, these local plans were joined by a general municipal zoning plan, in force since 1976 (Decree 322), and a number of specific federal regulations (land division legislation) and state regulations (environmental protection laws) (Schlee and Tângari 2008).

The overlapping of successive regulatory changes, conditioned by the selective valorization of urban land, the historical processes of social segregation, and the physical substrate characterized by coastal areas interspersed with mountain ranges, mangroves, bays, and marshes, generated the shaping of urban fabrics in diverse stages of consolidation in terms of their horizontal and vertical profiles (built density and high rise patterns) (Macedo 2009).

Setting out from this context, this article seeks to relate the configuration of the different public and private open space systems to the different levels of consolidation of the urban fabrics of Rio de Janeiro city.

The following questions were established for this phase of the research: what role do urban open space systems play in structuring the urban fabrics and in the configuration of landscape? How are they related to aspects of the physical substrate, to historical and contemporary processes of urban expansion, to the socioeconomic characteristics of the population, to urban mobility conditions, or to the definition of centralities? How are they classified and appropriated? How important are open spaces and landscape for planning decisions and municipal governance?

7.7 Articulation Between the Highway System, Urban Functions, and Centralities: Aspects of Urban Morphology

The city's highway connections are conditioned by the relief of the coastal plains, valley floors or landfilled terrain. Tunnels also exist connecting the districts separated by mountains. As well as the tunnels, transversal connections cross the hillsides and interconnect diverse urban areas via expressways. Urban centralities are concentrated along the main highway routes, where commerce, services and industrial activities are located. Residential uses are distributed in the center of the urban fabrics, segregated by income and conditions of urban land valorization.

Generally speaking, the city presents a compact but discontinuous urban fabric, delimited to the north by a chain of mountains belonging to the Serra do Mar, and to the south and east by the Atlantic Ocean and Guanabara Bay. The urban fabric is punctuated by forested mountain areas (Tijuca and Pedra Branca) and comprises a central core, originally defined by the localization of the port on the shores of Guanabara Bay, and urban sectors that have either developed along the shores of the bay and ocean to the northeast, southeast and southwest, or spread along the coastal plains and valley floors to the west and northwest.

The morphology of the urban fabric has been conditioned by the characteristics of the geo-biophysical substrate, resulting in a compact form of occupation, punctuated by the mountainous uplands that cut the urban fabric. It is worth adding that favela occupations occur in all these sectors, which follow the pattern of the sites in which they are inserted: in those areas with a more rugged physical substrate (slopes) and a higher land value, the favelas present medium rise building fabrics; in those areas with flat terrains and a lower land value, the favelas are mostly horizontal (Rio de Janeiro 2009). In all cases, though, land occupation is generally intensive with compact settlements and few open spaces.

In order to demonstrate the relation between the physical substrate and the urban morphology and as a guide for future studies, an analysis was undertaken at the level of the urban blocks, exploring the general characteristics of the urban fabric in accordance with the patterns of urban consolidation, vegetal cover, centrality distribution, and presence of open spaces for special use, such as cemeteries, military areas, roadside areas, and so on.

Based on the maps produced with the items above and the pattern of income distribution, we can study various aspects of spatial segregation, determined by the relation between physical substrate, morphology of the urban fabric, occupation patterns, and income profiles, thereby assisting the subsequent analyses described in the following item. This cross-checking of information allowed us to conclude that there is a higher consolidation of the fabric to the northeast, with a horizontal occupation by middle- and lower-income groups, and to the southeast, with high rise occupation by middle- to high-income groups, and greater heterogeneity to the west, with high rise sectors concentrated along the coastline, occupied by middle- to high-income groups, and horizontal occupation spreading along the inland areas by middle- to low-income groups.

We can also conclude that there is a higher incidence of non-consolidated fabrics with a higher frequency of vacant land to the west, a factor indicative of horizontal urban expansion. Forested mountain areas, taking the form of an arc, condition the profile of the urban fabric and have a strong impact across the entire city shape.

7.8 General Characteristics of the Open Spaces Systems

The current system of open spaces in Rio de Janeiro, as conceived by Magnoli and Macedo (Magnoli 2006a, b; Macedo et al. 2009a, b), is generally fragmented and diversified. In terms of public open spaces, their distribution in the urban fabric does not, generally speaking, respond to the real needs of the population as a whole, being concentrated in the wealthier residential areas located in the southeast and southwest sectors of the city, as described earlier. In these areas, the open space system is mainly structured along the coast of the ocean and lagoons and along the main roads inside the districts. As for private open spaces, these result from a combination of the distinct urban fabrics and their intra-block morphological characteristics, natural physical substrate, and urban legislation.

For analytic purposes and in accordance with research developed previously (Tângari et al. 2012b), open spaces—the focal point of this chapter—were classified into three categories: public and private urban spaces, environmentally protected spaces, and rural spaces. In turn, this subdivision was closely informed by urban legislation and land ownership profile.

Public and private urban open spaces also include those sites available to land development based on urban legislation. Environmentally protected spaces are those barred to land development and regulated by environmental protection legislation—Full Protection Units and Sustainable Use Units. Rural spaces are those not available to land development located outside the urban perimeter. No rural spaces are found within the limits of Rio de Janeiro municipality since the municipality's administrative border is located entirely within the urban perimeter.

The analysis presented in Fig. 7.2 was carried out for public open spaces, i.e., those situated outside the urban blocks and lots. The study was conducted at the

7 Open Space Systems in Rio de Janeiro: The Public and Private … 121

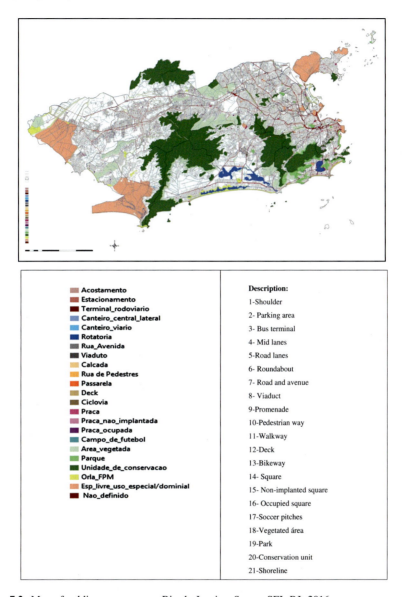

Fig. 7.2 Map of public open spaces—Rio de Janeiro. *Source* SEL-RJ, 2016

level of the urban block and by Administrative Region, at 1:2000 scale, based on the following classification:

A. Category: environmental open spaces, where leisure and recreational activities may also take place

Identified types:

– Conservation unit—in this research, corresponds to mountainous areas.
– Shoreline—mainland coastal zone, corresponding to the Permanent Preservation Areas (APP) adjacent to bodies of water and covered with plants, sand, stones and similar. Includes beaches and other types of shore.

B. Category: urban open spaces, related to the circulation of vehicles or pedestrians, where activities related to recreation, commerce, sports, culture, education, political actions and festivities also take place

Identified types:

– Shoulder—refuge lane located along the roadside areas of highways or urban roads.
– Promenade—sidewalk designed for a specific project or deriving from significant alterations with larger dimensions than normal. Includes sidewalks and paved areas running alongside beaches and other bodies of water.
– Mid lane—central or lateral area located along highways or alongside public roads, with or without vegetation.
– Road lane—residual area located along highways or alongside public roads, with or without vegetation.
– Bikeway—path designated for exclusive use of bicycles and non-motorized vehicles and barred to motorized vehicles.
– Deck—surface suspended over a body of water, including quays and marinas.
– Parking area—public area for parking vehicles, distinct from the parking spaces available on the roads.
– Walkway—raised path for preferential use by pedestrians and barred to motorized vehicles.
– Roundabout—island, generally circular in form, surrounded by roads, placed at intersections and returns, with or without vegetation.
– Road and avenue—traffic lanes between rows of buildings, usually including sidewalks.
– Bus terminal—set of bus bays and lanes located around the stops with shelters to protect pedestrians.
– Pedestrian way—intended for use by pedestrians and barred to motorized vehicles; includes roads closed to vehicle traffic, flights of steps, and public rights of way.
– Viaduct—raised vehicle lane visually marked from beginning to end of the ramp.

C. **Category: urban open spaces for use by pedestrians, allowing the realization of activities related to recreation, commerce, sports, culture, education, political actions and festivities**

Identified types:

- Soccer field—isolated informal open space where soccer is played. Does not include fields in squares and parks.
- Park—public open space officially designated as a park. Defined visually, with or without plants, larger than an urban square when considered within the municipal land use map.
- Square—area designated in a land development project as a public open space for recreational activities.
- Non-implanted square—area designated in a land development project as a public open space for recreational activities that has yet to be executed.
- Occupied square—area designated in a land development project as a public open space for recreational activities that has been used to build public equipment for health care, education facilities, or similar.

D. **Category: urban open spaces, related to administrative, transport, sanitation, educational or cultural infrastructures that may also be used for activities related to commerce, services, recreation, sports, culture or education**

Identified type:

- Open space of public ownership and use—publicly owned unbuilt spaces granted for special uses: railways, ports, airports, universities campuses, cemeteries, and so on.

E. **Category: urban open spaces, related to an area reserved for future expansion**

Identified type:

- Vegetated area—area predominantly covered by vegetation (shrubs or trees) able to be occupied, not subdivided, not belonging to the conservation units, private spaces, or publicly owned spaces.

The analysis carried by Administrative Regions of the Rio de Janeiro municipality, based on the study on the urban fabrics and centralities and on the categories and types described and localized above, afforded a preliminary conclusion concerning the overall distribution of public open spaces in the city:

- in the urban sectors to the north and northeast, where there are high densities of housing and medium- to low-income populations, we find a low number of squares, parks and soccer fields, and predominance of a dense road and railway network;

- in the center, where the historical portion of the city is located, there are squares, promenades and parks with a high frequency of commercial and service activities and a negligible residential concentration;
- distributed across the urban areas to the southeast and southwest, which concentrate the high-medium and high-income bands of the population, and situated between the mountain ranges and the coastline, there are various kinds of parks (recreational, conservation, sports, cultural). There are few squares, but the sea coastline predominates, used intensively by the population as a large linear and continuous park;
- in the urban sectors to the west along the coastline, with medium- and high-medium-income populations located in more heterogeneous form, squares exist as part of the land developments, but the use of open space is shaped by the continuous strip of beaches accessed by the population in general;
- in the urban sectors to the west between the mountain ranges, occupied by low- and medium-income populations located in more scattered form concentrated along the highway and railway routes, there are a larger number of squares, soccer fields, and also occupied and non-implanted squares, corresponding to neighborhoods with little investment or regulatory control by the public authorities.

7.9 Final Considerations

The present article has sought to extend the methodological instruments used for morphological analysis of the public open spaces and their distribution across the city of Rio de Janeiro. It has sought to relate the forms and uses of open spaces systems with the analysis of public and private spheres reflected in the urban landscape. The aim was also to assist other researchers seeking to associate studies on morphology, landscape, and planning with a focus on the open spaces, their regulation and proposals.

Based on the questions raised and the results obtained in the diverse studies presented in the article, we can conclude that public management of open spaces, dominated by isolated and uncoordinated forms of intervention directed toward some parts of the city, results from the combined action of economic sectors of private investment and the public administration, which has tended to concentrate resources in the wealthiest neighborhoods. From the social viewpoint, we observe that conditions deteriorate to the extent that public policies have failed to make progress in rebalancing public investments in housing, transport, public services and sanitation, generating the unequal occupation of the territory and the constant threat of major environmental disturbances and social vulnerabilities.

Iniquities in the distribution of land and income in urban contexts in Brazil have resulted in conflicts and contradictions that are clearly reflected in the construction of the landscape, in the distribution, appropriation and treatment of open spaces, and in the relation between these and the built environment. The more intensive and wide-ranging the investments made in this territorial and sociocultural substrate, the more conflicts and contradictions tend to deepen.

Although some possibilities for transformation can be foreseen, the following questions remain unanswered in this research: how do populations relate to these changes, from the viewpoint of their culture and the values and symbols associated with the landscape and the territory? How are public administrators anticipating the new demands for housing, transport, infrastructure and social equipment? How will environmental systems respond? And, finally, how will landscapes and open spaces appropriations be reconstructed in these situations?

Plans for future development of this research include elaborating, through the use of geo-referencing tools, quantifications that will enable a comparison of levels of urban densification, incidence of centralities and distribution of public and private open spaces within the regions, sectors, and districts of Rio de Janeiro municipality. Based on these preliminary results and in line with the proposed goals, the aim is to contribute to public planning and design policies, as well as to improve the balance of investments made at municipal level in order to improve urban environments and places.

References

Abreu M (1987) Evolução urbana do Rio de Janeiro. IplanRio/Zahar, Rio de Janeiro

Brasil (2000) Lei Federal No de 18 de julho de 2000, que institui o Sistema Nacional de Unidades de Conservação da Natureza SNUC. Brasília

Campos AA, Queiroga E, Galender F, Degreas H, Akamine R, Macedo SS, Custódio V (eds) (2011) Sistemas de espaços livres-conceitos, conflitos e paisagens. FAUUSP, São Paulo

Campos AA, Queiroga E, Galender F, Degreas H, Akamine R, Macedo SS, Custódio V (eds) (2012) Quadro dos sistemas de espaços livres nas cidades brasileiras. FAUUSP, São Paulo

Cardeman RC (2014) A transformação da paisagem em área de expansão urbana: Planejamento em Vargem Grande na cidade do Rio de Janeiro. Thesis, PROARQ-FAU/UFRJ, Rio de Janeiro

DaMatta R (1991) A casa e a rua: espaço, cidadania, mulher e morte no Brasil, 4th edn. Guanabara Koogan, Rio de Janeiro

Ferreira JSW (2005) A cidade para poucos: breve história da propriedade urbana no Brasil. São Paulo, 21 p. Source: http://www.usp.br/fau/depprojeto/labhab/index.html

Harvey D (2005) A produção capitalista do espaço. Annablume, São Paulo

IBGE (2011) Censo Demográfico de 2010. IBGE, Brasília

Macedo SS (2009) Urbanização, litoral e ações paisagísticas à beira d'água. In: Tângari V, Schlee MB, Andrade R, Dias MÂ (eds) Águas urbanas: uma contribuição para a regeneração ambiental como campo disciplinar integrado. FAU/UFRJ-PROARQ, Rio de Janeiro

Macedo SS (2012) O Arco Metropolitano do Rio de Janeiro: reflexões. In: Tângari VR, Rego AQ, Montezuma RCM (eds) O Arco Metropolitano do Rio de Janeiro – integração e fragmentação da paisagem metropolitana e dos sistemas de espaços livres de edificação. PROARQ/ FAU-UFRJ, Rio de Janeiro, pp 291–305

Macedo SS, Custòdio V, Gallender F, Queiroga E, Robba F (2007) Os sistemas de espaços livres e a constituição da esfera pública contemporânea no Brasil. In: Terra C, Andrade R (eds) Coleção Paisagens Culturais, vol 3. EBA-UFRJ, Rio de Janeiro, pp 286–297

Macedo SS, Custòdio V, Gallender F, Queiroga E, Robba F (2009a) Análise do Sistema de Espaços Livres da Cidade Brasileira – uma metodologia em construção: Estudo de caso para o município de São Paulo. In: Revista Paisagem e Ambiente – Ensaios, no 26. FAUUSP, São Paulo, pp 197–210

Macedo SS et al (2009b) Considerações preliminares sobre o sistema de espaços livres e a constituição da esfera pública no Brasil. In: Tângari V, Schlee MB, de Andrade R (eds) Sistema de espaços livres: o cotidiano, ausências e apropriações. FAU/UFRJ-PROARQ, Rio de Janeiro

Magnoli MM (2006a) Em busca de outros espaços livres de edificação. In: Revista Paisagem e Ambiente – Ensaios, nº 21. FAUUSP, São Paulo, pp 143–173

Magnoli MM (2006b) Espaço livre - Objeto de trabalho. In: Revista Paisagem e Ambiente – Ensaios, nº 21. FAUUSP, São Paulo, pp 177–200

Maricato E (2001) Brasil, cidades. Alternativas para a crise urbana. Vozes, Petrópolis, RJ

Reis Filho NG (2006) Notas sobre urbanização dispersa e novas formas de tecido urbano. ia das Artes, São Paulo

Rio de Janeiro (CIDADE) (2009) Secretaria Municipal de Urbanismo. Projeto "Ocupações Irregulares". CMP/CGPU/SMU/PCRJ, Rio de Janeiro

Santos M (1988) Metamorfoses do espaço habitado - fundamentos teórico e metodológico da geografia. Hucitec, São Paulo

Santos M (1997) Pensando o espaço do Homem. Hucitec, São Paulo

Schlee MB (2009) O (re)desenho paisagístico das cidades brasileiras (1986–1995). In: Abap: 30 Anos de Arquitetura Paisagística no Brasil. Farah Ivete, Schlee Mônica Bahia and Tardin Raquel. PROURB/ABAP, Rio de Janeiro

Schlee MB, Tângari VR (2008) As montanhas e suas águas: a paisagem carioca na legislação municipal (1937–2007). In: Cadernos Metrópole, vol 19. PUC-SP, São Paulo, pp 271–291

Silva RDO (2004) O lugar do espaço público na paisagem pós-moderna. Anais VII ENEPEA, Belo Horizonte

Tângari VR (1996) Paisagem una zona norte do Rio: o caso do Méier. In: Paisagem e Ambiente - Ensaios, n°8. FAUUSP, São Paulo

Tângari, VR (1999) Um outro lado do Rio: paisagem urbana da zona norte do Rio de Janeiro. Ph. D. thesis, FAUUSP, São Paulo

Tângari VR, Schlee MB, de Andrade R (eds) (2009) Sistemas de espaços livres: o cotidiano, apropriações e ausências. PROARQ-FAU/UFRJ, Rio de Janeiro

Tângari VR, Rego AQ, Montezuma RCM (eds) (2012a) O Arco Metropolitano do Rio de Janeiro – integração e fragmentação da paisagem metropolitana e dos sistemas de espaços livres de edificação. PROARQ/FAU-UFRJ, Rio de Janeiro

Tângari VR et al (2012b) Morfologia urbana, suporte geo-biofísico e o sistema de espaços livres no Rio de Janeiro. In: Campos AA, Queiroga E, Galender F, Degreas H, Akamine R, Macedo SS, Custódio V (eds) Quadro dos sistemas de espaços livres nas cidades brasileiras. FAUUSP, São Paulo, pp 195–227

Villaça F (1998) Espaço intra-urbano no Brasil. Studio Nobel, São Paulo

Author Biography

Vera Regina Tângari is an Associate Professor at the Federal University in Rio de Janeiro, Brazil. She graduated in Architecture (Instituto Bennett de Ensino, 1981), with a master's degree in Urban Planning (The University of Michigan, 1983), and a Doctoral degree in Urban Environmental Structures (University of São Paulo, 2000). Currently a researcher at the Graduate Program in Architecture and advisor of doctoral and master thesis and dissertations, her main research fields include urban landscape morphology, urban design and architectural design. She is also a member of the directory board of the Brazilian Association of Landscape Architects and associated to the Brazilian Architects Institute.

Chapter 8
The "Reinvention" of the City Through the Favelas

Cristóvão Fernandes Duarte

Abstract In Rio de Janeiro, *favelas* (Brazilian slums), with more than a century of existence, are highly incorporated to the urban landscape. It is important to mention that it was in Rio de Janeiro, in the last decade of the nineteenth century, that the term "favela" first emerged to designate (and discriminate) poor settlements built in the fringes of the formal city by the individual initiative of dwellers themselves. Initially considered precarious and temporary settlements, *favelas* turned into immense poor neighborhoods, as from the second half of the twentieth century, endowed with great cultural vitality and showing a clear critical consciousness related to the segregation and excluding processes associated with their origin. This article presents some thoughts on the resistance and consolidation of *favelas* and their leading role in the processes of the production and reproduction of spaces of the poor.

Keywords Slums · Segregation · Consciousness · Resistance · Production of space

8.1 Introduction

Favelas constitute a contemporary urban phenomenon associated with socio-spatial segregation processes imposed by the big cities uncontrolled growth and by the absence of wealth redistribution mechanisms that guarantee access to housing for the poorer people. Condemned, so to speak, to an "exile within their own city", these populations find in their self-built homes, entirely paid with their own and scarce financial means, a feasible surviving strategy.

English version by Denise de Alcantara Pereira.

C. F. Duarte (✉)
FAU-UFRJ, Rio de Janeiro, Brazil
e-mail: cfduarte@ufrj.br

© Springer International Publishing AG, part of Springer Nature 2018
L. Capanema Alvares and J. L. Barbosa (eds.), *Urban Public Spaces*,
The Urban Book Series, https://doi.org/10.1007/978-3-319-74253-3_8

Since the first favelas appearance in Rio de Janeiro, from the second half of the nineteenth century to the current decade,[1] the number amounts to 763 slums, sheltering an estimated population of 1.4 million people (IBGE, Census 2010). The favela phenomenon in the carioca[2] town is becoming larger and larger, and it is acquiring a degree of complexity that defies the comprehension capacity of experts themselves. Despite the effort of researchers, from the most diverse fields of knowledge, dedicated to the task of studying favelas, there persists a notorious consensus regarding the path still to advance on this matter (Table 8.1).

During decades, the common sense considered favelas as a temporary phenomenon, generated by a critical combination of imbalanced circumstances produced by the city's economic and demographic growth (Perlman, 2002). Thus, they were doomed to disappear as soon as the necessary conditions for the provision of large-scale housing for their dwellers were set. In this mix of tolerance and indifference, a sort of "invisibility pact" regarding favelas and urban poverty in a general manner was established.

If we consider favelas by their apparent features—formed by fragile and precarious dwellings settings; supported by unreliable foundations; built without specialized knowledge; and wedged on the city's steepest hillsides, or on flooded-like terrains along the shores of rivers and lagoons—it is likely that we get to the conclusion that those settlements were not really thought to last. For decades, they have been exposed to the cold and heat; to rains and flooding; to landslides; to collapsing and (accidental or criminal) fires; to lethal "lost bullets" from the shootings between police and crime groups; to prejudice and socio-spatial segregation; and also, to uncountable forced eviction attempts by police and bulldozers. Nevertheless, favelas resist, expand, and consolidate, strongly incorporated into the urban landscape; and nothing indicates, objectively, any possibility of reversion of this process (Fig. 8.1).

In some cases, the expansion of the favela phenomenon already surpasses the limits of localities traditionally identified as favelas, involving large areas of other neighborhoods, mainly those located in the city's periphery. Even in housing complexes, planned and built by the public sector to serve as exemplary alternatives to favelas, as in the cases of Cidade de Deus and Vila Kennedy[3] (just mentioning two of the most well-known cases), one can observe the general occurrence of morphological patterns characteristic of favelas, resulting from remodeling and expansions introduced individually by the dwellers themselves.[4]

---

[1]It is worth mentioning that it was precisely in Rio de Janeiro that the term "favela" first emerged, by the end of the nineteenth century, to designate (and discriminate) poor and informal settlements built in the margins of the formal city by initiative of the own dwellers.

[2]*Carioca* refers to anything from or anyone who is born in the city of Rio de Janeiro.

[3]The housing complexes of Cidade de Deus and Vila Kennedy were built by the government in the 1960s to house people removed from the more privileged areas of the city.

[4]Other examples of housing complexes that turned into slums can be found in Andrade, Luciana and Leitão, Gerônimo. Transformações na paisagem urbana: favelização de conjuntos habitacionais, in: A cidade pelo avesso; desafios do urbanismo. Rachel Coutinho Marques da Silva (org.). Rio de Janeiro: Viana & Mosley: Ed. PROURB, 2006, p. 114

8 The "Reinvention" of the City Through the Favelas

Table 8.1 Population growth in the city of Rio de Janeiro

Year	City population (A)	Favela's population (B)	B/A (%)
1950	2,375,280	169,305	7.13
1960	3,300,431	335,063	10.15
1970	4,251,918	565,135	13.29
1980	5,090,723	722,424	14.19
1991	5,480,768	962,793	17.57
2000	5,857,904	1,092,476	18.65
2010	6,323,037	1,393,314	22.03

Source IBGE Foundation; Demographic Census; Iplanrio, 2010

Where does all this energy come from? How could favelas, facing so many challenges, last for so long, multiplying through the territory with such vitality? What could be the reason for the resistance of the majority of dwellers to abandon their houses in the favela, even when threatened by drug trafficking and militia violence? How can we explain the general replication of the favela's urban morphology amidst the territory of the so-called legal city, transforming many neighborhoods and housing complexes spatial configurations into new favelas? How can we explain the contrast perceived between the vitality, diversity, and intensity of the routine experienced in favelas' public spaces in comparison to the monotony, emptiness, and fragmentation of other city neighborhoods' urban fabric? What is the secret of such success? Which lessons could (and should) we learn with favelas?

Certainly, the longevity of the socio-spatial urban segregation process is ultimately due to macroeconomic and structural reasons. The continued effectiveness of the economic model, based on income concentration, and the absence of a consistent and responsible public policy on the social housing field, intrinsically constitute good explanations in order to maintain those processes of social inequality production and unbalanced valorization of urban land for the large capital real-estate speculation, from which result, among other things, the favelas (Valladares, 2005).

However, we are interested here in debating other factors, specifically associated to the power of resistance demonstrated by favelas when facing these general processes, and their accepted leading role in the production and reproduction of spaces for the poor in the city of Rio de Janeiro. This is not a simple question, for which there are no readymade and conclusive answers. It relates to an extremely complex and diversified framework, engendered by distinct historic, socioeconomic, geographic, and cultural constraints. Some traces may be evoked in a preliminary effort to approach this phenomenon, though.

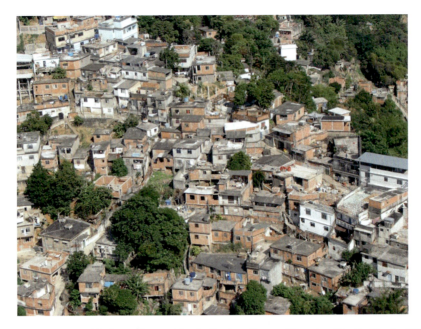

Fig. 8.1 Prazeres Hill, Santa Teresa, Rio de Janeiro. *Source* Photo by Claudia Brack, 2007 (author's collection)

8.2 The House in the Favela as a Locus for the Binding Desire and Thirst for Rights

The "recreation" of the city, promoted by the outliers, under the form of interstitial spaces of resistance and survival, in spite of the difficulties faced by its dwellers–builders, favored the consolidation of important solidarity and mutual protection networks. Established through neighborhood relationships and produced in the contiguous favelas' urban tissue, these networks play a crucial role for the survival strategies engendered by their dwellers. Analyzing the role of proximity in the space production processes, Santos (1999, p. 133) teaches us that contiguity is the foundation for solidarity. The possibility of knowing that one counts on neighbors' help and protection in good or bad times represents an asset of immeasurable value—be it to watch kids that play on the street, to appease domestic misunderstandings, to transport a sick relative in the middle of the night, or to organize a party or a memorial. These are just a few among so many other examples, especially regarding a poor community. In fact, the resulting social cohesion of these protection and solidarity networks was one of the crucial elements for the failure of eviction policies, continuously promoted by the government along the years.

An aspect related to spatial contiguity and always pointed out as a problem to confront, regards the high indexes of population density verified in poor settlements. It is important to mention, however, the difficulty in generalizing this type of diagnosis, due to the diversity of situations found in each favela. Even within the limits of the same favela, one can note the existence of distinct spatial gradients of population density and social groups' income. Aspects such as the increase in multiple storey buildings as well as local topographic characteristics usually demand deeper and more specific studies, in relation to the effects of human density analysis in favelas. What effectively compromises quality of life, and represents a public health problem, is not human density, as seen in the majority of favelas, but open-air sewage; garbage buildup in streets and vacant lots (without pickup and without treatment); the unhealthy conditions present in some dwellings. For all these problems, however, there are feasible and effective solutions, both from the technical and the economic points of view. The key for the comprehension of the relations established between population density and spatial configurations in favelas may be found, perhaps, in the concept of "compact city" proposed by Richard Rogers in the following passage:

> the model of the dense city doesn't need to be seen as a health threat. This means that we may reconsider the advantages of social proximity, rediscover the advantages of living in the company of others (...) For these reasons, I believe that we should invest in the idea of the "compact city" – a dense and socially diverse city, where economic and social activities may be superimposed, and where communities are concentrated around neighborhood units. (Rogers, Gumuchdjian, 2001, p. 33)

Another relevant issue refers to the fact that essentially all that is built in the favelas results from the economic investment and labor (in their free time) of the dwellers themselves, be it for the acquisition of the material used, or for their dwellings construction, accesses, equipment, and improvements made on the public space. The effective participation of the public sector for the improvements and urban infrastructure works in favelas, besides being contingent and limited spatially, started in very recent times. Thus, abandoning their own communities would be similar to renouncing to a good hardly conquered through over-work of the inhabitants' succeeding generations.

In addition, in the case of favela dwellers, the house may become, when necessary, a production unit, offering options for increasing the family's income. A series of small stores managed by the inhabitants emerge coupled with the house, such as bars, smalls shops, markets, video-rentals, printing shops, internet shops, beauty parlors, storages, sewing shops, among so many others, "that are maintained thanks to the local market constituted by the favela itself" (Silva, Barbosa, 2005, p. 97) (Fig. 8.2).

The self-construction of the dwelling unit can be compared to the construction of a life project, better yet, to a life project in construction. As the family grows, all the saved resources are gradually used for the dwelling's expansions and improvements. That is why the favelas are always a construction process. The unfinished aspect that most of the houses show in favelas reveals, in fact, the relentless capacity of their dwellers in the attempt to materialize the dream of a better future for themselves and their loved ones. A work in progress future that does not only takes too long, but also, many times, refuses to arrive. A future that is always wished for and obstinately foreseen in each small change introduced in the dwelling.

Fig. 8.2 Santa Marta Favela, Rio de Janeiro. *Source* Photo by Cristovao Duarte, 2009 (author's collection)

Thus, sufficient elements have been gathered in order to state that the house in the favela represents the essential starting point in the struggle for civil rights. In the impossibility of supplying, by their own means, access to other essential rights, the slum dwellers attempt to build their own shelter. It is something they can and know how to do. Once built the "shell" of the shelter, a struggle starts toward ownership formalization and secure access to water and energy supplying sources, telephone, sewage, and drainage systems; and for their rights to education, health, work, transportation, and so on. In this everlasting to be concluded, the individual shell-shelter in the favela becomes the house dwelling in the city, claiming, in the unfolding of collective social fights, the right to the city and to citizenship.

Therefore, the house is, simultaneously, the locus of desire and thirst bonded to the indivisibility, interdependency and universality of all rights associated to it.

8.3 The "City-Favela" as a Place of Gathering and Exchanging Among Strangers

We shall consider, in more detail, what the design of favelas' public spaces informs us about the processes above described. The first finding related to the geometric form of the urban fabric is the absence of a master plan previously formalized, capable of guiding the opening of streets in the territory. Streets, in general, are irregular and tortuous, as in cities characterized by processes of additive growth. This ultimately results from the addition of continuous single initiatives through time. A trademark, although not exclusive, of medieval and Islamic cities, examples of cities with irregular urban fabric multiply through History, as evidenced by favelas themselves.

The absence of a previously and formally designed project does not allow us, however, to classify them as spontaneous or organic. According to Rossi, "to say that the medieval city is organic, means an absolute ignorance of the political, religious, and economic structure of the medieval city, as well as of its spatial structure" (Rossi, 1977, p. 62). In fact, those cities, as well as the favelas, express a perfectly legible logic on their urban design, allowing us to infer that each addition or suppression carried out along their consolidation process was a consequence of the struggle among various interests at play, mediated, ultimately, by a collective (and procedural) idea of a city.

In the constitution of the favela urban fabric, a socio-spatial dialectic between the inside and the outside, the individual and the collective, the private and the public, is in charge of providing a spatial orientation and dimensioning of access paths amidst buildings, guarantying people's right of way, and supplying basic daily life needs at walking distance. Streets that promote and constrain daily socio-spatial practices are also constrained and promoted by the same actions (Santos, 1988, p. 67). Buildings participate on the constitution of streets that are, in their turn, constitutive parts of the buildings. If the construction of the houses results from the individual initiative of its residents, the constitution of the public space in the favela arises from eminently collective demands. As in the traditional or preindustrial city of additive growth, in the favela, the urban fabric is built in symbiosis between architecture and public space.

The spatial continuity of urban fabrics and the sense of esthetic unity are other characteristics shared by the traditional city and favelas. While the first phenomenon originates from successive aggregation of single initiatives, the second one stems from the articulation of different parts among themselves and with the whole, thus revealing an undeniable sense of coherence and harmony on the setting. In this sense, the spatial continuity of the favela urban fabric opposes the fragmentation processes present in the modern city. Similarly, the aesthetical unity of the city built as a human artifact preserves the idea of a community formed by different individuals (built collectively as the place of encounter and of exchange among individuals), while in the city product, a tendency to homogenize the public spaces prevails, resulting from eliminating and/or segregating the differences (Lefebvre, 1991, p. 82).

Recurrent comparisons between the road network in the formal city and in the favela usually accentuate the low accessibility of the latter, most of all, when the studied examples occur in hilly areas. Clearly, both the quality of the pavement (sometimes inexistent) and the improvised solutions for steeper paths (as, for example, the case of ramps and stairs), generally built without proper technical and financial means, contribute to reduce their efficiency. Nevertheless, if we consider the uses of those spaces and their forms of appropriation by the population, the intrinsic accessibility of the favela fabric, most of the times, reveals itself as satisfactory.[5] Favela's public spaces are meant for people, not for cars, as it happens in the city that surrounds them. Such distinction is tacitly recognized in the well-known oppositions between "favela" and "asphalt", largely used by the media in Rio de Janeiro, supposedly emphasizing favelas' precariousness. Identified with the asphalt, the city known to be legal truly admits that its large and well-paved streets are preponderantly made to motorized use and circulation. In fact, traffic jams (which result in a waste of time and money), other forms of usurping and privatizing the public space by car users, environmental pollution, and accidents with human casualties and car collisions, they all became usual happenings permanently incorporated into the "progressive" scenario of the asphalt city. The violence represented by the spaces for fast traffic flows, defined by the hegemony of motorized vehicles, makes the human body an anachronic instrument poorly adapted for survival in the city, confronting its limitations and fragilities with the machines' preeminence in a more and more hostile, threatening, and technicized environment (Duarte, 2006, p. 10).

Insisting on the comparison between the spatial configuration of favelas and traditional (or preindustrial) cities, regarding their urban design geometric irregularity, it is worth asking why it has never occurred to people to complain about the narrow and winding streets of the Alfama district, in Lisbon, for example; or about the Gothic District's alleys and passageways, in Barcelona; or still about the old stairways and terraces (that resemble the slabs built in favelas) in the Greek islands' villages and about the mazed patterns of Venice; nor about the intertwined pattern of Medina, in Fez. Just the opposite, these unique characteristics are the ones that turn these, and many other similar places, into remarkable touristic destinations, attracting visitors from all over the world.

We must therefore analyze the favela's road network accessibility vis-a-vis the generous offer of proper and safe spaces for daily socio-spatial practices, from

---

[5]The analysis refers only to the street pattern accessibility. Therefore, cases where topography represents land sliding or collapsing risks for existing dwellings are exempt here.

which results the intensity and vitality perceived in the forms of appropriation of the public space by dwellers. According to Silva and Barbosa:

> In favelas, streets are spaces for festivities, leisure, affective encounters, for work, for play. (…) In favelas there are also dangers, mainly due to the violence imposed by police and armed criminals. Nevertheless, the streets are still spaces for approaching, for developing a sense of belonging and for engagement in individual and collective causes. There is still life in the streets, with the presence of the unexpected and the suppression of the absolute domain of the private over the public. (Silva, Barbosa, 2005, p. 98)

A kind of collective corporeal intelligence, which also translates into an urban competence for the rationality and economy of means and resources, presides dimensioning and interconnecting the streets in a favela. The human body enacting as an instrument for spatial mediation and appropriation allows the maintenance of people and things flows as a socio-spatial practice regulated by the unity and coherence of the uses of time and space. In favelas, built at human scale, the flow of things is still subdued to the people's flows.

The collective appropriation of space (use value) as opposed to the idea of property (exchange value), establishes the public space in the favela as the time–place of encounter and exchange (material and symbolic) between the different (Lefebvre, 1972, p.179). The social production of presence and visibility in the public space also represents the expansion of political awareness and the bonds of belonging. In this sense, the public space of the favela is a space lived intensely as a space of affection, conflict, and struggle for the affirmation of fundamental rights, in permanent tension with the abstract, cold and rationalized spaces of the surrounding city.

8.4 The "Reinvention" of the City Stemming from Popular Spaces

As mentioned in the beginning of this essay, during a long time, problems raised by the favela generation process in Rio de Janeiro were underestimated or, up to a certain point, ignored. The conservative utopia of an "orderly", rich and technologically sophisticated city, seemed to be the desired (and even "promised") future for the carioca city. Moreover, this was the city known and recognized by its natural landscape beauties, by its importance as the previous Federal Capital, by its core condition for the intellectual and artistic avantguard of the country, and by its vitality as a production and diffusion node for popular and erudite culture, among many other factors. The credo, engendered by the collective imagination also prevailed (and above all) in the city's public management throughout time, defining, according to these ideological premises, its urban policies, which prioritized public investments and co-opted the professional competence of technicians and public agents. It was, in other words, about reducing the "inevitable" historic process that would lead Rio de Janeiro to be a "First Class" city, or, at least, to make it similar to the prosperous cities of the developed countries, to the commonsensical eyes.

The adopted prescription consisted, thus, in the import and technocratic replication of urban governance models implemented in the mainstream capitalist big cities. Meanwhile, the real problems were ignored or, simply, "swept under the carpet", where they were accumulated without any perceived solution. The results of this process are well known. As the city expanded, the problems also expanded. The production of massive social inequalities was not interrupted or mitigated. On the contrary, we saw an exponential growth of urban poverty and socio-spatial segregation, as an inevitable counterpart of the brutal income concentration, brought off by the ruling classes in the last decades.

The most recent edition of the above-mentioned mistakes corresponds to the urban transformations carried out in the city preparing it for the 2016 Olympic Games. Governed by the speculative market interests, the Olympic agenda adopted by the city administration produced a set of mega-interventions disconnected from each other, lacking proper urban planning, or at least a global plan concerned with the future governance of the so-called Olympic legacy. Regarding the favelas, actions for urbanization, land use regulation, and quality of life improvements originally anticipated for the slum communities did not happen. Instead, we watched the military occupation of favelas through the "Pacifying Police Units" (UPPs), and a perverse reedition of eviction practices that seemed to be, not long ago, discarded or reserved for dwelling units proved to be in risk areas only.

Little by little, the certainty of a prosperous first-class future destined for the "Marvelous City" fades. Alternatively, another representation of the common sense emerges, stating that the city (now seen as a megalopolis for its unforeseen and assumed overgrowth)[6] has become a chaotic, threatening, and out-of-control organism. Although recently established, this new symbolic representation likewise persists in serious ideological misconceptions that not only naturalize political and economic processes that created (and fed) the existing problems, but also reject, by aprioristic discredit, any attempts at its solution.

The historic path that started with miraculous attempts at "solving" inexistent problems (in an invented city) until the premature capitulation through a fallacious assumption about the inutility of any attempts at transforming the current scenario (in face of an apparently out-of-control city) has collected tremendous and successive failures.

The search for appropriate solutions implies, firstly, the creation of channels for active popular participation, and the establishment of strategies for the mediation among the stakeholders, including technicians, public agents and managers, businessmen, communities' leaderships, and other forms of citizenship representation. We must understand that the solutions to be proposed shall contemplate the city that is in front of our eyes, mostly composed by the poor, the spatially segregated and the excluded from citizen's rights. This shall be, therefore, the primary focus of

---

[6]The population of Rio de Janeiro Metropolitan Region is estimated in approximately 12 million people (IBGE, Census 2010).

actions that cannot be procrastinated and that shall address the serious problems experienced in the city.

More than ever, it will be necessary to advance urbanization policies in favelas, amplifying their scope, strengthening their results and overcoming past mistakes. The universalization of citizenship rights, guarantying universal access to housing, work, transportation, health, education, and leisure, is the irrevocable precondition for the transformation of potential allies into effective partners for building a more democratic and equitable city (Fig. 8.3).

In this process, there will be certainly much to learn with favelas and their dwellers-builders, starting with the rediscovery of proximity, copresence, and contiguity advantages. The city of encountering people is also the city of meeting the most diverse urban functions. The simultaneity and convergence that result from the collective and common uses of space in the favelas allow the production of bonds of identity and belonging that point to new horizons of meaning that allow us to think about the political sharing of existences built in common by the social use of public space.[7]

The solution for the favelas is not off of them, but within the recognition that favelas represent the "reinvention" of the city itself, understood as a place for gathering and exchange among different individuals, as we intended to picture in this essay. A reborn, rejuvenated, loosen up, and undeniably joyful city. A city built as a response to the social exclusion and spatial segregation processes, but also as an alternative and clairvoyant form of self-protection from the directions taken by the big city which surrounds it. Once reflecting and mirroring an unequal society, the existing socio-diversity (Santos, 2000, p. 21) of favelas features, nowadays, a leading role in the solution for the problems faced by the city as a whole.

Moreover, at the same time that we see the rebound of violence in the daily war between the police, the militia, and the drugs and guns trafficking cartels, favelas reaffirm themselves in the carioca landscape as immense neighborhoods of poor people, endowed with great cultural visibility. They show a clear critical consciousness regarding the segregationist and excluding processes associated to their origin. At the national and international scenario, they raise an extensive production of documentaries, films, photos, music, books, academic dissertations, made by, mostly, the inhabitants of favelas themselves, as well as, numerous cultural initiatives linked to the hip-hop movement. They recognize favelas not for their historic issues and needs, but by their exceptional qualities, including those from an urbanist point of view, as places of conviviality and production of identities, that refuse their condition as ghettos or spaces of segregation within a broken city.

In times stamped with uncertainties and oblivion utopias, when the future of humankind is threatened by the depletion of resources and global warming, and by the insanity of wars and fundamentalisms (both economic and religious); when our ability to desire becomes meaningless and undersized, and it is reduced to a

---

[7]I owe this idea to Professor Jorge Luiz Barbosa, to whom I am grateful for the always fruitful dialogue on the theme of favelas.

Fig. 8.3 Santa Marta Favela, Botafogo, Rio de Janeiro. *Source* Photo by Cristovão Duarte, 2009 (author's collection)

rampant consumerism and to the pursuit of selfish fulfillment; perhaps favelas have something valuable to teach us. We must learn again to dream dreams of shared happiness. Less selfish and more democratic dreams that, once come true, may include the possibility of others' fulfillment. More sustainable dreams and, for this reason, more feasible and durable ones, that may point to the direction of a more humane and solidary future.

References

da Silva RCM (org.) (2006) A cidade pelo avesso; desafios do urbanismo. Viana & Mosley, Ed. PROURB, Rio de Janeiro

Duarte CF (2006) Forma e movimento. Vianna & Mosley: Ed. PROURB, Rio de Janeiro

Lefebvre H (1972) La revolucion urbana. Alianza Editorial, Madri

Lefebvre H (1991) O direito à cidade. Ed. Moraes, São Paulo

Perlman J (2002) O mito da marginalidade: favelas e política no Rio de Janeiro. Paz e Terra, Rio de Janeiro

Rogers R, Gumuchdjian P (2001) Cidades para um pequeno planeta. GG, Lisboa

Rossi A (1977) A arquitectura da cidade. Edições Cosmos, Lisboa

Santos CNFD (1988) A cidade como um jogo de cartas. Universidade Federal Fluminense, EDUFF, Niterói. Projeto Editores, São Paulo

Santos M (1999) A natureza do espaço: espaço e tempo: razão e emoção. Hucitec, São Paulo

Santos M (2000) Por uma outra globalização: do pensamento único à consciência universal. Record, Rio de Janeiro

Silva JS, Barbosa JL (2005) Favela: alegria e dor na cidade. Editora SENAC Rio, Rio de Janeiro

Valladares LDP (2005) A invenção da favela: do mito de origem a favela.com. Ed. FGV, Rio de Janeiro

Author Biography

Cristóvão Fernandes Duarte graduated in Architecture and Urbanism (School of Architecture and Urbanism—FAU, 1983), received his master's degree in Urbanism (Graduate Program in Urbanism - PROURB, 1997) and his Doctorate on Urban and Regional Planning (Institute of Urban and Regional Planning and Research—IPPUR) 2002, all three at the Federal University of Rio de Janeiro, where he is now an associate professor at FAU. He is in charge of several research projects at the Graduate Program in Urbanism and at the Professional Master in Landscape Architecture, focusing on urban design, urban renewal projects and contemporary landscape and urbanism.

Chapter 9
In the Guise of a (Global) Comprehension: A Multidimensional Analysis of Urban Public Spaces Through Selected Authors

Lucia Capanema Alvares

Abstract This chapter proposal is two folded: As it explores the model discussed in the introductory chapter, by Capanema Alvares and Barbosa, and sees how well it works as a tool to analyze urban public spaces and to bridge the arguments made by the authors present in this book, it also tries to unveil the global nature of events that lie in the core of these very Brazilian cases. As such, it is an ending chapter; hopefully, however, it will come to open new ways of looking at urban public spaces with the criticisms and contributions of our readers, which will be most welcomed.

Keywords Urban public spaces · Framework · Socioeconomic
Sociocultural · Socioenvironmental

9.1 The Proposed Model as an Analytical Tool

As we tried to introduce and systematize as big a number of relevant issues as possible in our introductory chapter without losing sight of parsimony, Ana Fani Carlos dialogues with all of them content wise.

First comes the body, and then the family, the neighborhood, and the city. In an inter-scalarity based on the body, she parallels and completes the arguments of Fernandez and Brandão (2010) and Swyngedouw (2010) in the opposite (inner) direction, bridging the body and the global world. Given the "intertwining of scales", there is no solution without questioning capitalism as a model for the world and the role states play in conceptualizing and perpetuating the model.

As the body engages in the dialectic of being passive and/or subversive, it can reject all "coercion exerted by private ownership" in a "practice that is sociospatial in nature", bridging the socioeconomic, the sociocultural, and the socioenviron-

L. Capanema Alvares (✉)
Programa de Pós-Gradução em Arquitetura e Urbanismo,
Universidade Federal Fluminense, Niterói, Rio de Janeiro, Brazil
e-mail: luciacapanema@gmail.com

© Springer International Publishing AG, part of Springer Nature 2018
L. Capanema Alvares and J. L. Barbosa (eds.), *Urban Public Spaces*,
The Urban Book Series, https://doi.org/10.1007/978-3-319-74253-3_9

mental pillars of the city. Focusing on the relationship between the body and the city, Grosz (1992) highlights a worldwide modern phenomenon, the marginalization of some (chosen) bodies:

> The question is […] to examine how different cities, different sociocultural environments actively produce the bodies of their inhabitants as […] bodies with particular physiologies, affective lives and concrete behaviors. […] The city orients and organizes family, sexual, and social relations insofar as the city divides cultural life into public and private domains, geographically dividing and defining the particular social positions and locations occupied by individuals and groups. […] These spaces, divisions, and interconnections are the roles and means by which bodies are individuated to become subjects. […T]he city's form and structure provide the context in which social rules and expectations are internalized or habituated in order to ensure social conformity, or position social marginality at a safe or insulated and bounded distance. (Grosz 1992, p. 250)

This very sociocultural insulation provokes different responses, as have shown Carlos through the poor youths, Barbosa and Damasceno Pereira through the appearances of the different, and Torraca through the poor's engagement in a circular violence.

The body that lives in a city divided into "areas of work, of private life, and of leisure"—where leisure, together with culture, is increasingly privatized (by the global capital) and commercialized as a commodity and where access to housing is limited—is differentiated by class and feels as if it was an alien. Here, the issues of mobility and porosity play a major socioeconomic, sociocultural, and socioenvironmental role, depriving the citizen from his or her rights. At this point, Carlos exceeds the model, for her argument goes beyond human rights, and embraces Lefèbvre's right to the city (1991).

When Mike Davis' cornerstone book, City of Quartz, came out, he already pointed that in "the valorized spaces of […] super-malls, […] public activity is sorted into strictly functional compartments, and circulation is internalized in corridors under the gaze of private police" (1990, p. 226), conforming what he called the "panopticon mall" (p. 240) in the city of Los Angeles. These shopping spaces were and are designed after behavioristic guidelines in order to format consumer habits, homogenize choices, and stigmatize the different. When discussing how the urban poor cope with homogenization and stigmatization, Carlos brings us the unexpected youth use of their bodies to affirm their right to be different in a consumerist society in São Paulo's panopticon malls of the twenty-first century.

As she unveils the contemporary aspects of our consumer (modern) world, she calls attention to some very capitalist characteristics. She sees a society "under the sway of the financial world and sustained by the state"—in which people respond to market demands and identities get lost in the construction of an exacerbated individualism—as the main reason for the conflicts that search for "another society", linking the exterior dimension (dominated by the global capital) to the socioeconomic dimension of local relations (where, according to Torres Ribeiro, the market replaced politics and economics replaced the state) and to the sociocultural dimension (where identities thrive to exist, get recognized, and sustain memory).

9 In the Guise of a (Global) Comprehension: A Multidimensional … 143

The limitations imposed on city inhabitants through what Habermas calls technical rationalities (political-administrative) reduce their creative powers and destabilize everyday life, but citizens have managed to reach public spaces, in the wave of the world protest movements, questioning "this life", a life "subsumed under exchange value." For Carlos, and here disagreeing with Torraca, the street demonstrations introduced democratic practices insofar as they were struggles for "another possible world" (in the way which conflicts should work and along the lines Irazábal discusses (2008).

The consumption world is, moreover, about stigmatizing the non-subject, and identifying the poor with everything that is backward, out of date, dirty, and violent, justifying the hygienist policies, as in Torraca's walls. Even the new "Class C", as Serpa also sees it, now precariously included in the consumption world and submitting itself to a capitalist program, has only changed status "from a peripheral population to a space-consuming population" that moves to newly and poorly built gated communities, mimicking the middle classes, and spend their free time in shopping malls or in the "domain of private life."

This reproduction of patterns, guided by the capital need for expansion, brings deleterious consequences to both sociocultural, as Carlos discusses, and socioenvironmental dimensions, as investigated by Tângari. Insofar as commodities determine relations between people, humanity no longer finds fulfillment in "creative freedom", but in consuming. And in showing it through spectacle.

Since global capitalism is the hegemonic force, the political-administration dimension only converges with it, removing the obstacles to its accumulation through changes in a "class-based planning" legislation and through "channeling and ranking investments in the city", what relates the external dimension to Tângari's arguments concerning local planning in Rio. Back in 1990, Davis already denounced that urban redevelopments had "transformed public parks into temporary receptacles for the homeless and wretched" (1990, p. 226) in Los Angeles, very much like Capanema Alvares (2014) found in the 2010s Rio de Janeiro. Together these strategies not only reduce the meaning of public spaces as places of sociability (sociocultural), as Serpa also argues but create segregated spaces (in the socioeconomic realm). Segregation is the contradiction of the encounter; it is a "form of deprivation", the "negative of the city."

The encounter, in Carlos, is central to construct identities and collective histories (sociocultural dimension) in the public sphere—what dialogues with Barbosa and Damasceno Pereira—but this construction has been hindered by the surveillance powers of the state, as Torraca points out. In another point of agreement with Torraca, Carlos states that segregation can appear "in the discourse of exclusion, which suggests policies of inclusion […] or as a poverty trademark, which demands policies for its eradication." By eliminating the encounter of the different, our model poses, the political-administrative dimension will prevent conflict and fear from surfacing as in Simmel (1903), Durkheim (1979) or Bauman (2007), and UPS will not serve as public sphere for the *vita activa*.

When introducing "The politics of oneself and politics with many others", Barbosa and Damasceno Pereira discuss the inherent conflictual relations between the two scales (as in Carlos' body inter-scalarity) and seem to elect the difference-unit dialectic as their focus of analyses, as Bauman (2007) and Heller (2004) do within the sociocultural dimension: "the 'we' of the differences in being and the unity for guaranteeing shared common rights." For the authors, "to acknowledge the body [...] is the exercise of 'another politics,' in which life itself is a political act", echoing Carlos.

Like Barbosa and Damasceno Pereira, Epstein has noted *a propos* city fear, that "the subject's identity cannot be constructed, materialized, or repeated without, at the very least, a psychical and spatial acknowledgement of an Other whose relationship to the subject will always be imbued with the power dynamic implied by the simple statement "You and I" (Epstein 1998, p. 216). Since "'to be' and 'to appear' are one", when subjects elect their appearances in UPS, they are challenging the "common sense that makes them invisible to differences", and are forcing their visibility, as well as the recognition of alterities and of all "individuals in their differences." Differences that are not welcomed by our contemporary cities' totalitarian 'arch-semiotic', as Davis (2006) has observed in downtown Los Angeles.

According to our focused authors, as subjects seek to "free themselves from the [hegemonic] norm", they construct ephemeral and individual practices as "style and aesthetics of existence", present in the social movements and cultural expressions (as pictured by the authors and in Carlos' *rolezinhos*), but may also embrace more collective and continuous practices, as pointed by Serpa (2013) when discussing strategies of cultural production that question the ruling classes hegemony, and in Duarte's favelas. In Holston's terms they are

> insurgent forms [...] found [...] in everyday practices that, in different ways, empower, parody, derail, or subvert state agendas, [...] engage the problematic nature of belonging to society, and [take place in] sites of insurgence because they introduce into the city new identities and practices that disturb established histories. (1998, pp. 47–49)

As a paradigmatic example of aesthetic collective and enduring practices within the sociocultural dimension, Woods (1998) describes the Blues Epistemology, "a self-referential system of social explanation" (p. 83) born out of the resistance to the US plantation regime implemented in the sixteenth century and crystallized in opposition to the Reconstruction governments of the late 1800s. A true "theory of African American aesthetics" developed in the 1920s and 1930s, this epistemology

> became the channel through which [Southern] African Americans grasped reality [...] and organized against it. [...] The indigenously developed folk culture, its orature, its ethics, its tradition of social explanation, and its prescriptions were [their] basic representational grid". (p. 83)

The tensions pointed out by Barbosa and Damasceno Pereira with the "quotidian standards—consumable and consumed" make reference not only to manifested conflicts, but also speak to Torraca's "circularity of violence" engendered by political-administrative instances, her "autophagic" (self-destructive) nature of daily life, and to the stigma on young blacks from favelas, "subjects that repeal oppressive norms and perverse naturalizations established in the city" also addressed by Torraca.

As much as the authors see external influences in hegemonic forces that "turned the city into machines of inequality reproduction", they also envision "counter-hegemonic movements", both in Foucault's aesthetic of existence, regarding the subject's quotidian practices in the city and in Arendt's spaces of appearances, when citizens "constitute and maintain spaces of collective manifestations." Despite the philosophers disagreements in a number of issues, Foucault's subject conducts (2010, 2011)—"including the power relations that act upon the bodies" (again echoing Carlos)—seem in tune with Bourdieu's (1987) habitus (strategic positioning according to expectations) as well as with Katz (1984), for whom, along Arendt's lines (1991), the self is only realized politically in the appropriation of the public sphere. Altogether, they hit the bulk of the sociocultural dimension.

But "styles of existence" do more than daily constituting selves; they also "seek a life more creative, active and full of possibilities", or "another type of life" (as in Carlos), when they exist in the presence of others and propose negotiations in the city, as Arendt (1991) established in our sociocultural dimension, and can be seen in Duarte's favelas, the true polis conformed by citizens, or in the "reverse city"—a city of rights built out of the rejection of the hegemonic.

In the socioeconomic dimension, "the claim to the right to life shows up as a claim to the right to the city", once again associating human rights to Lefèbvre's superior call (1991). Mediated by the socioenvironmental dimension, the "space of appearance", or the "process of experimentation and creation that allows replacing the granted citizenship for a *vita activa* citizenship", is the great potentiality envisioned by Queiroga for multifunctional spaces. This interdisciplinarity is well understood by the authors when they state that "in the public space, social, economic, and cultural issues engender the subject's sensible experiences." Altogether these authors incidentally respond to Holston's call: "What planners need to look for are the emergent sources of citizenship—and their repression—that indicates [...] a continual reinvention of the social, the present, and the modern and their modes of narrative and communication" (1998, p. 49) or in Miraftab's words, "their own terms of engagement" (2009, p. 41).

Torraca sees Rio as a divided city since at least the beginning of the twentieth century, but stresses the recent external forces and ideologies that have made it yet more segregated. The "cornered democracy" concept is a representation of the public spaces division "between the democratic asphalt and the permanent state of exception imposed on the slum" made true by oligarchic elites within the political-administrative instances. Reflecting the self-destructive character of the consumer society, this "autophagic democracy" perpetuates an aesthetic of violence or what she calls the "circularity of violence." A democracy based on material goods consumption leads to the "self-consumption of democracy in the process of constructing reality, [...] opening space for dealing with democracy destruction." The aesthetic that emerges from this autophagic democracy in socio-spaces is one of segregation, memory annihilation, inequalities, and divisions, affecting the socioeconomic, the sociocultural, and the socioenvironmental dimensions of the city.

When Planet of Slums came out in 2006, Davis asked us if the great slums of the world were not volcanoes waiting to erupt. The author then envisioned that "the future of human solidarity depends upon the militant refusal of the new urban poor to accept their terminal marginality within global capitalism" (p. 201). In different forms, according to Davis, the urban poor would be bound to respond with violence to their criminalization, in a circular movement toward more and more violence. Similarly to other US cities, he also noted in Los Angeles (Davis 1992) a "security offensive, [a] middle-class demand for increased spatial and social insulation" (p. 227) and—contrary to the Eastern Europe falling walls—a growing social apartheid that had been materialized, through the adoption of a "deliberate socio-spatial strategy" (p. 229), in the construction of walls all over the city. Later, Balko (2013) drafted the recent US history of police militarization, stressing that gross funding was channeled to the "War on Terror" as a response to September 11, not unlike Rio's militarization using the 'war on drugs' discourse.

Torraca now denounces how social movements and unrests coming from the slums endure both semantic and concrete apartheid processes through walls that separate them from the city and through what Davis called MOUT, "Military operations on Urbanized Terrain" (2006, p. 203), forging a circularity of violence. As Rousseau has stated, "violence is justified against anyone who is excluded from the social contract because he threatens the perpetuation of sovereign power that is assumed as the defender of order, peace and stability" (Vardoulakis 2013, p. 153). According to Ford, and reminding René Girard's 'Violence and Sacrifice', "Violence must be answered with more violence. [V]iolent intensity suggests that the only response to violence is more violence, a circularity of violence that does not allow its victims to be released from its burden" (2010, p. 84). In that sense, Rio slums seem to have 'evolved' towards the "distinctive battlespace of the twenty-first century" (Davis 2006, p. 205), placing the political-administrative dimension in diametrical opposition to the sociocultural and socioeconomic dimensions.

Having as one of her main objectives evidencing the horizontal sociocultural movements vis-a-vis the vertical corporate-state movements, Torraca moves on to analyze the 2013 Brazilian riots and recognizes that the reduction of social inequalities and of social violence in the popular governments of Lula and Dilma (2002–2016), had seemed to bring the country's political-administrative institutions to a mature democracy. However, as middle classes complaints in the virtual world made viral, the consequent conflicts manifested in UPS shook the country and the traditional media, all taken by surprise. Concerning social movements in UPS, Douzinas (2013) reminds us that "[u]rban space offers ample opportunity for political action" as has been demonstrated by "iconic cases [of early modernity] urban riots: American Civil Rights movement, May 1968, [Athens] 1973, Prague, Bucharest, Tehran and Cairo uprisings, to name a few, [in which] the 'street' has confronted and unsettled urban legality" (p. 139). Paving Torraca's line of reasoning, he also noted it was "strange that the widespread uprising that took place in Greece in December 2008 surprised and shocked politicians and mainstream commentators" (p. 139).

In Rio, the violent police reactions to the general public followed its training in the slums, and the sociocultural grammar of public spaces went upside down: "the social division lived daily by the inhabitants of the city made itself present in the riots" when the "democracy of the asphalt" was treated as the "bare life of the slum." The population response was immediate: more and more people wanted to join the spectacle, until the hegemonic media regained control over the after-truth, and re-imposed the corporate entrepreneur city, ready for FIFA and COI mega-events and for the coup d'état that impeached the left-wing elected president. Most 2010s manifestations around the world (from the Arab Spring to the numerous Occupy movements) have presented a number of resemblances and many inspired the 2013 Rio riots (Benayon, Capanema Alvares and Souza 2014), but the June 2013 protests in Istambul were some of the most similar to the Rio riots, with the absence of a centralized leadership, the mainstream media downplaying it at the beginning, the crucial role played by the alternative media in the Web, the engagement of both leftist and right-wing citizens and the excessive use of police force. Unlike the Brazilian case, the Turkish rallies were not co-opted by the mainstream media and the corporate interests to guide the masses through a rally process that led to a coup d'état, showing how UPS 'making history' (Irazábal 2008) events can be of inter-scalar importance in the political-administrative realm.

In and of itself, the media globally fuels the circularity of violence. On the one hand, and very much like in the Iraq and Afghanistan wars, Mirzoeff's (2011) "military-visual complex" technologies have been used to broadcast surreal images of UPPs and military troops invading slums, creating an idea of a desirable efficiency in chasing outlaws amidst poor people houses. On the other hand, "rioting, [in] its own aesthetic" (Douzinas 2013, p. 139), is transformed in spectacle by the mainstream media, argues Torraca, echoing Douzinas (2013) and Balibar (2007), when the latter discusses the riots in French urban peripheries:

> An implicit understanding with photographers and mainstream media offers publicity to the insurgents and dazzling photos and stirring stories to the press. As Etienne Balibar put it, the mass media have become 'passive organizers' of the riots because of their news value. But there is a price to pay. The 'virtual violence' they display '*transforms* real endemic social violence, to which it responds, *into spectacle*, thereby at once making it *visible* in its intensity and invisible and its everydayness'. (Douzinas 2013, p. 140)

Torraca goes on to denounce that these inter-scalar interests, together with a long history of police violence inherited from the military, sought much more than hygienist policies; they aimed at imposing an "oligarchic rule of law" in Rancière's words (2014), a "permanent state of exception", as in Agamben (2004), on the poorer parts of the divided city, "producing and reproducing violence uninterruptedly to attend exclusively to private [real estate] interests" while making sure it constituted a "spectacle of the real" that reassured its own circularity, having as excuses a "war on drugs" and the mega-events to come. As such, external 'examples' were used as a means to eliminate the encounter between the different, proposed by Arendt (1991), Habermas (1981), and Bauman (2007) and explored by the previous chapters. Contrary to the possibilities of self-expression and advocacy presented by Barbosa and Damasceno Pereira, and along the lines of Carlos' urban deprivation and stigmatization, for Torraca "public spaces have been demarcated as spaces of exclusion, [...] preventing the construction of a subjectivity of the economically colonized", and further reproducing the roots of prejudice in a "spectacle of empty bodies controlled by terror", as Barbosa and Damasceno Pereira's invisible bodies also recalled.

This state of exception paradigm serves the entrepreneurial city—global interests included—but goes far beyond an administrative issue, impeding not only the encounter that gives life to the sociocultural dimension of a city, but also the development of all that is, in socioeconomic terms, close to the right to the city. But that also gives rise to an aesthetic of resistance, as Barbosa and Damasceno Pereira, and also Carlos, have pointed out. Through UPS appropriations, artistic events and activities in favelas "rescue political practices [from a] consumerist kidnapping of lives and dreams", and offer, as in Duarte, a "resistance to the circularity of violence imposed by the state."

Serpa's chapter explores how the sociocultural dimension touches the other dimensions at different scales, since leisure has changed globally and locally for different reasons. He starts by assuming leisure spaces and work spaces form a "dialectical and inseparable pair"; thus, the socioeconomic dimension is herein tied to the sociocultural dimension: as the "logics of productive work" have changed towards freeing people "from labor for reproductive work" (for better or for worse), there will be changes in the demands for UPS, as well as for different housing and transportation systems. As much as the author sees the new Class C self-employment changing the use of and the demand for urban public spaces, Roy (2005) views informality as "a mode of urbanization, [...] a system of norms that governs the process of urban transformation itself" (p. 148), contradicting De Soto's (2000) "heroic entrepreneurship" ideal, which is at the very basis of neoliberalism: by 'freeing' the poor to be entrepreneurs rather than the old-fashioned proletariat (Roy 2006) the new rules "obscure the role of the state and even render it unnecessary" (Roy 2005, p. 148). Again, Roy's observations point to the inter-scalarity and the external dimension influences in planning.

Serpa sees a number of reasons why, despite all time-saving technologies (in Harvey's (2014) words), human beings are still subsumed to the intensified time given by machinery: as labor and consumption became two sides of the same coin, the more the person works, the greedier he or she becomes, as stated by Arendt (1991). Class attachment and consumerism lead to one another. Since consumption and its derived satisfaction are ephemeral in nature, society has become a composition of "episodes and fragments", therefore focused on short-term objectives; no "narratives of identity and life history" make sense anymore. This little attachment to places, to groups, to belonging, not only hinders personal experiences of sociability—leaving only abstraction to a long-term fulfillment—but represents a form of deprivation of urban life, as perceived by Carlos. In other words, the local sociocultural dimension has not been advanced by the changes in external capitalism factors concerning changes in work-leisure relations.

This global phenomenon realizes itself in two fairly different ways, certainly more acutely diverse in the Global South: while the upper classes may enjoy more leisure based on consumption, "many workers set themselves as individual entrepreneurs" in order to guarantee some cash flow stability. Brazil, in particular, witnessed a sizeable increase in the so-called Class C in the twenty-first century, which meant a number of low wage workers being able to open their own small businesses. In any case, and according to De Masi (2000), free time still cannot be much appreciated in our current society, for people are not used to value it, are not used to "entertain themselves"; the socioenvironmental dimension therefore tends to be more or less disregarded in those settings. On the contrary, this external phenomenon may bring a number of socioeconomic consequences with the increase of telework: transportation, commerce, and services will have to respond to different demands, both location and time wise, affecting land use value, housing standards, health-related issues, and the like.

But if and when the time for "creative idleness" comes, UPS, together with private places of encounter, will be core spaces, as cities will have to answer the demands of those "who rest and have fun" (in De Masi (2000) words), local or incoming tourists. The socioenvironment dimension will be most affected in all of its aspects (it is worth noting that Queiroga found an increasing demand for UPS in twenty-first century Brazil, though the cited study did not discuss class or income cohorts).

By means of two case studies, Serpa found out that among the mid-low income classes in Brazil, "ascension in the social structure implies the indebtedness and impoverishment of the social capital available" to those who become individual or family entrepreneurs, and "ascension takes place more from the insertion in consumption" than from living the public sphere. As already stated in Carlos, this class fraction mimics the middle classes and spends its free time in shopping malls or in the "domain of private life." Worse yet, by switching the television it turns itself into easy prey to the mainstream media twisted construction of reality, as Torraca warns us. According to Serpa's assessment, the Brazilian new Class C, as shaped by late capitalism and the neoliberal canons of flexibilization and self-entrepreneurship, "is far from reaching the 'idleness' envisioned by De Masi: [...] it does not engage in cultural enlightening activities; [in fact,] there has been a good deal of impoverishment of the[ir] social capital" (in this volume). Not unlike the contemporary western self-employed low and middle classes, Brazilians tend to spend their free time consuming marketed goods and TV shows. In other words, in order to climb the socioeconomic ladder, this group not only lowers its sociocultural possibilities, lowering, as a consequence, its recognition and demand for UPS, but also relinquish its basic human rights concerning work hours and its right to the city. They become "super-exploited [workers], with no tradition of class solidarity", i.e., citizens deprived of an urban life.

While emptying public spaces of meaning, this phenomenon has also been partly supporting some dynamism in Third World and Eastern economies. In China, where it plays a substantive role, leisure studies call for civilized, healthy and rational use of free time in order to foster a competitive society (Rolandsen 2011);

in Taiwan, leisure also seems to be seen as a resource, but a resource to be shared and put to the best community interest (Liu and Zhang 2006). In both cases, the demand for socioenvironmental amenities tends to increase.

If there is no clear demand for UPS, the political-administrative dimension may as well not provide or care for them, what would mean a scenario of socioeconomic interests, fueled by external factors, ruling alone socioenvironmental and sociocultural possibilities, as Tângari fears. But Serpa optimistically reminds us that, on the other hand, "more people working at home and sparing the fatigue" of long journeys to work, "can release new energies [...] at the neighborhood scale", generating greater citizen participation and interest in UPS. Then again (in Torraca words, which Carlos seems to agree), while "leisure has become a possibility of seizing gains, the ludic and art can help subvert relationships from their current stablished forms"; that would call for a "new form of social and spatial organization of society and cities" as stated by Serpa.

Potential is the guiding concept in Queiroga's chapter. While acknowledging that both theories and practices from the Global North have influenced Brazilian UPS readings and projects towards gated communities and indoor private activities, he points out that, coming from a different socioeconomic and sociocultural reality, there has been a concrete demand for leisure and civic areas for public use in the country.

Reminding us that while in Arendt's terms "work and labor are activities proper to the private sphere" (agreeing with Serpa on the leisure conceptualization), political action, in a broad sense, can only take place in a general public sphere (in Habermas' terms 1981)—the locus of *vita activa*. In his conceptual system concerning the public sphere and public spaces, the category "public space" highly converges to our UPS concept; while he conceives the term focusing on land use, we do it focusing on access, meaning that Queiroga's public spaces, different from UPS, encompass public owned spaces that preclude public access and appropriation, while excluding private property with free access to people. These nuances will have some importance in sociocultural and socioenvironmental aspects. Most important, however, are the notions of temporary and hybrid public spaces, meaning that through appropriations, spaces may change in character and use in real life, developing socioeconomic, sociocultural and socioenvironmental roles to different degrees in time. A number of authors have stressed the socioenvironmental potential of multifunctional spaces in the developed world, as they offer recreational areas that can play crucial environmental roles, like mitigating floods (see for example, Siekmann et al. 2012), while others have pointed to the sociocultural relevance of such spaces, as their

> amenities often appeal to diverse community members, including activists, artists, academics and social entrepreneurs, allowing them to act as incubators for new ideas, knowledge exchange, shared experience and experimentation. This connection of diverse communities can inspire innovative thinking and provide opportunities for collaboration and partnerships across traditional boundaries". (Multi-functional Spaces 2017)

Moreover, Brandt and Vejre (2004) have pointed to the multidisciplinary character of such spaces, as they see, among other functional classifications, the one based on their economic, ecological and cultural functions. Some of the most recognized multifunctional spaces are the trendy High Line, built in 2009 on top of an old rail line in New York, and the Granville Island in Vancouver.

In large and mid-size Brazilian cities, the long external influence toward the road mode of transportation resulted in open spaces for public use dominated by the road system, with more than double the areas dedicated to "squares, parks and the like", showing a socioeconomic dimension predominance. While a number of pedestrian streets have been implemented, mobility is still the driving force behind new pedestrian lanes and bikeways.

Housing needs, as Tângari also discusses, have been politically situated opposite to dedicated leisure spaces and environmental protection areas, as if they were in necessary struggle and not complementary parts of human rights in the city. Queiroga sees that we have to avoid "the tendency to treat social and environmental issues in isolation", but as "public policies in general fail to recognize it", there has been few attempts at promoting socioeconomic aspects together with conservation and fruition; lately, the political-administrative dimension has bended toward environmental aspects, as other studies have shown how urban landscapes can contribute to city entrepreneurship and city marketing.

While in Brazilian poor neighborhoods the streets have always played multi-functional roles (mostly serving commercial and leisure activities, as Duarte shows) in central areas the 'appropriation of squares, streets, and avenues has undergone decades of decline." For Queiroga, however, multifunctional spaces "reveal an excellent strategy for exploiting available resources." Both genuine and policy-driven appropriations are taking place in a number of ways, to the advancement of the sociocultural dimension: through providing leisure activities as a necessary complement to work, through turning leisure into consumption, through staging spectacles for city marketing, through conflictual demonstrations, and/or as "potential tools for organizing social and cultural events 'towards another kind of globalization'", in tune with all previous authors hopes and visions.

In his final statements, Queiroga argues that lived open spaces are under constant transformation, no matter the plans initially made for them. More than questioning planning we ought to recognize that "structural relations between State, capital and work are not fixed, they become established within a dialectical process". In other words, the local dimensions are not only intertwined, but also and altogether, are open to change.

It is very clear for Tângari that "the organization of Brazilian society" (en-compassing both socioeconomic and sociocultural dimensions) is expressed "in the configuration of open spaces", whether they may be public or private, and serve economic, cultural or environmental ends. Dialectically, open spaces are respon-sible for creating identities and collective memories. Her main question, thus, focuses on how space is manifested in society.

Unfortunately, she sees the political-administrative dimension as a dominant force in the production of public spaces, ignoring class struggles when imposing the capitalist logic based on vehicle circulation, to the detriment of "sociability and encounters." Another aspect of this domination is reflected in the "tensions and conflicts between the process of occupation and the environmental substrate", in which housing needs and environmental protection are made to clash.

Unveiling external and corporate capital influences over city planning, she argues that, since the 1980s, the real estate market, through the "standardization of landscapes, [the] adoption of imported models [and the assignment of] value to new localities" has been structuring the current levels of spatial segregation in Brazil. With the proliferation of gated communities for high-income sectors in the urban fringes, the poorer either joined them in the surrounding undeveloped areas, settled in the "outer peripheries without infrastructure, or the environmentally fragile areas not yet occupied." In any case, those occupations configured environmental social injustices, creating zones "contrary to the idea of the constitution of a democratic public space, a space of social participation, [generating] individualization, spatial segregation and high environmental costs." Not surprisingly, the "induced", the "spontaneous", and the "controlled" growth, all inductive of socioeconomic conflicts of interests, are "embedded in the legal instruments that regulate urban occupation." Along with the political-administrative dimension, the market and the mainstream media make believe that the real struggle is between low-income settlements and protected areas.

Taking Rio as an emblematic example of Brazilian cities, Tângari shows that when the geo-biophysical substrate is more valuable as a socioeconomic asset, the pressures on the socioenvironmental dimension will cause unequal distribution of UPS and will forge, again, environmental social injustices. Her research project aimed at exploring the "relationship between landscape construction, [...] the geo-biophysical substrate" and the socioeconomic dimension (considering the influences of both capital and the different fractions of labor); it also aimed at understanding how recurrent the spatial segregation patterns have been, "irrespective of the size of the city [or] the population" and of planning instruments and political-administrative structures. Her results, backed by other studies concerning the whole country, show that six similar patterns (like high concentration of land or low supply of public transportation, for example) have been systematically adopted, regardless of the substrate and the sociocultural characteristics, in order to ensure unequal cities. In Rio's real estate market, in particular, (except for newly developed fringes where there are vast non-occupied green areas), high-income settlements and quantity and quality of UPS go hand in hand and vice versa. In a quali-quantitative approach and taking historical, social, and political aspects into consideration, Tângari demonstrates how the poorer urban areas are historically bound to lack quality public spaces that could enhance their inhabitants' citizenship, demonstrating in Rio de Janeiro what Fernández-Álvarez (2017) has recently found in Mexico City regarding green public spaces. While Fernández-Álvarez's results show that green public spaces distribution is biased against young populations with low levels of education and high levels of poverty living in densely populated areas, Tângari found that throughout the twentieth century public policies have shaped the metropolitan area so that a low number of squares, parks, and soccer pitches, and the predominance of a dense road and railway network are positively related to high densities of housing and medium to low-income populations in the urban fringes. That is how, echoing our previous authors, the common citizen is deprived of an urban life, how he or she is seen as bare life, how the circularity of violence is linked to the real estate market, the entrepreneur city, and their external allies.

Despite different roots and inspirations, the socioenvironmental injustice that might be a trademark of modern urbanization history in the Global South has reached worldly attention and has been a major focus of academic research since the 1990s, as Bolin et al. (2000), Turner and Wu (2002) and Carruthers (2008) have demonstrated. Turner and Wu (2002) argue, moreover, that a growing body of literature places "the sources of environmental injustice in a complex process through which structural factors such as capitalism, policies and regulations, and social stratification" interact with private and governmental decisions that shape public policies throughout the world (Turner and Wu 2002, p. 18), warranting our multidimensional analyses. We, in this volume, are thus trying to break the chains of localized discourses and tactics, as Carruthers has called for (2008).

Notwithstanding her findings, Tângari also hopes that planning will be able to "assist in the proposal of projects designed to regenerate and manage public space" toward a more egalitarian society.

Despite and against all odds, favela "populations find in their self-built homes, entirely paid with their own and scarce financial means, a feasible surviving strategy." With this statement Duarte opens the last and most cheering chapter, finally giving the reader some concrete hope in the city. As much as these populations' position in the city is near the bottom, their history is based on political-administrative and socioeconomic segregation translated into the territory, as Tângari has shown. Their sociocultural appropriation of space and resources, and their sociabilities have, however, made a difference. Amidst a historical "mix of tolerance and indifference", where no human rights are considered, "favelas resist, expand and consolidate", mingling in. They are here to stay. As Miraftab reminds us, "the deep informality of third world cities is not their failure, but as Simone (2004) suggests, a triumphant sign of their success in resisting the Western models of planning and urban development" (2009, p. 45).

In the "Carioca" (Rio's) specific case, the alleged city's proneness to be a "first class" international destiny led administrators to "import and technocratic(ally) replicat(e) urban governance models" (showing the external influence), which only concentrated income in the hands of a few and deepened the socioeconomic and sociocultural segregation in the last decades. More recently, international tourism and the mega-events industry brought a badly planned legacy and excused a real state project based on the "military occupation of favelas through the 'Pacifying Police Units' (UPPs)", also denounced by Torraca.

Duarte wonders, interested "in debating [the factors] associated with the power of resistance [and the favelas'] leading role in the production and reproduction of spaces for the poor", why their inhabitants resist evictions and how they manage to keep a vibrant environment while their regular and formal neighbors have become dull and fragmented. The answer starts with land appropriation based on use value and not on exchange value, which becomes solidary, contiguous, and cohesive, leading to likewise sociocultural relations; their low standards of living are mostly due the political-administrative dimension with its entrepreneurial ties that do not extend public services and facilities to these areas, and not to high densities. Another dominant factor is their solidary spending and investing structure: together they build their homes, their businesses, and by extension their public space, which become commonly appropriated. Their right to work is exercised in their own houses or out in the public space, whereas their rights to housing and to the city constitute a tough struggle, from land ownership to mobility, and to education and health services. The absence of expertise (political-administrative) planning opens the way to a "sociospatial dialectic" process involving "the inside and the outside, the individual and the collective, the private and the public" (as in Mauss 1904–1905 and in Vernant 1990), and the construction of public space "arises from eminently collective demands."

The dichotomies we, as outsiders, create between favelas and "the asphalt" (to employ Torraca's terminology) are mostly located in the difference between having or not political-administrative regulations and provisions, between what we are used to and the different. Coming from different socioeconomic and sociocultural dynamics, we see the violence of the militia, but we do not see the violence of "car users (and their) environmental pollution" or "the violence represented by the spaces for fast traffic flows, defined by the hegemony of motorizes vehicles [...] in a more and more hostile, threatening and technicized environment". In favelas, on the contrary, "streets are spaces for festivities, leisure, affective encounters, for work, for play" (Silva and Barbosa 2005 *apud* Duarte), despite the danger and fear imposed by the state police and the criminals.

Within the sociocultural dimension, the symbolic appropriation of UPS in favelas permits a rather different "production of presence", less violent to its inhabitants (as Carlos and Torraca wish) and "of visibility", accounting for those that are invisible in the asphalt (as Barbosa and Damasceno Pereira have argued), as opposed to the "abstract, cold, and rationalized spaces" of the regular city.

In a world "reduced to a rampant consumerism and to the pursuit of selfish fulfillment" (as in Heller 2004, and in Carlos), "perhaps favelas have something valuable to teach us", says Duarte. Some of the lessons he amassed include "the creation of channels for active popular participation", "the universalization of citizenship rights", "the production of bonds of identity", and "the political sharing of existences built in common by the social use of public space."

As for our proposed model, we argue that it faired reasonably well as an analytic tool, knitting together the texts herein presented and a number of authors and cases from around the world, thus offering a comprehensive enough perspective, though in need of incorporating more variables and blurring its dimensions rigidity, as our contemporary time demands. Above all, it missed to clearly address, more than human rights, Lefèbvre's right to the city (1991).

References

Agamben G (2004) Estado de Exceção. Homo Sacer, II, 2nd edn. Boitempo, São Paulo

Arendt H (1991) A condição humana, 5th edn. Forense Universitária, Rio de Janeiro

Balibar E (2007) Uprisings in the Banlieues. Constellations: Inter J Critical Demo Theory 14(1):47–71

Balko R (2013) Rise of the Warrior Cop: the militarization of America's police forces. Public Affairs, New York

Bolin B et al. (2000) Environmental equity in a sunbelt city: the spatial distribution of toxic hazards in Phoenix, Arizona. Global Environ Change Part B: Environ Hazards 2(1):11–24. University of Melbourne, Victoria, Australia

Bauman Z (2007) Vida líquida. Jorge Zahar, Rio de Janeiro

Benayon JS, Capanema Alvares L, Souza RF (2014) Indignation and expectations in the Brazilian protests 2013: a statistical reading. Annals of the III Enanparq, São Paulo

Bourdieu P (1987) Choses Dites. Éd. de Minuit, Paris

Brandt J, Vejre H (2004) Multifunctional landscapes—motives, concepts and perceptions. In: Brandt J, Vejre H (eds) Multifunctional landscapes: volume 1 theory, values and history. WIT Press, Southampton, pp 3–32 (Advances in Ecological Sciences, Vol. 1)

Capanema Alvares L (2014) Espaços livres públicos (elp): uma análise multidimensional de apropriaçoes e identidades. Espaço e cultura (uerj) 1:179–202

Carruthers DV (2008) Environmental justice in Latin America: problems, promise, and practice. MIT Press, Cambridge, United States of America

Davis M (1992) City of Quartz: excavating the future in Los Angeles. Vintage Books, New York

Davis M (2006) Planet of Slums. Verso, London

De Soto H (2000) The mystery of capital: why capitalism triumphs in the west and fails everywhere else. Black Swan Books, London

De Masi D (2000) O ócio criativo, 2nd edn. Sextante, Rio de Janeiro

Douzinas C (2013) Philosophy and resistance in the Crisis. Polity Press, United Kingdom

Durkheim E (1979) Da divisão do trabalho social. Abril Culturual, São Paulo

Epstein D (1998) Psychoanalytic Directions for an Insurgent Planning Historiography. In: Sandercock L (ed) Making the invisible visible: a multicultural planning history. University of Califórnia Press, Berkeley, pp 209–226

Fernández-Álvarez R (2017) Inequitable distribution of green public space in the Mexico City: an environmental injustice case. Economía, Sociedad y Territorio 17(54):399–428, Toluca, México

Fernández VR, Brandão C (2010) Escalas y políticas del desarrollo regional. Buenos Aires, Davilla y Miño

Foucault M (2010) Governo de si e dos outros: curso no Collège de France (1982–1983). São Paulo, Editora WMF Martins Fontes

Foucault M (2011) A coragem da verdade: curso no Collège de France (1983–1984). São Paulo, Editora WMF Martins Fontes

Grosz E (1992) In Colomina B, Bloomer J (eds) Sexuality & Space. Princeton Architectural Press, Princeton

Habermas J (1981) The theory of communicative action. Lifeworld and system: a critique of functionalist reason vol 2. Beacon Press

Harvey D (2003) The new imperialism. Oxford University Press, Oxford

Harvey D (2014) SIMPURB: Conferência de Encerramento. In: Oliveira FG, Freire DG, De Jesus GM, De Oliveira LD (Org.) (eds) Geografia Urbana. Ciência e Ação Política. Rio de Janeiro, Consequência, pp 45–64

Heller A (2004) O Cotidiano e a História. São Paulo, Paz e Terra

Holston J (1998) Space of Insurgent Citizenship. In: Sandercock L (ed) Towards Cosmopolis. John Wiley and Sons, New York, pp 37–55

Irazábal C (2008) Ordinary place/extraordinary events: democracy, citizenship and public space in Latin America. Routledge, New York

Katz R (1984) Empowerment and synergy: expanding the community's healing resources. In: Rappaport J, Hess R (eds) Studies in empowerment: steps toward understanding and action. Hayworth Press, New York

Lefèbvre H (1991) O direito à cidade. Moraes, São Paulo

Liu HM, Zhang Y (2006) Evolution of the leisure Ethic in Western Countries. Studies Dialect Nat 4:91–95, Beijing, China

Mauss M (1904–1905) Essai sur les variations saisonnières des sociétés eskimo. Étude de morphologie sociales. l'Année Sociologique (tome IX)

Mirzoeff N (2011) The right to look. A counter history of Visuality. Duke University Press, Durham & London

Miraftab F (2009) Insurgent planning: situating radical planning in the global south. Planning Theory 8:32–50

Multi-functional spaces. Community Research Connections. In https://crcresearch.org/solutions-agenda/multi-functional-spaces. Accessed on 26 Nov 2017

Rancière J (2014) O Ódio à Democracia, 1st edn. São Paulo, Boitempo Editorial

Rolandsen UM (2011) Leisure and power in Urban China: everyday life in a Chinese City. Routledge, New York

Roy A (2005) Urban informality: toward an epistemology of planning. J American Plan Assoc 71(2), Spring

Roy A (2006) Praxis in the time of empire. Plann Theor 5(1)

Serpa AP (2013) O espaço público na cidade contemporânea. Contexto, São Paulo

Siekmann M et al (2012) Multifunctional land use in urban spaces to adapt urban infrastructure. In: Leal Filho W (ed) Climate change and the sustainable use of water resources. Climate Change Management Series, Springer, Berlin, Heidelberg

Simmel G (1903) The sociology of conflict. Am J Sociol 9:490–525. Available from: www.brocku.ca/MeadProject/Simmel/Simmel_1904a.html. Accessed: 15 may 2014

Silva JS, Barbosa JL (2005) Favela: alegria e dor na cidade. Editora SENAC Rio, Rio de Janeiro

Simone A (2004) For the City yet to Come: Changing African Life in Four Cities. Durham, NC: Duke University Press

Swyngedouw E (2010) Globalización o glocalización? Redes, territorios y reescalonamientos. In: Fernández VR, Brandão CA (eds) Escalas y políticas del desarrollo regional. Buenos Aires, Davilla y Miño

Turner RL, Wu DP (2002) Environmental justice and environmental racism: An annotated bibliography and general overview, focusing on U.S. literature, 1996–2002, Berkeley. Workshop on Environmental Politics, Institute of International Studies. University of California, Berkeley

Vardoulakis D (2013) Sovereignty and its other: toward the dejustification of violence. Fordham University Press, New York

Vernant JP (1990) Mito e Pensamento entre os gregos. Paz e Terra, Rio de Janeiro

Woods C (1998) Regional blocs, regional planning and the blues epistemology in the Lower Mississippi Delta. In: Sandercock L (ed) Making the invisibile visible: a multicultural planning history. University of Califórnia Press, Berkeley, pp 78–99

Author Biography

Lucia Capanema Alvares holds a degree in Architecture and Urban Planning from the Federal University of Minas Gerais (1988), a master's degree in City and Regional Planning—Memphis State University (1992), a Ph.D. in Regional Planning—University of Illinois at Urbana Champaign (1999), and has a post-doc in Urban and Regional Planning at the Institute for Urban and Regional Planning and Research, IPPUR-UFRJ (2011). Currently an associate professor at the Graduate Program in Architecture and Urban Planning of the Fluminense Federal University, she has co-authored the book *A Construção do Turismo: Megaeventos e outras estratégias de venda das cidades* (2014), alongside authoring numerous chapters and papers both nationally and internationally.

Index

A
Aesthetic of existence, 43–46, 145

B
Body, 27–30, 46, 47, 55, 92, 122, 134, 135, 141, 142, 144, 153

C
City, 2, 4–7, 11–14, 16, 18–20, 22, 27, 29, 31–35, 37–41, 43, 44, 46, 48–55, 57–59, 61, 62, 66–68, 74, 75, 77, 80, 92–94, 97–102, 104, 106, 112, 113, 115, 118–120, 123, 124, 127–137, 141–149, 151–154
Classification, 82, 102, 118, 122, 151
Consciousness, 80, 127
Creative idleness, 73, 74, 78, 80, 81, 85, 86, 149

D
Democracy, 2, 5, 18, 50, 57–67, 69–72, 145–147
Difference, 2, 5, 7, 8, 22, 31, 43, 44, 46–49, 51–55, 59, 62, 77, 85, 115, 116, 134, 144, 153, 154

E
Entrepreneurship, 21, 78, 81–83, 148, 149, 151

F
Framework, 2, 21, 95, 98, 117, 118, 129
Free spaces, 3, 4, 91

H
Hegemonic city, 8, 13, 14, 20, 27, 35, 44–46, 48, 53, 55, 59, 96, 106, 143–145, 147

L
Leisure, 4, 11, 13–17, 33, 67, 74–76, 80, 81, 83–86

M
Metropolis, 4, 10, 16, 32, 34–36, 40, 74, 80, 81, 86, 112
Multifunctional spaces, 100, 145, 150, 151

O
Open spaces, 5, 11, 16, 20, 21, 92, 94–96, 98–106, 110–113, 115, 117–120, 123, 124, 151

P
Police violence, 60, 61, 147
Popular appropriations, 4, 12, 135, 154
Production of space, 14, 34, 85, 86, 114
Protest movements, 61, 143
Public and private spheres, 4, 35, 117
Public policies Brazil, 58, 60, 92, 102, 104, 113, 124, 151
Public policies, 2, 19, 32, 37, 58, 60, 92, 102, 104, 113, 124, 151–153
Public space, 7, 10, 12, 13, 15, 18, 20, 22, 30–32, 34, 35, 37, 40, 44, 46, 51–55, 58, 59, 62, 66–68, 71, 74, 80, 91, 93–97, 99–102, 105, 106, 110, 129, 133–135, 137, 143, 145, 148, 149–154

R
Reality construction, 70
Resistance, 4, 12, 40, 59, 62, 64, 65, 67, 68, 71, 129, 130
Right to the city, 12, 36, 41, 53, 101, 132, 142, 145, 148, 154

© Springer International Publishing AG, part of Springer Nature 2018
L. Capanema Alvares and J. L. Barbosa (eds.), *Urban Public Spaces*,
The Urban Book Series, https://doi.org/10.1007/978-3-319-74253-3

Rio de Janeiro, 19, 46, 47, 57–59, 61–66, 70, 71, 75, 100, 111, 113–115, 118–120, 124, 125, 129, 134, 138, 143, 152

S
Segregation, 2, 12, 22, 35, 37–39, 41, 112, 113, 115, 116, 118, 127, 129, 136, 137, 143, 145, 152, 153
Self-creation, 44
Slums, 16, 57–59, 61–64, 67, 70, 71, 147
Sociocultural, 2, 9, 10, 13, 15, 16, 18, 21, 32, 117, 125, 141, 142
Socioeconomic, 9–11, 15, 16, 18, 20, 21, 113, 117, 119, 141, 142, 145, 146, 148–154
Socioenvironmental, 112, 145, 149, 150, 152, 153
Socio-spatial segregation, 109, 128
Space reinvention, 43
Spaces of appearance, 44, 51

U
Urban identities, 1–3, 20, 21, 41, 49, 67, 69, 137, 142, 143, 151
Urban landscape, 30, 96, 110, 112, 115, 127, 128, 151
Urban Public Spaces, 1–4, 8, 11, 13, 73, 86, 87, 141, 148
Urban space, 2, 6, 12, 20, 27, 28, 32, 34, 35, 37–40, 86, 91, 92, 104, 110–112, 120

W
Work, 3, 7, 10, 11, 15–17, 35, 39, 51, 54, 55, 66, 73, 74, 76–79, 84–87, 92, 99, 105, 106, 111, 117, 131, 135, 137, 141, 142, 148–151, 154